VIF Perspective

INDIA'S FOREIGN POLICY AND NATIONAL SECURITY STRATEGY

Editor
C D Sahay

Vitasta
LET KNOWLEDGE SPREAD

Published by
Renu Kaul Verma
Vitasta Publishing Pvt Ltd
2/15, Ansari Road, Daryaganj
New Delhi - 110 002
info@vitastapublishing.com

In association with
Vivekananda International Foundation
3, San Martin Marg, Chanakyapuri, New Delhi 110021

ISBN 978-93-86473-39-4

First Edition 2019
3rd Reprint 2021
MRP ₹695

Cover and layout by Vits Press
Printed by Vikas Computer and Printers

Contents

This book is dedicated

to

Vice Adm KK Nayyar, PVSM, AVSM

Former Vice Chief of Indian Navy and
Founder Chairman of the
Vivekananda International Foundation

List of Contributors

Dr Arvind Gupta is at present the Director, Vivekananda International Foundation (VIF). He has earlier held the positions of the Deputy National Security Adviser, Secretary, National Security Council Secretariat (NSCS), Director General the Institute of Defence Studies and Analyses (IDSA). He has also been the Joint Secretary, NSCS, on deputation from the Ministry of External Affairs (1999-2007). He is the author of the book, *How India Manages Its National Security*, published by Penguin.

Swaminathan Gurumurthy is a well-known public personality, a legal and financial professional, investigative journalist, writer, academic and activist. He is a Visiting Faculty at the IIT, Bombay, and Distinguished Professor of Legal Anthropology at the Palkhivala Centre for Legal Anthropology, Sastra University. He is also Trustee and Executive Committee member of the Vivekananda International Foundation.

CD Sahay is a Senior Fellow and Center Head for Neighbourhood Studies and Internal Security Studies at the VIF. He is a Former Secretary (R), Cabinet Secretariat. He has decades of experience in dealing with national security issues and international terrorism.

Vice Admiral Anil Chopra has been the Commander-in-Chief of Indian Navy's both the combatant commands, i.e., the Western and the Eastern Naval Commands, besides the Chief of the Indian Coast Guard. In 2017, Admiral Chopra was appointed to the National Security Advisory Board, Government of India.

Lt Gen Gautam Banerjee, PVSM, AVSM, YSM, is a former Chief of Staff, Central Command, and a former Commandant of the Officers' Training Academy, Chennai. Author of six books and over hundred papers on defence and strategic matters so far, he is a Senior Fellow and Editor at the Vivekananda International Foundation.

Ambassador Kanwal Sibal is a former Foreign Secretary, Government of India. Earlier, he has served as India's Ambassador to Turkey, Deputy Chief of Mission in the United States, Ambassador to Egypt, France,and, finally, Ambassador to Russia. A former member of India's National Security Advisory Board, he is also on the Board of the New York East-West Institute and the Advisory Board of the Vivekananda International Foundation.

Ambassador Rajiv Sikri is a career diplomat, having retired in 2006 as Secretary, East, in the Ministry of External Affairs. He has served as India's Ambassador to Kazakhstan. He is the author of *Challenge and Strategy: Rethinking India's Foreign Policy* (SAGE: 2009), and has contributed numerous articles to edited books, journals, newspapers and magazines.

Tilak Devasher is a former Special Secretary, Cabinet Secretariat, Government of India. He is the author of the book titled, *Pakistan: Courting the Abyss.*

Ambassador Gautam Mukhopadhaya is a former diplomat who served as the Ambassador of India to Syria, Afghanistan and Myanmar. He has also worked in the UN Headquarters at New York as a Consultant on Social Development, and has been a visiting scholar at the Carnegie Endowment for International Peace.

Lt Gen RK Sawhney, PVSM, AVSM, is a former Deputy Chief of the Army Staff and a former Director of Military Intelligence. He is presently the Centre Head and a Senior Fellow (National Security and Strategic Studies) at the Vivekananda International Foundation.

Ambassador Sanjay Singh has served as India's Ambassador to Iran and as the Secretary (East) in the Ministry of External Affairs. He is associated with various think tanks on issues related to foreign affairs and has been the President of the Association of Indian Diplomats.

Ambassador Anil Wadhwa is a career diplomat having served as Secretary (East) in the Ministry of External affairs, and Ambassador of India to Italy, San Marino, Thailand, Oman, Poland and Lithuania. He has also served with India's Permanent Mission at Geneva and worked on deputation with the Organisation for the Prohibition of Chemical Weapons in Hague, Netherlands.

Foreword

Vivekananda International Foundation is a prominent and distinctive think tank based in Delhi. Guided by the message of Swami Vivekananda (1863-1902), the VIF conducts research on a wide range of subjects covering international relations, national security, foreign policy, issues of defence, governance, economics, history and civilisation. The objectives of the VIF research is to promote nation-building, encourage harmony in diversity, prioritise conflict avoidance and generate environmental awareness. An able team of researchers, defence, security and foreign policy experts, prominent academics and eminent citizen helps VIF in its activities. The VIF message is reflected in its numerous publications.

As the world becomes multipolar and India begins to take its deserved place in the comity of nations, there is an urgent need to develop an Indian vision and narrative. Such a narrative should be based on India's own experience of dealing with the world over several millennia and Indian wisdom contained in numerous ancient texts. We have to remind ourselves that the world will not take us seriously unless we project a distinct Indian identity.

In the last few years, Prime Minister Modi has been

projecting India at the world stage effectively by highlighting the themes of *Vasudhaiva Kutumbakam*, *Sarve Bhavantu Sukhinaha*, of dialogue and harmony, power and restraints, growth and cooperation. The challenge before us is to connect these themes effectively into a wholesome and effective narrative backed by appropriate means and resources.

More than a hundred years ago, Swami Vivekananda had the courage and audacity to project the universalism of Hinduism to the outside world. Even though India was colonised and oppressed, he strongly believed that India's civilisational message was of relevance to the entire world and mankind.

India is on the cusp of another phase of a social, political, economic and cultural renaissance. We need to develop a vision for India's place in the world and also a framework for foreign policy suitable for meeting emerging challenges.

In 2017, the Vivekananda International Foundation started a series of publications under the general title of 'VIF Perspective'. The first book brought together thoughtful essays and articles on a variety of subjects ranging from India's Nuclear Deterrence to Climate Change.

There is a great deal of uncertainty in the world today. The world is becoming multipolar. The challenge before India is to ensure that it finds a voice in the changing world. Under Prime Minister Modi, India's foreign policy has been characterised by intense global engagement and several innovations. India is today much respected across the world. India's Act East policy, Neighbourhood First policy, security and growth for all are some of the pioneering initiatives. Defence, security and technology cooperation as well as engagement with the vast

Indian diaspora are some of the hallmarks of the emerging foreign policy. A foundation has been laid for India's deeper and more meaningfull engagement with the world.

Analysing these trends, the VIF is happy to present to the readers a volume titled *India's Foreign Policy and National Security Strategy*, a collection of articles and essays analysing India's foreign and defence policy. The VIF believes that India needs to build an Indian Narrative on these issues which should be based on India's experience and cultural and civilisational values. Two of the eleven essays in the volume deal with these aspects. It is hoped that the readers will like the volume.

Dr Arvind Gupta
Director VIF
New Delhi, August 2018

Editor's Note

Last year Vivekananda International Foundation (VIF) had launched a new publication titled, VIF PERSPECTIVE-*Securing India*, bringing together a compilation of well-researched papers by a group of highly regarded professionals, covering a range of issues of national concern. The objective was to generate and stimulate well-informed debate in shaping strategic opinion.

Encouraged by the overwhelming response of our readers, it was decided not only to continue with this initiative but also to strengthen it further by enlarging and deepening the areas and contents of coverage.

In so doing, we carefully selected a wider range of issues of current relevance that directly or otherwise impact India's quest for emergence as a major power in the subcontinent and beyond, ensuring the wellbeing of its citizens in a peaceful environ, both internally and in the regional context. The challenges faced by India are enormous and multi-faceted but by no means insurmountable.

As we undertake this exercise to examine India's approach to addressing these multi-faceted challenges, it may not be out of place to mention that the present National Democratic

Alliance (NDA) government led by Prime Minister Modi has just completed four years in office with less than one more left to go before the next elections are due in mid-2019. These four years have witnessed new and path-breaking initiatives in almost every area of state activities, both in the internal and external fields.

In the international arena, special mention need be made to the Government's 'Neighbourhood First' policy under the extended concept of 'Sab ka Saath-Sab ka Vikaas', the 'Act East' initiative, building closer ties with major powers like USA, EU, Russia, China, the 'Make in India' campaign, active participation in regional and multi-national fora like the 'Quad', BRICS, BBIN, Shanghai Cooperation Organisation (SCO), interactions in the Middle East and the Gulf, inviting Foreign Direct Investments (FDI), outreach to the Diaspora etc. Even repairing relations with Pakistan was accorded high priority till the western neighbour deliberately derailed the process by escalating the level of trans-border hostilities and militancy well beyond the level of tolerance.

In this issue of the PERSPECTIVE, we have selected some key aspects of the initiatives and their impact in transforming India's policy approaches. In the eleven articles included in this volume, we have started the discussions with Dr Arvind Gupta's article on civilisational impact on the evolution of India's strategic culture and a new Indian narrative. He has argued in favour of India building its own narrative on contemporary issues that combines tradition with modernity.

Continuing on a related theme, Shri S Gurumurthy traces the rules of war in Hinduism and Islam, contending that the Hindu civilisation stands out almost uniquely for its noble war ethics that deeply impact human behaviour in normal times, and in times of war.

The hard power aspects of building a stronger and secure nation, begins with my own assessment on strengthening India's internal security architecture into a robust entity to ensure effective response to terrorism and other destabilising developments like Left Wing Extremism and insurgency in the Northeast.

In the other two article in this section, Gautam Banerjee critically analyses the role, responsibilities and structure of India's Higher Defense Organisation (HDO), highlighting the need for a responsive and contemporised mechanism for better management of national defence and military security. Anil Chopra highlights the need to correlate India's national aspirations and military expenditure to strengthen the military instruments for greater international prestige and fulfilment of its international aspirations.

And finally, discussions on India's diplomatic initiatives and imperatives is led by Kanwal Sibal examining the impact of Prime Minister Modi's 'Neighbourhood First' approach to strengthen peace, tranquillity and prosperity – a policy initiative that will take time to succeed as smaller neighbours will always explore ways to balance disparities in size and power by resisting a close embrace.

Tilak Devasher in an incisive examination of Pakistan's looming water crisis, points out that as its ground water resources dwindle, Pakistan will seek to enhance water extraction on either side of the border and try to pre-empt India from fully harnessing its share of water from its eastern rivers.

Examining the recent developments in Afghanistan, RK Sawhney and Gautam Mukhopadhaya suggest that India should lift its game in Afghanistan through greater commitment to Afghanistan's unity and security, and people-centred investment partnership under an invigorated regional diplomacy.

Moving eastward, in his article on India's 'Act East Policy', Rajiv Sikri argues in favour of building stronger economic relations with ASEAN, expanding it to include security dimension and finally evolving it into a larger Indo-Pacific strategy, essentially to cope with the rise of China which poses significant strategic challenges in India's immediate neighbourhood, including the Indian Ocean region.

Seen in this context, implications of emergence of QUAD (Quadrilateral Security Dialogue) as a new platform for strategic cooperation has been dealt with by Anil Wadhwa who looks at the changed geo-political scenario in the Indo-Pacific region and China's aggressive actions, quest for port acquisition and setting up of bases in the Indian Ocean littoral countries as a major challenge to rules-based order, and a free, open, transparent and balanced Indo-Pacific region.

And finally, Sanjay Singh reviews the situation in West Asia, marred by conflicts in Syria and Yemen, extremist violence and widening sectarian divisions leading to continued regional instability and external interventions by global powers. These are of concern to India, given its extensive economic activities, quest for energy and people-to-people ties with the region.

The final outcome of the study is presented as VIF PERSPECTIVE – *India's Foreign Policy and National Security Strategy*. I gratefully acknowledge the unstinted cooperation of all the authors and reviewers, the editorial team and the core group of support staff without whose tireless efforts this publication would not have been possible.

I would also like to thank the Director, VIF for his abiding trust and support. I would be failing in my duty if I were not to place on record the enormous contribution of my colleagues in the VIF Editorial Committee for their guidance through incisive scrutiny of articles, and the administrative staff for helping me and my team in resolving the glitches as these kept cropping up all through the exercise.

With these words, I commend this VIF PERSPECTIVE for your reading pleasure. I look forward to your comments and suggestions that will help us to further improve our efforts.

CD Sahay
Editor, VIF Perspectives and Senior Fellow, VIF
New Delhi, August 2018

India's Strategic Culture
Need for an Indian Narrative

Arvind Gupta

This paper argues that as India takes its place in the comity of nations, there is a need for it to build its own narrative on contemporary issues. In order to do so, India should delve into its ancient culture, which is a deep reservoir of knowledge and wisdom. It is possible to build a narrative which combines tradition with modernity. The paper further seeks to refute the perception that India lacks a culture of strategic thinking.

India's World View

AS INDIA rises politically and economically the questions being asked are:

What is India's vision for the world?

How can India contribute to world peace and stability?

How will it deal with the tremendous social, economic and political turbulence in this globalised world?

With the conflict between modernity and tradition becoming sharper, materialism and individualism leading to atomisation of society and its institutions, how will India navigate these choppy waters?

These very pertinent questions are being discussed increasingly in academic seminars, conferences and literature. However, the answers are not clear. Many observers continue to remain unconvinced that India has a coherent story to narrate to the world.

The Chinese have unfolded their world view through a series of official documents, presidential addresses and pronouncements followed by roadmaps. Much of this is rooted in the Buddhist precepts, even though it is a communist state. In contrast, despite India having a rich and continuously practiced cultural and philosophical tradition, it is not being applied in terms of national interest under a well thought out strategy.

As India grows and reclaims its place in the comity of nations, there is an imminent need for India to build its own narrative on contemporary issues. People want to understand as to what has India to offer by way of new ideas and concepts in an interconnected world. Till 1991, India had a socialist big economy model for economic growth and development, after which she switched over to the capitalist market economy mould. However, the Indian economic model in practice, which is based on traditional social capital, has yet to win global recognition and has not offered an alternative to existing theories as yet, which can be detrimental to national interest.

Western countries have for long shaped the global narrative for several centuries now, which has been having certain very long-reaching impact and strong influence world over, on Indians as well. China, a rising power, is delving deep into its past and building its grand narrative based on Confucianism, tailored to modern needs. Russians also have an especially Russian narrative of their own. They regard themselves as having been a saviour of Europe in the last one thousand years. A homegrown Indian narrative, which is born out of the native wisdom, rooted in its tradition, based on its value systems, suited to its culture and based on its vast repertoire of literature and philological tenets is imperative. Very often the Indians, influenced by the Western values of materialism and consumerism, are defensive about their own culture, which is more expansive and assimilative. Culture must inform the Indian narrative for it to be convincing.

At the turn of the 20th century, India saw a powerful nationalist movement in favour of the indigenous or *swadeshi*. Many eminent Indian thinkers, Vivekananda, Rabindranath Tagore, Aurobindo, Sister Nivedita, MK Gandhi, KM Munshi, amongst others have emphasised the need for Indian history to be written from an Indian perspective.

Vivekananda wanted Indians to take pride in Hinduism and its universal values and in their culture. He was of the view that on that basis alone new India will arise and awaken.

Rabindranath Tagore talked about the need for writing the history of India from India's perspective. In his address to students and teachers in 1903, titled, 'The History of Bharatvarsha', he said, 'By not viewing Bharatvarsha from Bharatvarsha's own perspective… we get demeaned ourselves… what our ancestors did, this we do not know, therefore we do not know what we ought to aim for'.[1]

Likewise, KM Munshi stressed upon the need for writing Indian history by the Indians. He wrote, 'The central purpose of a history must, therefore, be to investigate and unfold the values which age after age have inspired the inhabitants of a country develop their collective will and express it through the manifold activities of their life. Such a history of India is still to be written'.[1] He lamented that the histories written of India decried the Hindu social system, ignoring the fact that the very same social system developed the tenacity, thus arming the people to 'survive catastrophic changes for millennia'. Strong social system developed in India over a long period imparted the Indian society the resilience and capacity to withstand the changes.

Ananda Coomaraswamy was an ardent cultural nationalist who saw culture as a vehicle for national awakening. He lamented that the Western culture had vulgarised the Indian culture and that the Indian education system had no place for Indian culture. Indian students coming out of the Indian education system were strangers in their own land. He also criticised British authorities for neglecting Indian culture.[3]

Philosopher KC Bhattacharya talked about the need for 'Swaraj in Ideas'. More recently, S Gurumurthy has been a strong supporter of the role of Indian culture in developing an Indian model of economic development.[4] The prevalent notion of secularism has prevented Indians from taking pride in their culture. Gurumurthy quotes Daya Kishan Thussu, Professor of International Communication and Co-Director of India Media Centre at the University of Westminster in London, from his book, *Communicating India's Soft Power: Buddha to Bollywood*: 'In a nutshell, the distinctive characteristics of India's soft power is based on its traditions of public reasoning and religious tolerance, its culture of argumentative heterogeneity and philosophy of peaceful coexistence.'; and further, 'Secular India is afraid of opening the locker of ancient India fearing that the pseudo-secular foundation of Indian secularism will crumble'.[5]

Rajiv Malhotra, an Indian-American scholar, argues that Western scholars, who are aware of the superiority of Indian thought, are engaged in imbibing ideas from Hindu culture without acknowledgment in their own culture and sanitising them by stripping them of their religious and philosophical context.[6]

In the changing situation, the government is conscious of the Indian approach to development. A Cabinet Resolution of 2015 by which NITI Aayog, a think tank and a truly advisory body was set up, talks about the need for finding India's 'own strategy of growth'. It says, 'The new institution has to zero in on what will work in and for India. It has to be a Bharatiya approach to development'. The resolution quotes Mahatma Gandhi, Tiruvalluvar, Deen Dayal Upadhyaya, Sankardev and Ambedkar in the text.[7] In this connection, the concept of 'Social Capital' which encompasses the collective will of people manifested through family, caste, community and mutual association is mentioned. Social capital reduces the reliance on the state to provide social security and thus reduces its burden.[8]

The truth, however, is that we have failed to develop an Indian approach to resolving our problems. Even our history has been written and interpreted in the Western framework. The Western writers who wrote the earlier histories of India, had European history and historical standards as their benchmark. Laudable as some of their efforts might have been to learn Sanskrit and other Indian languages in order to learn about India, their Western biases are visible. While some of them made laudatory references to Indian culture, others have been extremely derogatory. The context of Indology studies of that time was colonialism. Europeans saw themselves in the superior role of civilisers and educationists. They failed to appreciate the variety and depth of Indian philosophy and its richness because these ideas differed from the Western ideas rooted in materialism. Missionaries tried to preach their religion as an adjunct to the colonial rulers. Macaulay wanted to churn out an army of English-speaking *babu*s who would propagate and defend the values of the British Raj.

The result of all this activity was that the history of Indian people written by the Europeans was one-sided, with the ulterior motive of undermining the Indian culture and propagating Western cultural and material superiority. The effort was to enslave the Indian mind by inculcating in the Indians a sense of inferiority vis-a-vis what was regarded as a superior Western culture. It is regrettable that even in post-independent India, there have been few efforts to base Indian policies in Indian culture. The result is that our minds have remained enslaved, in awe of the Western civilisation and its material achievements.

India has been an unbroken and flourishing civilisation for more than 5,000 years. No other civilisation can claim such long continuity. The present-day Greek, Egyptian, and Romans have little in common with their respective ancient civilisation. On the other hand, it is a remarkable fact that Indians relate to their ancient civilisation very well. It is important to understand that the Indian civilisation has not only survived so long but has also contributed significantly to the world culture in philosophy, sciences, religion, architecture and literature. Ancient Indian treatises, like the *Veda*s and the *Upanishad*s and the epics like *Mahabharata* and *Ramayana*, are a fount of ideas. India's soft power is undisputed. Clearly, India has the possibility of delving deep into its past and look for ideas which can be applicable today.

Some people hold the view that looking to a long gone, though glorious, past for solving contemporary problems is a futile and regressive exercise. But this need not be so. The present has been built on the foundations of the past. The past cannot be ignored as it holds lessons for today and tomorrow. A synthesis of cultural past and contemporary present is perfectly possible.

The reality, however, is that many Indians of today's generation, including the educated ones, have precious little knowledge of what India was. They do not have the knowledge of Sanskrit and other classical languages in which these texts were written or spoken. Western education has also decried Indian culture as mumbo-jumbo and inferior to Western culture. This has created a sense of inferiority among Indians about their past. Most Indians do not take pride in their heritage and are quite oblivious of it. This manifests in the great deal of insensitivity of both, the public and the government, towards the archaeological sites that are disappearing fast due to neglect and ignorance. The disappearance of ancient languages, dialects and the entire cultural eco-systems should be a matter of great concern for all Indians.

India has given birth to some of the world's major religions like Hinduism, Buddhism, Sikhism, Jainism etc. The followers of Christianity, Islam, Zoroastrianism, Judaism etc. also live in India without any coercion or constraints. Unlike the principle monotheistic religions of the world, the Hindus have been tolerant in their approach to all religions, having accommodated and assimilated many sects. The culture and religions of the vanquished have been taken in the mainstream Hindu religion. This inclusiveness is a unique aspect of Indian culture. Religions like Buddhism and Jainism arose as a reaction to orthodoxy in Hinduism and yet the Hindus relate positively to these religions. Ancient Hindu thought holds, *Ekam Sat, Vipra Bahudha Vadanti,* that is, 'Which exists is one: Sages call it by various names'. Such an understanding allows for the existence of multiple approaches to the ultimate truth which is one.

In the last century and a half, India has produced many thinkers who argued and contributed to the renaissance of Indian culture, which must continue. The tolerance of the Hindus comes from its strong core, wherein lies the belief that divinity is reflected in every human being, and thus, there is a spiritual connection between every individual. That is why Hinduism has survived for so long. Hinduism is a confident religion with a long tradition of self-reflection, self-correction and assimilation of ideas from other schools of thought. Some resent this tendency in Hinduism to assimilate external influences, as in their view, this dilutes the very essence of Hindu religion. Others feel that the core of Hinduism is strong and assimilation has only helped the religion to survive and flourish and maintain the essential unity of the different sects of the religion.

The unique Hindu qualities of tolerance and assimilation have been noted by many Western scholars. Scholars note that there is unbroken continuity in Indian civilisation since 3,000 BCE at least. A wide variety of belief systems are encompassed within the Hindu religion which respects reason, debate and scholarship. It, therefore, stands to reason that rather than looking for ideas only in Western scholarship, one can turn to this ancient but vast repository of knowledge and wisdom for identifying universal ideas which may provide guidance for solving today's challenges.

The Chinese are turning to the texts written in the era of Warring States, roughly contemporaneous with Kautilya, for ideas on their foreign policy and security. Why cannot India, which has much wider sources to draw upon, do the same?

Sources of Indian Thought: The Indian Narrative

The ancient Hindu texts are a rich source of ideas. The universalism of some of the Indian thinking is striking and has impressed modern philosophers and thinkers. The Vedas, *Brahmana*s and the *Aranakya*s provide the foundation of ancient Indian thought. A brief description follows.[9]

Vedas or Samhitas: These are the most ancient of the Vedic literature. They go back to at least 1100 BCE or even earlier. There are four Vedas or *Samhita*s – the *Rig Veda, Sama Veda, Yajur Veda and Atharva Veda*. Their teachings are considered eternal. They deal with a variety of topics ranging from deep philosophical questions about nature and the universe to rituals and ceremonies.

Brahmanas: These are commentaries on the Vedas. They discuss the meaning of the various concepts propounded in the Vedas. They also go into the recensions of the Vedas. Each of the Brahmanas is associated with one of the Samhitas or its recensions.

Aranakyas: These are associated with the Vedas and the Brahamanas. They deal with rituals, ceremonies and their interpretations. Some of them have philosophical discussions as well.

Upanishads: These are philosophical works of great significance. The teachings of the Upanishads provide the basis of Hindu thought. They speculate over the concept of *atman* – soul, *brahman* – the absolute, what is the origin of the universe etc. Of a vast Vedic corpus, the Upanishads have left deep impact on the Hindu thought.

Vedantas: *Vedanta*s, or the end of the Vedas, reflect ideas that emerged from the speculations and philosophies contained in the Upanishads. It does not stand for one comprehensive or unifying doctrine. Rather it is an umbrella term for many sub-traditions,

Vedangas: They represent the additional fields of study and include many sciences such as phonetics – Shiksha, poetic meter – Chandas, grammar – Vyakarana, etymology and linguistics – Nirukta, rituals and rites of passage – Kalpa, time keeping and astronomy – Jyotisha. All of these have influenced the various schools of Indian philosophy.

Upavedas: Several technical works are included such as Archery – Dhanurveda, associated with the Rigveda; Architecture – Sthapatyaveda associated with the Yajurveda; Music and sacred dance, drama and dance etc. Gandharva veda associated with the Samaveda; Medicine – Ayurveda, associated with the Atharva veda.

Puranas: The *Purana*s are a vast repository of myths, legends, genealogies and lore. There are 18 Maha Puranas – Great Puranas and 18 Upa Puranas – Minor Puranas, with over 400,000 verses. They are considered *Vaidika* – congruent with Vedic literature. The *Bhagavata Purana* has been among the most celebrated and popular text in the Puranic genre. Though mixed with mythology, the Puranas give a glimpse of ancient Hindu India.

Epics: The Ramayana and the Mahabharata are the most celebrated epics of Hindu culture. They have a venerable place in the average Hindu's daily life and influences his or her thoughts deeply. Their importance cannot be overstated. The key takeaways from the Mahabharata are: fight for rights, good prevails over evil and wars have to be fought after planning. The Ramayana lays out the conduct of the king, his subjects, the opponent, the principles of the war etc. The wars for a just cause must be fought, high personal moral standards are a must and good will prevail over evil.

Bhagavad Gita is the finest jewel of Indian thought. Though

a part of the Mahabharata, in the form of a dialogue between Krishna and his friend and disciple Arjuna, the Bhagavad Gita has universal messages for the individual relating to his or her conduct. The importance of Karamyoga – Action, Jnanyoga – pursuit of knowledge and Bhaktiyoga – devotion and surrender to God has been underlined. The Bhagavad Gita has provided guidance to countless generations, influencing some of the greatest thinkers in India and outside. The book distils the basic message of the Vedas and the Upanishads.

Schools of Indian Philosophy: The Hindu philosophy has six major schools, namely, *Vaisesika* of Kanada, *Nyaya* of Gautama, *Samkhya* of Kapila, *Yoga* of Patanjali, *Purva-Mimansa* of Jaimini and *Vedanta* or *Uttara Mimansa* of Vyasa. These are orthodox schools as they follow the authority of the Vedas. Jainism and Buddhism are regarded as heterodox schools because they reject the authority of the Vedas.

Dharamashastras: The rich Dharmasastra literature espouses the moral, ethical and legal code of conduct for the individual as well as for the rulers. The literature can be divided into three categories, namely, *Dharmasutra*s (600 BCE), *Smriti*s (1-800CE) and *Dharmanibandha*s (1100-1800 CE). Several commentaries have also been written on the subject of dharma. The *Dharmasutra* literature is rooted in the Vedas but there are non-vedic dharmasutras also. The examples of dharamsutras of the later kind include *sutras* ascribed to Buddha, Brahaspati, Kanuva etc.[10]

India has long tradition of innovation in political and economic governance. *Manusmriti* (1000 BCE), the oldest such treatise, lays down the code of conduct to be followed by rulers and individuals in different walks of life. It has been signally significant in influencing social, political and economic thought.

Although it has been criticised as being patriarchal, the basic code of behaviour laid down in Manusmriti was logical for the times it was written in. Kautilya's *Arthashastra* and many other subsequent treatises have built upon Manusmiriti.

India has a long tradition of political institutions. India was divided into several republics. They had their way of choosing the monarch and establishing the various institutions of governance. Some of the terms used those days like *Sabha, Samiti, Parishad* etc are current even today. Among major works of political science, *Shanti Parva* of Mahabharata, *Dandaniti* of Usanas, *Arthashastra* of Kautilya, *Nitisara* of Kamundaki, *Viduraniti, Panchatantra, Hitopdesha* etc. can be counted. The *Thirukkural* (1st century BCE) in the Tamil language is often considered the Veda of the Tamils. It draws parallels with the Vedas and Manusmriti.

KP Jayaswal (1881-1937) in his book *Hindu Polity: A Constitutional History of India in Hindu Times*, carried out an extensive study of the growth and evolution of Hindu law, jurisprudence and political systems over centuries. His masterly early 20th century work, based on the study of Vedic literature as well as inscriptional and numismatics records, covers the study of sovereign assemblies in Vedic times, Indian republics, Hindu monarchies, the *Janapada*s and *Mahajanapada*s or regional assemblies etc.[11] He describes at length the characteristics of the political institutions like the king, the council of ministers, and administration of justice, economics and other institutions. Jayaswal mentions several works of antiquity dealing with the principles of governance and politics. He points out that governance was studied much before Kautilya wrote the *Arthashastra* (300 BCE) which mentions the names of at least twenty authors before him.

Vivekananda and Aurobindo

Vivekananda is the major figure who introduced to the West the essentials of Hindu religion, particularly Vedanta, and helped generate a new awareness of Hinduism in the world. His contribution towards the resurgence of Hinduism in modern times is unmatched. He emphasised the primacy of spiritual life, inner strength and the essential unity of all religions. In 1897, he founded the Ramakrishna Math Mission, which reinterpreted Hinduism in contemporary light. Vivekananda introduced the West to the essentials of Hindu thought and helped to generate a new awareness of Hinduism in the world. He believed that Hinduism would give a new spiritual impetus to the world.

Aurobindo's political philosophy could be called spiritual nationalism. He stressed those aspects of Hindu tradition that spoke of spiritual evolution through complete surrender of human consciousness to the Supreme Being.

At the philosophical and psychological level, Hinduism provides a world view in which the universe is a family, *Vasudhaiva Kutumbakam*. The individual is a reflection of the ultimate reality; truth always prevails and the search for truth is paramount. There is non-duality at the level of ultimate reality but multiple ways to reach that reality. The cycle of birth and rebirth continues and the task before the individual is to overcome this cycle. Goals by themselves are unimportant and there is no time frame to arrive at the goals. The primacy of action is established and the attachment to the goals is discouraged. In the Hindu world view nature is to be respected, feared, worshipped and propitiated.

At the social level, the ruler and the ruled have duties to each other. The ruler should rule in accordance to dharma and should take care of the wellbeing and welfare of the people. The duties of every individual are defined in accordance to their skill and capability. The conduct of the ruler should be above board and in accordance with the dharma. Hierarchy is to be respected. But it is not immutable. The Varna system divided the society in accordance to the professions and trades practiced. This was a division based on the considerations of efficiency. The social rigidities that crept into the caste system, bringing in the issue of birth et al happened over a course of time. These were distortions which many social reformers have tried to purge. Casteism is the scourge of Indian society. The efforts to bring social reforms should continue in this direction.

Does India have a Strategic Culture?

It is surprising that with so much of richness and depth in ancient Indian thought, a question is still being asked whether India has a culture of strategic thinking. Tanham (1992), in a study sponsored by RAND Corporation, argued that India had primarily defensive thinking due to the geography, its cultural belief systems, the legacy of British colonialism and India's preference for strategic autonomy.[12] In his opinion, India, unlike China, never had a grand strategy. To be sure, his question was in the context of national security and military power but the debate has expanded to the larger questions about the Indians' ability to think strategically for their country. Tanham did not say that India does not have a strategic culture, but what he said was that Indians have a defensive mindset. However, many analysts interpreted his argument as an assertion that Indians cannot think strategically. Tanham's argument got support from many influential strategic thinkers like K Subramanyam who were frustrated that Indian foreign policy was all defensive, timid and cautious.

However, there have been opposite views too. In 2006, Rodney Jones[13] published a study for Defence Threat Reduction Agency, for their Advanced Systems and Concepts Office, in which he comes to the conclusion that Indians do have a strategic culture with distinctive traits. He wrote, 'India's strategic culture is not monolithic, rather is mosaic-like, but as a composite is more distinct and coherent than that of most contemporary nation-states. This is due to its substantial continuity with the symbolism of pre-modern Indian state systems and threads of Hindu or Vedic civilisation dating back several millennia'. He identified the following elements of Indian Strategic Culture:[14]

Philosophical and mythological foundation

- The sacred permeates the Indian identity;
- Goals are timeless, not time bound;
- India's status is a given, not earned;
- Knowledge of truth is the key to action and power;
- World order is hierarchical, not egalitarian.

Instrumental implications

- India's external visage is enigmatic;
- Self-interest expressed externally is impersonal and absolute;
- Contradictions in the real world are natural and affirmed;
- Force has its place, but guile may trump force;
- Actions have consequences, good intent does not absolve injury;
- Trust is in right knowledge and action, it is impersonal, and hard to build or replenish;
- Security is sedentary, as it encompasses a geographic setting and way of life;

- Strategy is assimilative, where appearances change, reality is constant.

Jones is not the only one to identify the elements of Indian strategic culture. Many people are revising their thinking about Indian culture and thought. Kissinger, in his *World Order* (page 114), devoted several pages to the Hindu concept of the Hindu world order and outlined its important features. Kissinger noted that Hindu cosmology operates on a vast timescale in which kingdoms would rise and fall and universe would be destroyed and recreated. Referring to the Bhagavad Gita, he further noted, 'This central work of Hindu thought embodied both an exhortation to war and the importance not so much of avoiding it but of transcending it. Morality was not rejected, but in any given situation the immediate considerations were dominant, while eternity provided a curative perspective'.[15] He quoted from the Arthashastra, Ramayana, Mahabhararta and Bhagavad Gita to prove his point. The debate in the literature now seems to indicate that most analysts do think that India has a strategic thinking which is defensive. Many argue that an old civilisation could not have survived without having a strategic culture.

India is a multicultural society with a rich tapestry of cultures, languages and thinking. The ancient Indian texts, not just of Hinduism but also of Buddhism and Jainism as well as texts in several languages, provide a vast storehouse of Indian strategic thinking. It is also argued that the Arthashastra is a broad-based treatise on statecraft, some of whose tenets are of universal significance and relevant today. More recently, the works of Vivekananda, Aurobindo and Gandhi have also supported the view that Indians can think strategically.

Ancient Indian thought dwelt at length on the nature of warfare. The Hindu concept of war is very different from the concept of war in the West. In Western history, war has been associated with 'un-relieved barbarism'. In contrast, Kautilya, writing in 3rd century BC, talked about three kinds of victories in war. The first category of victory was *Dharma Vijaya* in which the victor was content with the submission of the defeated and did not eye his territory or wealth. The second category was *Lobha Vijaya* in which the victor gained land and money from the defeated King, and the third category of victory was the *Asura Vijaya* of the barbaric victor who robbed the defeated King of his son, wife or life. According to Gurumurthy, the third kind of victory was 'abhorred and detested in ancient India'.[16] The conquered states were allowed to preserve their political, social and cultural identity. The ancient Hindu texts are replete with emphasis on morality and ethics in warfare.

Even in post-independent India, there is no dearth of examples of Indian strategic thinking. India has fought five wars in the last 70 years. It has been involved in out-of-area contingencies militarily in Sri Lanka and Maldives in the mid-1980s. It has undertaken numerous humanitarian assistance and disaster relief operations in Iraq, Yemen, Libya, Sri Lanka, Nepal and Maldives, and conducted many counter-insurgency and counter-terrorism operation in difficult areas and has been a part of the UN peacekeeping efforts. Non-alignment was a successful strategy adopted to keep India out of the messy Cold War conflicts. Successive Indian prime ministers have displayed a sense of realism to deal with the challenges of security and development. The signing of a nuclear agreement with the US in 2008 was a piece of strategic thinking. The present government's approach to the Indo-Pacific region, the policy of 'Security & Growth for All' or the Act East Policy are also strategic initiatives. Therefore, the criticism that India lacks strategic thinking is untenable.

A Prime Minister Showcases Indian Culture

During his travels and interactions abroad, Prime Minister Narendra Modi has been putting forward the ideas of Indian culture for the world. A notable example of this was India's outstanding success in getting the United Nations General Assembly - UNGA to declare June 21 as International Day of Yoga. This is in recognition of Indian culture and its contemporary relevance. Yoga is spreading fast across the world among all sections of global population. It is the many ideas such as this which forms an Indian narrative.

The PM has frequently mentioned the idea of *Vasudhaiva Kutumbakam* – world is a family in his speeches. Underlying the basic unity of mankind, this is a powerful idea at a time when despite globalisation the world is fragmenting. At the World Economic Forum Summit meeting in Davos in 2018, he said:[17] 'As a representative of India, Indian-ness and Indian heritage, the subject of this forum for me is as contemporary as it is timeless. It is timeless, because in India, from time immemorial we continue to believe in uniting mankind and not in dividing them or creating fissures. In the ancient books, written thousands of years ago in Sanskrit, Indian philosophers have propounded the thesis of *Vasudhaiva Kutumbakam.*[18] It means the whole world is one family. In essence, we all have been joined with each other like a family and our destiny links us with a common thread. Today, this concept of *Vasudhaiva Kutumbakam* is even more relevant in bridging the gaps and distances.'

Modi pointed out how the Indian tradition of respecting and preserving nature is relevant today. On the issue of climate change, the Indian Prime Minister went straight to the heart of the problem – greed-based exploitation of Mother Nature has led to the conflict between man and nature:[19] 'On several occasions, you must have heard of deep synergy with nature in the Indian tradition. In our ancient texts written thousands of years ago, man was described as: *Mata Bhumi, Putro Aham Prithvya* i.e., we the human are children of Mother Earth. Why is there a kind of war between Nature and Mankind if we are the children of mother earth?' He went on to say, 'In the beginning of one of the most important religious texts called Upanishad, a seer has described to his disciples the changing nature of the world: *Tena Tyaktena Bhunjitha*. It means that one should enjoy the worldly pleasures with austerity and one should never covet what belongs to others. Around 2,500 years ago, Lord Buddha has given primacy to the concept of *Aparigraha*, which means using things as per the necessity, in his teachings. The concept of "trusteeship" propounded by Mahatma Gandhi, the father of the Indian nation, was also in favour of using and exploiting things as per the need; he straightaway opposed the idea of greed-based exploitation'.

PM Modi linked the growing wave of protectionism with the philosophy of Gandhi. He said:[20] '....And the growth of global supply chains has also stopped. The solution to this worrisome situation against globalisation is not in isolation. Its solution lies in understanding and accepting the change, it lies in making smart and flexible policies with the changing times. India's Father of the Nation Mahatma Gandhi had said, "I do not want that the walls and windows of my house to be closed from all sides. I want the breeze of the cultures of all the countries to freely move in my house. But at the same time it will not be acceptable to me that this wind blows away my feet off the ground." Following Mahatma Gandhi's this philosophy and contemplation, today's India is welcoming the life-providing waves of the world with full confidence and boldness.'

The Prime Minister invoked the ancient Indian wisdom to say that India will always be a force for harmony: 'Not only this, a predictable, stable, transparent and progressive India will continue to be the good news in an otherwise state of uncertainty and flux.' An India where enormous diversity exists harmoniously will always be a unifying and harmonising force. Not for us, not only for our country, since ancient times the Indian society, the thinkers and sages and monks of India have dreamt that: *Sarve Bhavantu Sukhinaha, Sarve Santu Nirmaya, Sarve Bhadrani Pashyantu, Makashchid Dukha Bhag Bhavet* – which means all of them become happy, all of them are healthy, there is welfare of everybody and nobody should suffer. And they have also shown the path to achieve this ideal and to realise this dream. *Sahnavavatu, sahnaubhunaktu, sahveeryam karvaavahe, tejaswin adhitmastu ma vidvishavahe.* This old Indian prayer, which goes back to thousands of years, means that we all work together, walk together, our talents flourish simultaneously and there is never any hatred between us.

The great Indian poet of the last century and Nobel laureate Gurudev Rabindranath Tagore had imagined such a heaven of freedom, 'where the world has not been broken up into fragments by narrow domestic walls'. Let us together create such a heaven of freedom where there is cooperation and coordination and not divide and fracture. Let us all rid the world of its cracks and unnecessary walls.

Credit goes to PM Modi for having articulated the fundamentals of Indian thinking at the global stage not for pontificating, but for analysing the true nature of today's problems and suggesting ways to tackle them. The ancient Indian thinking, suffused with spiritualism, without discarding materials, stresses on the need for a balance between the two.

A lot is said and written about the Sustainable Development

Goals suggested by the UN. The balance between development and environment is at the core of sustainable development goals. The implementation of these goals is a major task. In the Indian thinking, the King is advised to ensure the *yoga kshema* or the welfare of his subjects. Indeed, that is his primary duty. If all states agree to this basic truth, it should be possible to achieve sustainable development of mankind.

Conclusion

The above survey has sought to show that India has a rich tradition of strategic thinking and it is possible to cull out the kernel of Indian strategic thinking from ancient Indian texts. Indian culture is rich and encompasses a variety of shades besides Hinduism. This survey has been limited to only Hinduism because that is the oldest culture of the land. But, its inclusive nature has accommodated many other shades of thinking which form the composite Indian culture. Buddhism and Jainism are examples. The Tamil Sangam literature is also a rich source of Indian thought. Later on, the Bhakti movement, the Sufi culture, Sikhism and many sects and regional variations have enriched the Indian culture. It is necessary to delve deep into the regional varieties and shades of Indian culture to identify the sources of Indian strategic thinking. It is superficial to say that Indians lack the culture of strategic thinking. It is possible to build a strong Indian narrative based on the values of Indian culture from both the ancient and modern Indian thought.

Sri Aurobindo summed it up aptly:[21] 'India can only survive this new, powerful world with fresh divine creations of her own spirit, cast in the mould of her own spiritual ideals. She must meet it by solving its greater problems, through solutions arising out of her own deepest and largest knowledge.'

References

1 Indian Strategic Thinking: Keynote Address by Dr Arvind Gupta, Director VIF, at Seminar, 'Exploring the Roots on India's Strategic Culture' at IDSA, on October 5,2017, URL: http://www.vifindia.org/directorremarks/keynote-address-by-dr-arvind-gupta.

2 Munshi, KM (1951), 'Foreword' to *Vedic Age* by R. C. Majumdar, Department of Ancient Indian Culture, BharatiyaVidyaBhavan.

3 See, Ananda Coomaraswamy: A Case for Cultural Nationalism in Anirban Ganguly, *Debating Indian Culture*, DK Printworld, New Delhi, 2013, pp.33-42.

4 S Gurumurthy, Case for India Specific Economic Model. Culture and Development, Vivekananda Kendra.

5 S. Gurumurthy, http://www.newindianexpress.com/opinions/columns/s-gurumurthy/2016/nov/19/sri-sri-ravi-shankar-the-soft-power-exponent-of-india-1539708.html.

6 Rajiv Malhotra, *Indra's Net*, Harper Collins Publishers India, pp.12-13.

7 Quoted in S Gurumurthy, 'Case for India Specific Economic Model', *VIF Perspective: Securing India*, Wisdom Tree, New Delhi 2017.

8 Ibid, page 41.

9 See the *Encyclopedia of Hinduism*, India Heritage Research Foundation, Mandala Publications, New Delhi, 2013.

10 See, *Encyclopedia of Hinduism*. Also see PV Kane, History of Dharmashastra,
Bhandarkar Oriental Research Institute, Pune, 1962.

11 KP Jayaswal, *Hindu Polity: A Constitutional History of India in Hindu Times*, Chaukhambha Sanskriti Pratishthan, Delhi, Delhi Edition 2005.

12 Tanham, George K, Indian Strategic Thought: An Interpretive Essay, Santa Monica, Calif.: RAND Corporation, R-4207-USDP, 1992. As of March 08, 2018: https://www.rand.org/pubs/reports/R4207.htmlGeorge K Tanham.

13 Rodney W Jones, India's Strategic Culture, Prepared for: Defense Threat Reduction Agency Advanced Systems and Concepts Office, 2006. https://fas.org/irp/agency/dod/dtra/india.pdf

14 Ibid. p.5.

15 Henry Kissinger, WorldOrder, p.114, URL:https://is.muni.cz/el/1423/podzim2017/MVZ253/um/H_Kissinger_-_World_Order, accessed on April 12, 2018.

16 S Gurumurthy, 'Religious Faith and Modern Civilisation' in Joshi et al. (2008), Transcending Conflicts: Indian and Eastern Way, New Delhi: Global Foundation for Civilisational Harmony (India)., pp. 516-517.

17 Prime Minister's Statement on the subject 'Creating a Shared Future in a Fractured Word' in the World Economic Forum (January 23, 2018), URL:http://mea.gov.in/Speeches-Statements.htm?dtl/29378/Prime_Ministers_Keynote_Speech_at_Plenary_Session_of_World_Economic_Forum_Davos_January_23_2018.

18 This phrase originally appears in the Maha Upanishad (VI.71-73), a minor Upanishad belonging to the so-called group of Visnu Upanishads. I thank Dr Arpita Mitra of VIF for drawing my attention to this.

19 Ibid.

20 Ibid.

21 *Complete works of Sri Aurobindo*, Vol. 20, P - 43

Hinduism: The Noble Rules of War

Their Impact on Indian Civilisation

S Gurumurthy

In history, the best in peoples, cultures, religions may manifest in normal times but their worst manifests in times of war. Nothing is more explicitly indicative of the civility and nobility or barbarism and inhumanity of a civilisation than the war ethics which it had followed or the lack of it. In the Western paradigm war is the time when everything, right or wrong, is considered fair. This is where the Hindu civilisation stands out almost uniquely with its noble war ethics. Therefore, as to why the Indian civilisation faced invasions and defeats at hands of Islamic conquerors can be answered only through study of the power of religion over human behaviour in normal times, and in times of war.

Hindu Theological and Philosophical Position on War

TO ANSWER the question as to why the Indian civilisation faced invasions and defeats at the hands of various Islamic conquerors, a study of the powerful drive of religion over human behaviour in normal times and particularly in times of war is warranted. In the Western paradigm, war is the time when every wrong thing is considered fair. This is where the Hindu civilisation stands out almost uniquely with its noble war ethics—which it followed until almost the CE 16/17 Century.

Particularly at a time in the history of all civilisations when wars were mere expressions of barbaric qualities in human endeavours, if a civilisation had high ethical standards for wars and had by consensus enforced them, then it had to be something very different from the civilisations elsewhere. The Hindu civilisation rested on soft power rather on hard power. It, in a way, ignored hard powers save with the exception of Chanakya and Chandragupta in the distant past and Samarth Ramdas and Chhatrapati Shivaji in the recent past. The trust on soft power and the neglect of hard power was at a cost.

There are two aspects to this discussion. What is the traditional theological and philosophical position on wars and war ethics in the Hindu civilisation as compared to the relative position of the Abrahamic civilisation, particularly the Islamic position? Second, how was the actual conduct of the Hindu civilisation as compared to the Abrahamic on the battlefield? This will hold key to the question why the Indian civilisation lost out on the battlefield so often, particularly in the initial stages of the Islamic invasion.

War as 'unrelieved barbarism' in Western History

A leading work on the nature of laws of war commenced the discussion on the rules of war in ancient and modern Western history, thus: 'There is evidence that some ancient civilisations prohibited certain methods of warfare: agreements on the treatment of the prisoners of war were concluded in Europe around 1400 BC. The Manu Laws of India prohibited, around 500 BC, the use of poisoned weapons and other inhumane methods [citing 'A Swedish Working Group study of Conventional Weapons, their Deployment and Effects from Humanitarian Aspects, Recommendations for the Modernisation of International Law, Stockholm 1973, 11']. But elsewhere, barbaric practices often accompanied victory in war. The maxim '*vae victis*' implied that the vanquished nation could expect little mercy.'[1]

The *Encyclopedia Britannica*, obviously ignoring or unaware that noble rules of war existed in history outside Europe, thus described the state of the rules of war in ancient times, 'In early history, war appears to have been a matter of almost unrelieved barbarity. Practically no restraints were observed in methods of war; there was little discrimination between combatant and non-combatant; and torture, slavery, death, and confiscation of property awaited conquered forces and population'.[2]

So, wars were never confined to just an issue between combatants and anything—be it property, temple or other assets and anybody including women and children—belonging to the enemy were the targets. The Encyclopedia goes on further to say: 'Yet the identifiable features of the present law can be traced back to the ancient times in different parts of the world. As a rule, however, the mitigating features of the law represented only an ideal and so it was actually applied only during wars between kindred peoples or like civilisations. Such were the conditions that persisted through ancient times into Middle Ages, until, prompted by religion and ideas of chivalry on the one hand and by the increase of rationalist and humanist sentiment on the other, a substantial body of law had come into being by the late middle ages. Such laws governed certain aspects of war, at least among fellow religionists. Most noteworthy of these early laws was the insistence that prisoners, if they were Christians captured by Christians, could no longer be enslaved.'[3]

What the Encyclopedia regards as mitigating features were confined to merely an agreed restraint against enslavement of the prisoners of war and it was restricted to only Christian prisoners of war captured by Christian victors! It was more a clannish restraint founded on religious identity. So, it was at best an intra-Christian dictum, with the barbaric rules being continued to apply to non-Christians.

On the other hand, when we examine the Hindu paradigm of war, we find it conceptualised and institutionalised the noblest rules of war and integrated it with the acceptability of the state, which observes the rules and delegitimises a state which deviates from it. While the Western-Abrahamic concept of war is victory at any cost, the Hindu rules of war postulate that victory obtained by the noble rules of war was only celebrated and the victory obtained by unethical methods was never accepted, decried as unmeritorious, while barbarism in wars was unknown.

Introduction to the Hindu Concept of War & Victory

It may be stated with conviction, that the concept of war and victory in ancient Hindu civilisation is in total contrast to what the Western civilisation bears testimony to, based on an entirely different philosophy and outlook.

Ancient Hindu texts had classified conquests into three types: Namely, *Dharma Vijaya* [ethical victory]; *Lobha Vijaya* [lustful victory]; and *Asura Vijaya* [barbaric victory]. *Dharma*

Vijaya, that is victory obtained by ethical rules, was the ideal which the Hindu kings were expected to follow and they usually did, says AL Basham in his famous work, *The Wonder That Was India*.[4] The basis of *Dharma Vijaya*, ethical victory, is *Dharma yuddha*, that is, ethical warfare. Unless the warfare is ethical, the victory cannot be ethical. The essence of *Dharma yuddha*, which leads to *Dharma Vijaya* is that, 'in the convention of *Dharma yuddha*, the adversary is never taken unawares', says Balshastry Haridas in his seminal work, the *Glimpses of Vedic Nation*.[5] This is totally in contrast to the traditional and even modern war rules of elsewhere in the world. The contours of what constitutes *Dharma yuddha* as set out are:

- if the adversary had no shield, he was never attacked; the fight took place between two persons who had the same weapons;
- if one was a horseman, he would never think of attacking a charioteer;
- when an adversary was injured, he ceased to be an enemy and he was attended to as an injured;
- it was considered a disgrace for a warrior to stoop down or abandon the morals of his profession;
- for a warrior, death is considered to be preferable to ignominious victory;
- the belief was that, victory which is built upon fraud, treachery, betrayal or cheating would entail, at some time, total destruction of the family and the dynasty;
- the captives – men, women, and girls – would be unmolested;
- after one year these prisoners were permitted to return to their homes;
- even slaves in the war and plunder of wealth were

expected to be returned to the rightful owners after a lapse of one year;

- the victorious kings were never permitted to plunder the wealth of the defeated people, destroy their properties, and occupy their territories; and so on.[6]

At the outset, these illustrative norms are adequate to capture the quality and character of wars in ancient India. Even the Great Ashoka's Kalinga War was in terms of the Hindu rules of war, an unrighteous war and victory. On the basis of the concept of *Dharma yuddha* as understood in ancient Hindu texts, Balshastry Haridas refers to Prof VR Ramachandra Dhiksitar's seminal work, *War in Ancient India,* where on the question about Ashoka's repentance, Dhikshitar asks: What is that repentance except that he waged in Kalinga an unrighteous war involving the slaughter of innocent; and that he took a vow from that day to resort only to righteous war.[7] Thus, on the test of what is *Dharma yuddha* even Ashoka's Kalinga war, despite his claims that his victory was *Dharma Vijaya*, is not regarded as such.

The great Indian treatise on statecraft, *Arthashastra* written by Kautilya Chanakya who, at times, is wrongly bracketed with (Machiavelli), explained the qualitative difference between the three victories, thus: First, *Dharma vijayin*, the ethical victor, is the one who is satisfied with mere submission or obeisance of the defeated king; Second, *Lobha vijayin*, the lustful victor, is the one who is satisfied with gain in land and money from the defeated king; Third, *Asura vijayin*, the barbaric victor, is the one who is not satisfied with land and money of the defeated king only, but robs the defeated king of his son, wife and life. This being barbaric was abhorred and detested in ancient India. *Nitivyakhyamrta*, an ancient Indian exposition of rules of justice, defines the three categories of conquests almost in the same words. This shows that, in the first two kinds of conquests, the conquered states retained their own institutions, organisations and governments undisturbed by conquests. Ashoka characterises his war and conquest as *Dharma Vijaya*, ethical victory. Likewise, Pravarasena II and Samudragupta's conquests are all noted as *Dharma Vijaya*.[8]

In the ancient Hindu civilisation, on the accepted principles of war morality and war ethics that was only considered legitimate, a king could not wage a war against another simply because he had a large army. A king could wage war with another king only if the other had misbehaved with his people or for similar justifiable reason. He could not wage war merely to conquer. Kings aspiring to be called *Samrat* or *Chakravartin* or Emperor performed the *Rajasuya* and *Ashwamedha Yagnas* in ancient times.[9]

The Ashwamedha Yagna is the horse sacrifice. At the start of the Yagna, the horse is worshipped and then allowed to roam all over the country for one year, protected by an army and when it returns safely after doing so, the Yagna is completed and the king who performs the Yagna becomes the Emperor – *Samrat*. If anyone stops the horse *en route,* it is only then that war endues. There are records of this. For instance, a general by name Udayachandra, of Nandivarma Pallavamalla about ninth century AD, defeated Prithvivygraha, King Nisadha who had accompanied the horse in a horse sacrifice.[10] The Pallava King Sivaskandavarman of Kanchipuram in Southern India, 70 km from Chennai, performed the *Agnistoma*, *Vajapeya* and the *Ashwamedha Yagnas*.[11] The historic data of kings who performed *Ashwamedha* Yagna and other sacrifices are given in the magnum opus, *The History of Dharma Shastra* (Ancient Indian and

Medieval Religious and Civil Law, Government Oriental Series Class B No 6, by the late Dr Pandurang Vaman Kane, Bandarkar Oriental Research Institute, Pune, 1973 Vol III).[12]

India's Ethical Rules of War vis-à-vis the West's

The wars in ancient Hindu tradition were, thus, based on high and noble principles. And this high ethical underpinning to wars was integrated to the concept of a geographical, cultural and political India founded on the principle of '*Dharma*', which existed and functioned in India from ancient times. '*Dharma*: The essentially untranslatable Sanskrit word for one of the central principles of Indian religions, covering the ideas of cosmic, natural and social order.'[13] The rules of war were an integral part of *Rajdharma,* statecraft, which was in turn integral to the overarching concept of Dharma. Dharma constituted the normative social, religious and political order in Hindu civilisation, and it was founded on the principle of duty, individual and collective. The discussion here is however limited to the rules of *Dharma* in wars.

The origin of ethical rules of war is in the *Rig Veda*, the most ancient Hindu text in the world. 'The Rig Veda sets down the rules of war [at 6-75:15] and says that a warrior will go to hell if he breaks any of them.

- do not poison the tip of your arrow;
- do not attack the sick or old;
- do not attack a child or a woman;
- do not attack from behind.[14]

The Mahabharata, one of the most ancient Hindu epic, lists certain rules of war agreed between the combating sides, – such as one warrior should fight only with someone on the other side similarly equipped, one should not kill a soldier who is already in combat with another, or who has turned his back from fight or one who is without armour. Similar position is commended by intellectual and moral authorities – rishis – like Apasthamba, Gautama, Yajnavalkya, Manu, Sankha, Baudhayana, Brhat-Parasara, Sukra and *itihasa*s [texts] like Ramayana and in Shanti Parva, Drona Parva, Karna Parva, Sauptika Parva volumes of the Mahabharata.

Some of these will bear comparison with the conventions of Geneva and The Hague conferences.[15] The forbidden actions in war are: not killing any one who has lost his horse, charioteer, or weapons, turns away from battle, sits down, climbs a tree in flight etc, citing Rishi Gautama, an ancient Hindu law giver.[16]

More, one should not fight with treacherous weapons, or with barbed or poisoned weapons, weapons with points of blazing fire; not fight one who runs away, or folds his hands, or is sleeping, or is naked or disarmed, or is seriously wounded, or whose weapons are broken, or is merely an onlooker or is not taking part in the battle, or is in fear or has turned to flee; not kill or fight one who is taking water or meals, or taking off his shoes, nor kill a woman or female elephant, nor a charioteer, nor should one who is not a king kill a king—citing Manu, the foremost Hindu law giver.[17]

Baudhayana, another famous law giver, and Shanti Parva of Mahabharata forbid the use of poisoned or barbed arrows. Shanti Parva stipulates that the wounded soldier should be treated with medicine and should be allowed to go when he is healed. These rules, though ideal and not probably followed in every case, are more humane as compared to modern warfare.[18]

In ancient times, non-combatants were not molested, to which Megasthenes bears testimony when he says, 'tillers of soil even when the battle is raging in the neighbourhood are undisturbed by any sense of danger, for the combatants allow those engaged in husbandry to remain quite unmolested'.

The rule of war in *Gada yuddha* [mace fight] was that no blow was to be struck below the naval, a rule which Bhima violated when he struck Duryodhana with his mace in his thigh. At the end of Mahabharata war, Duryodhana recounts all bad deeds of Krishna and the Pandavas to which Krishna responds with the numerous breaches of war morality such as slaying of Abhimanyu by many engaging him at the same time, contrary to the rule that battle has to be one-to-one between equals.[19] But these were breaches of the ethics on both sides, the ethics being acknowledged to be legitimate.

The rules of Hindu warfare observed in the battle field summarised from the different texts referred against each in *War In Ancient India* by VR Ramachandra Dhikshitar[20] are:

1. A warrior in armour should not fight with a warrior who is not clad in mail – [Mahabharata. Shanti Parva 95.7];
2. One should fight with only one enemy; and should stop fighting when the opponent becomes disabled. [Ibid];
3. If the enemy is clad in mail, his opponent should put on armour. Chap IV. 91. [Ibid. 96.3];
4. A cavalry soldier should not attack a warrior on a chariot, but a warrior on a chariot could attack a warrior on a chariot. Similarly a cavalry-man could resist another cavalry-man. The general rule is that warriors should fight with only their equals [Ibid. 8-9];
5. Poisoned or barbed arrows should not be used [Ibid 10];
6. A weak or wounded man should not be killed [Ibid 11];
7. He, whose weapon is broken or whose bow-string is cut or who has lost his chariot should not be hit [Ibid 12];
8. A warrior who requests to be excused saying, 'I am

thine', or joins his hands in supplication, or throws off his weapon, must not be killed. But he can be captured as a prisoner of war [Ibid 96.3];

9. A king should fight with only another king and should not fight with warriors of inferior status [Ibid 96.7];
10. If a Brahmin enters the field to bring about peace between contesting parties, both should stop fighting. And no injury should be inflicted upon such a Brahman [Ibid 8];
11. Aged men, women, children, the retreating, or one who holds a straw in his lips as a sign of conditional surrender should not be killed [Ibid 98.70-72];
12. The panic-stricken and scattered foe should not be hotly pursued [Ibid 74. *Boudhayana Dharma sutra* 1.10.8];
13. No one should kill the sleepy or the thirsty, or the fatigued, one whose armour has slipped, a peaceful citizen walking along the road, one engaged in eating or drinking, the mad and the insane, one who went out of the camp to buy provisions, a camp follower, menials and the guards at the gates [Ibid 100.27-9; Manu VII. 92];
14. In case of insufficient supply of numbers in a particular division or divisions in the army, substitutes may be used. An elephant may be opposed by five horses or fifteen men and four horses; one horseman may be opposed by three footmen; and three horsemen by one elephant rider [Agni Purana 242.38];
15. It is forbidden to kill a Brahman by caste or by profession, or who declares himself to be a Brahman, or cow or an out-caste [Gautama X];
16. He should not be killed who gets upon an eminence or tree, who is eunuch or a war musician [Manu VII. 90.93] *Silappathikaram*, a Tamil classic, refers to

warriors escaping from the battle field in disguise. Most of them were allowed to run away, though some of them were captured and sent off to far off lands. When these captives were presented before the Pandya and Chola kings they spoke disparagingly of Senguttuvan, the Cheran King, as having transgressed the limits of fair fighting [Silappathikaram XXVI];

17. It is further prohibited to fight those who do not offer to fight, who hide themselves in fear or who go to the field as spectators [Ramayana: Yuddha kanda 80.39] Mahabharata also affords ample proof that spectators were admitted into the battle field during the scene of action and they were not injured or harmed;
18. Fruits, flower gardens, temples and other places of worship were left unmolested [Agni Purana 236.22];
19. Megasthenes who was in India in the 4th century BC says: 'Whereas among other nations it is usual in the contests of war to ravage the soil and thus reduce it to an uncultivable waste, among the Indians, on the contrary, by whom husbandmen are regarded as a class that is sacred and inviolable, the tillers of the soil, even when the battle is raging in the neighbourhood, are undisturbed by any sense of danger, for combatants on either side in waging the conflict make carnage of each other, but allow those engaged in husbandry to remain quite unmolested. Besides they neither ravage an enemy's land with fire nor cut down its trees.';
20. Nor would an enemy coming upon a husbandman at work on land do him any harm, for men of this class being regarded as public benefactors, are protected from all injury [Arthashastra XIII.4];

21. Prisoners of war were generally accorded generous treatment. Sometimes the captive agreed to become the slave of the captor for a period of one year after which he became a free man. [Mahabharata. Shanti Parva 96.4-5];
22. If maidens were among the prisoners of war they were courteously treated and were induced to marry persons of the captors' choice. If they declined the offer, they were sent back to their homes under proper escort. [Shanti Parva 96.5] In the recent Vijayanagar Empire history, Krishnadevaraya returned the wife of the defeated Gajapati ruler. [Sewell. *A Forgotten Empire* p. 320];
23. Usually the defeated king was reinstated on the throne. But if the enemy king had met with his death in battle, his son or nearest relative was installed on the throne on terms of being a subordinate alliance. [Arthashastra VII ch 16; Manu VII. 202 ff];
24. The subjects of the vanquished monarch were allowed to retain their own laws and customs [Ibid XIII.ch5];
25. The conqueror in most cases was satisfied with the acknowledgement of his overlord-ship and did not trouble himself as long as his sovereignty was not challenged [Vishnu Purana III 30-31; Jayaswal: *A History of India* AD 150 to AD 350];
26. A wounded opponent should either be sent to his own home or if taken into the victor's quarters, he should have his wounds attended to by skilled surgeons. After he gets well cured he should be set at liberty [Shanti Parva 95.17-18] Women were appointed to nurse the wounded. In the camp, were found surgeons with surgical instruments, machines, remedial oils, and bandage cloth handy, in their possession. After

defeating the enemy the victor should show mercy to them and sympathise with them by comforting them, taking hold of their hands affectionately and even shed tears before them so as to secure their devotion. [Shanti Parva 102.34-39] This was true of the soldiers of his own army or of the enemy [Ibid 95.17-18];

27. It was a custom to fight during the day and cease fighting during the night. This was also the practice in the Mahabharata war and a practice in all righteous wars. According to Clausewitz [Vol. 1 p 231] when the army retired for rest, all feelings of animosity were to be suspended and both the contending parties were to behave like allies.

Such noble rules of war could neither be conceived in the West of Greco-Roman times, nor that had turned Christen. Even the modern rules of war lag behind the rules of ancient Indian rules of war. The story of nobility of the Hindu civilisation's rules of war does not end here and goes further to how the defeated kings and defeated nations and peoples are to be treated under the rules of war followed by Hindu civilisation.

Conquests are Ethical, Conquered King continues to Rule

What about the treatment of the conquered kings, and his country and the people in ancient Hindu warfare? *Dharma Vijaya* or ethical conquest, consists in persuading other kings to pay obeisance to avoid wars. It is also considered *Dharma Vijaya* when after a war the defeated king is returned his throne by the victor with honour. In ancient Hindu texts, the second kind of conquests, the *Lobha Vijaya* or the lustful victory in which the conquered king was robbed of his wealth and territory, was not spoken of highly and the last one, *Asura Vijaya* or barbaric victory where the conquered king was robbed of his wife, son and family was completely unacceptable. That is why the Indian tradition including the Puranas are full of stories of battle against *Asura*s who aspired for or achieved *Asura Vijaya*. The Hindu civilisation distinguished between different categories of victory or conquests based the ethics of warfare which it had commended. Since wars were fought on the basis of strict norms, the result of the wars, the conquests, too were not different. As the wars were ethical, the conquests and victories could only be ethical and not otherwise.

The Mahabharata holds up a high ideal of ethical victory. In Bhishma Parva of Mahabharata, it is said that, 'conquerors do not secure victory so much by their army and prowess as by truthfulness, freedom from cruelty and observance of dharma and energetic actions'. Shanti Parva states that, 'it is better to die rather than obtain victory by wicked actions'. Even Kautilya says that the conqueror should not covet the territory, wealth, son, and wife of the slain in the battle; that he should reinstate the son of the deceased king on the throne of his father; that the emperor who kills or imprisons the kings that submit, and covets their lands, wealth, sons, or wives provokes the circle of states and makes them rise against himself.

Rishi Yagnavalkya, another ancient Hindu law giver, stipulates that it is the duty of the conqueror to protect the conquered country in the same way as he does his own country and the conqueror is to respect the customs of the conquered country, its laws and the uses of the families in the country. *Visnudharma sutra*, a law text, enjoins upon the conqueror not to uproot the usages of the conquered country, to establish in its capital some kinsman, of the slain king and not to destroy the royal family unless it be of low birth. Manu is identical in his views. Shanti Parva in Mahabharata and Katyayana, another law giver, commend that even when the vanquished king is at fault, the conqueror should not ruin the country for the fault of the vanquished since he did not commit his wrong doings with the consent of this subjects. *Rajnitipaksha,* another law text, draws from this conclusion that the ministers with whose consent the war was started may be harassed by the conqueror.

Sukranitisara, yet another law text, requires the conqueror to support the well-behaved son and the queen of the vanquished king or to give a fourth of the conquered kingdom to him and only 1/32 part of it to the kin, who is not endowed with good qualities, but the conqueror may appropriate the whole treasury of the conquered.[21] This is what Agni Purana, one of the 18 Puranas, says on the duties of the victorious king: The victorious king should honour the defeated king and treat him as his own son. He should not fight with him again. The wives of the defeated king would not belong anyone else, but to the defeated king. The wives of the defeated king should be protected by the conquering king. The victorious king should honour the customs and manners of the conquered country.[22]

The advice to re-install the vanquished kings was generally followed by ancient conquerors and emperors. Rudradaman (150 AD) was known as the establisher of kings who had lost their territories to him. Samudragupta was famed for having re-established several royal families that had lost their kingdoms to him.[23] Likewise the treatment of war widows and women of the hostile kingdom in ancient times were generally in conformity with the traditions captured in the ancient literature. Chhatrapati Shivaji who had to fight unconventional, guerilla warfare against the Islamic rule which was annihilating Hinduism, maintained highest standards in treatment of the women of the defeated kingdoms, and also in respecting the religious sentiments of the people.[24] Likewise, Prithviraj Chauhan treated Mohammed Ghori in the same way the Hindu traditions commanded him to treat defeated kings.[25] Undoubtedly, the war ethics of the Hindu civilisation demonstrated the highest human values which are not adhered to in the modern world today. In a bygone era where winning wars by any means, particularly in the name of God or religion was considered not only justifiable but also mandatory, the Hindu civilisation maintained highest standards in wars and generally never deviated from its ethics of war. Even modern global war conventions fall short of the standards which the Hindu civilisation had set for itself and practised, even when it faced Islamic and later colonial forces.

Hindu War Ethics Unparalleled

In the introduction to his work, *The Wonder that Was India*, AL Basham says, after severely indicting India, which was admittedly 'a cultural unit', for the 'internecine wars', 'cunning and unscrupulous' state craft of its rulers, 'flood, famine, and plague' that killed 'millions of people', 'inequality of birth' with 'religious sanction' where the lot of the humble was generally hard: Yet our overall impression is that in no other part of the world were the relations of man and man and of man and the state, so fair and humane. In no other early civilisation were slaves so few in number and no other ancient law book are their rights so well protected as in the *Arthashastra*. No other ancient law giver proclaimed such noble ideals of fair play in battle as did Manu. In all her history of warfare Hindu India has few tales to tell of cities put to the sword or the massacre of non-combatants. The ghastly sadism of kings of Assyria, who flayed their captives alive, is completely without parallel in ancient India. There was sporadic cruelty and oppression no doubt, but, in comparison with conditions in other ancient cultures, it was mild. To us the most striking feature of ancient Indian civilisation is its humanity.[26]

Incorrect Notion that Hindus were Never a Nation-State

Integral to the theory and practice of Hindu warfare, it is necessary to dispel the impression that the Hindus had no concept of nation or state and therefore they did not engage in warfare of the kind which the other civilisations engaged in. This is required for the limited purpose of establishing that the Hindu civilisation not only thought far ahead of the Christian and Islamic civilisations, but also had in practice and in place, a pan Hindu and pan-Indian state. This is so, because unless the fact of the Hindu civilisational concept of a State is established, wars within the Hindu civilisation would be regarded and even dismissed as merely an intra-civilisational and inter-Hindu tribal clashes. The idea of a super state federating or affiliating under it large number of smaller states was known to Hindu civilisation; but it was qualitatively different from the present concept of nation-state that evolved in the last few centuries in Europe. The present idea of nation state is just couple of centuries old. In the modern sense no nation-state existed earlier.[27]

In ancient India, the idea of suzerainty extending over many kingdoms was known in times of even the Rig Veda[28] and had been fully developed before the composition of the ancient texts of *Aitareya Brahmanas* and *Saptaha Brahmanas*. The first one mentions the names of twelve emperors of ancient India and the latter thirteen. Another ancient text, *Amarakosa*, states that a king before whom all feudatories humble themselves is called a *Chakravartin* - [Emperor]. The word *Chakravartin* was derived by Kshirasvamin as 'the one who wields lordship over a circle of kings or who makes the circle i.e., a kingdom, abides by his orders'. The word *Chakravartin*, though not as old as *Sarvabhauma*, is as old as the Upanisads.

Yet another ancient Hindu text, *Maitri Upanishad* mentions a list of fifteen *Chakravartins*! Kautilya defines the land of the *Chakravartin* as the territory on the earth spreading towards the north from the sea to the Himalayas which is thousand yojanas – [a yojana is equal to 1.6 kms] when measured as a crow flies. The same idea occurs in another text of equal antiquity *Kavyamimamsa,* written by Rajasekhara. Shanti Parva in Mahabharata speaks of a ruler who brings the whole earth under one umbrella.

This ideal of *Chakravartin* was set before them by all ambitious and energetic Indian rulers from ancient times. The result was that constant wars took place. A galaxy of historical emperors – Chandragupta, Ashoka, Pusyamitra, Bhavanaga, Pravarasena Vakataka, Samudragupta, Harsha – emulated such mythical heroes and emperors as Mandhata and Bharata and practically realised this ideal.[29] Thus, wars were unavoidable in ancient times. But, these wars were not tribal warfare like in most other civilisations. They were based on principles broadly recognised as *dharma* in the Indian civilisation. Also the wars were not between tribal chieftains but between established kingdoms based on high principles of moral and ethical principles and rule of law. (emphasis added).[30]

The geography of the Indian civilisation was also defined in the ancient Hindu texts. *Matsya Purana* first gives the dimensions of *Bharatavarsha* from South to North, from Kanyakumari to the origin of the River Ganga, as one thousand yojanas equivalent to 1,600 kms, when measured upwards across the boundaries, and that on all its borders *Mlecchas*, *Yavanas* and *Kiratas,* approximately meaning aboriginal people, dwell to its east and west and that the King who conquerered the whole of *Bharatavarsha* was a *Samrat.*[31] The same description is found in *Brahmanda Purana* almost in the same words in Chapter 16. The date of *Brahmanda Purana* is estimated to be earlier to 700-1000 AD.[32]

Sukaranitisara (I.183-87), another ancient Indian text, graded kingdoms starting from *Samanta* which had an income of 1-3 lakhs of karsas collected without oppressing the people, at the lowest level to *Rajan*, to *Maharaja*, to *Samrat*, to *Virat*, to *Sarvabhauma* who wielded suzerainty over the whole of the earth, meaning Bharatavarsha, and had an income of 11-50 crores equally qualitatively good revenue not collected by oppression.[33] The general view prevalent among West-centric historians that the Hindu civilisation never organised itself into an empire is not a correct presentation of the Hindu civilisational or political history. There is every reason why the Indian models of statecraft and war rules should be regarded as worthy of being cited or benchmarked and compared to the war rules of others in the Western world.

Kautilya's Advocacy of Acquisitive Wars Unethical?

Basham's view on Arthashastra as a treatise that encourages empire-building is not unfounded, 'The whole work is written for a king who aspires to become an emperor on the Mauryan model, and such a king is not advised to embark on war lightly. There are many ways of gaining power, intrigue and assassination being options among them, and these should always be resorted to in preference to war, which should only be looked on as a last resort. If the king suffers defeat, he must submit in the hope that he will be allowed to retain his throne as a vassal and ultimately again achieve independence and conquer his former overlord. The Arthashastra says nothing about fair play in battle, and evidently looks on conquest of the demonic variety as the most profitable and advisable. Though in one passage, not in keeping with the main tenor of the work, it suggests allowing the conquered king to remain as a vassal, it ends on a note of humanitarian imperialism. The victor must do everything in his power to conciliate the conquered people; if their economy has suffered badly from the war, taxes must be remitted; ministers of the defeated king must be won round, and law and order restored as quickly as possible; when in the conquered country the king should wear the local dress and follow the local customs. Evidently, from the point of view of Arthashastra, the main motive of war is gain and buildup of a great empire'.[34]

Basham's proposition that Arthashastra advocated conquest which was the *Lobha Vijaya* or conquest for greed is correct as that is what sanctions conquest and annexation. But, the most significant point to note is that Arthashastra never accepted barbaric warfare or *Asura Vijaya* which was the accepted war model of all other civilisations[35] But even the rules of Arthashastra which sought a compromise between *Dharma Vijaya* and *Asura Vijaya*, were rejected within a couple of centuries of the emergence of Kautilya's treatise by the mainline Hindu scholars charging that the Arthashastra prescriptions were 'wicked'. The more orthodox texts, according to Basham, take a different view, different from Arthashastra. According to them, 'the major motive of war is glory, not gain; further homage and not annexation was the rightful fruit of victory'.[36]

As Basham had mentioned, Kautilya's Arthashastra which justified the means by the ends, never became legitimate and in fact was de-legitimised in the first half of seventh century itself. Kautilya seems to be the follower of the dictum of Brhaspati who held that there was a difference between the code for the ordinary man and that for the King. A strong State being absolutely necessary for the administration of the country, Kautilya commends 'all kinds of sinister methods' for 'liquidating the enemy such as 'intrigues, unscrupulous use of poison, desperadoes and prostitutes, magic and charms'. 'His motto seems to have been that the ends justified the means. This earned for him the hatred of scholars like Bana'.[37]

A striking aspect of the Hindu civilisation is that, thanks to critiques such as *Kadambari Bana*, Kautilya's commendations on *Rajdharma* and war, justifying means through ends, did not make great impact on the Indian psyche and slowly it ceased to be a popular and acceptable work. The authority says: 'In the *Kadambari Bana,* first half of the 7th century, we have a striking reference to Kautilya's treatise as a cruel work' because it contains advice that is 'very wicked'. This shows how Kautilya's work had already become unpopular in North India, before the first half of the 7th century, on account of its vigorous advocacy that end justified the means. This explains to some extent the paucity of manuscripts of the Arthashastra in the whole of India, particularly in North India, from where only a fragment of the manuscript of the work has been recovered. There is probably a reference to the Kautilya by the author of the *Matsya Purana* on the issue of wrong war models. If this is to be accepted, Arthashastra would have to be pushed back at least some centuries before 250-300 AD the probable date of *Matsya Purana.*[38]

Noble Rules of War Impeded Empire-building in India

Unlike in the Greek-Roman history or in the Abrahamic tradition or in the Hellenistic-Abrahamic mix, sovereignty in ancient India had a different meaning, and that could be the basis of the Western historians' misreading of ancient India. Sovereignty in the ancient Hindu tradition did not invariably or necessarily result in acquiring control over vassal kings in all their affairs. Generally the supreme ruler did not hanker after territory as much as having his superior prowess acknowledged.[39] In this sense the ancient Indian State, at the pan-Indian level – that is what was then known as Bharatavarsha – was a loose, but clearly acknowledged cultural and political identity, rather than a nation-state in the modern sense of the term. In this sense, the position of the comparatively less rigid Holy Roman Empire, even though in intimate religious association with the dispensation of the Roman Catholic Church, may be drawn as a parallel without, of course, the binding authority of the Roman Catholic Church.

Henry Kissinger[40] traced the development of the political Europe from the medieval times, says that even with the overall supremacy of the Roman Catholic Church as the umbrella, the Holy Roman Empire could not achieve central control as a result of which the different states could turn independent over a period. The *Chakravartin* in ancient India was not a central authority, but an acknowledged superior king, an Emperor. The descriptions of *Digvijaya* in Mahabharata show that there was no aggrandisement for acquiring fresh territory but all that was desired was to make several kings submit and pay tribute or offer gifts. Arjuna says in the *Sabha Parva* that he would bring tributes from all kings and the conquered kings were generally represented as submitting and making gifts to the conqueror.[41] The Allahabad Pillar inscriptions reflect identically what Arjuna says in Mahabharata – that the kings and tribal chieftains fully gratified Samudragupta's commands by paying tribute and obeying commands.[42]

Basham faults the noble war model as one of the reasons for not empire building. He noted, 'The intense militarism of ancient India did not lead to the building of a permanent empire over the whole subcontinent. In this respect, the early history of India contrasts strikingly with that of China, where from the third century BC, a single empire was to rule, and division was the exception. In India, the Mauryas succeeded in creating a unified empire for a century, and in the heydays of the Guptas much of North India was under one hand, but these were exceptions as numerous factors prevented the unification of the recognised cultural unit of Bharatavarsha, which so many monarchs desired. But one of the main factors which prevented the unification of India was the martial tradition itself'.[43]

The important aspect of Basham's study is that Bharatavarsha was a cultural unit, capable of being welded into one single nation-state and that so many monarchs of India desired to bring the whole of Bharatavarsha under one political control; but that did not happen because of their martial tradition which restrained them from acquiring control over the defeated kingdoms. Basham also indicates that another reason why empire building in India did not materialise after the Maurya effort, was that, 'For the post-Mauryan king the idea of empire was something very different from that to which the West is accustomed'.[44] Basham goes on to explain the noble martial, that is war, traditions of India.

Basham's theory that the empire building in India was impeded by the noble model of warfare is a significant statement that constitutes a complete answer to critiques who bench mark the nation-state building models of the West. He says, "According to Arthashastra there are three types of conquest: righteous conquest, conquest for greed, and demonic conquest, in Sanskrit: *Dharma Vijaya, Lobha Vijaya* and *Asura Vijaya* The first was a conquest in which the defeated king was forced to render homage and tribute, after which he or a member of his family was reinstated as a vassal. The second was a victory in which an enormous booty was demanded, and large portion of enemy territory was annexed. The third involved political annihilation of the kingdom and its incorporation in that of the victor. The two latter types are generally disapproved by all sources except the Arthashastra. Thus, the Mahabharata declares: 'A king should not attempt to gain un-righteously, for who reveres the king who wins un-righteous victory? Unrighteous conquest is impermanent And does not lead to heaven'.[45]

Basing his theory on the now discredited Aryan invasion, Basham says, 'The idea of "righteous conquest" or "conquest according to the Sacred Law" may have developed among the Aryans soon after their occupation of North India, as an expression of their solidarity against the dark-skinned natives'.[46] This is to give credit to the so-called Aryan invaders for the noble war models of India. (The Aryan invasion theory is now totally discredited.) But, he contradicts his view in the next sentence: 'It is', that is, the concept of righteous war, 'evident though not explicitly stated in the Vedic literature'[47] Had the Aryans developed righteous war as a measure of conciliation how could it not find place in the Vedic literature which was pre-Aryan-Dravidian interface? So Basham's hypothesis without evidence that righteous warfare was the Aryan conciliation with the Dravidians seems to be clearly unwarranted.

Yet Basham's view that the concept of the righteous, which was prevalent in no other civilisation, was an impediment to empire building in India, Bharatavarsha, which is a significant contribution to how the Indian civilisation evolved as one of the greatest civilisations of the world without being obsessed with empire building through wars. Basham also explains how even as this adversely impacted on empire building, those who ignored the righteous law, emerged empire builders, thus: 'The Kings of Magadha, from Bimbisara onwards, ignored' the concept of righteous war 'and annexed territory without compunction', but the doctrine that war should be waged for glory and homage rather than sordid aims such as wealth and power grew in importance with the fall of the Mauryas, and was accepted by the quasi-feudal medieval order. 'Demonic conquest' still took place from time to time, notably under the Guptas, but 'righteous conquest' was the ideal which the Hindu kings were expected to follow, and it is evident that they usually did. (emphasis added)[48]

However, in retrospect, it would appear that empire building in India, which would have brought political unity on the lines of what the West believes today to be nation-state, consistent with the cultural entity of Bharatavarsha, would have been possible in India if only India had not rejected the Kautilya's prescriptions of war for greed and annexation. Other civilisations not only followed the lower, the second and the lowest, third grades of war, namely conquest for greed and barbaric conquests for annexation of the enemy kingdom, but also emerged as empire builders and nation builders. While the Hindus who followed ethical warfare and therefore did not build empires like the Europeans did, are faulted for not building empires!

Hindu War Ethics in Practice till 16-17th Century

The noble rules of war are institutionalised in the principle of *Raj dharma* or statecraft which is integral to the higher principle of *dharma*. Dharma is the un-legislated normative principle of life governing all in this ancient land. Such a normative state craft abiding by the principle of dharma is inconceivable outside the geography, history and culture of India. So wars, victory and defeat in the alien model and the ancient Indian model here are two different and divergent paradigms.

The ancient Indian model made wars rare and therefore the kings normally did not have a regular standing army except for defence and law and order purposes. It is only those who develop the ambition to emerge as the *Chakravartin*, the Emperor, who assembled the regular army. Thus, any alien appraisal of the Indian statecraft and wars cannot understand the normative standards by which the people in this country were governed.

Those who came to conquer India had no model of war based on ethics. That was why a Mohammed Ghori who was defeated several times was not killed by the victor, Prithviraj Chauhan. The host civilisation applied its normative standards even in war with the aliens who had no normative standards even in religion! For them victory was the target, how it was achieved never mattered. Again, as late as during the Western colonial conquest of India, ancient India's noble principles of war were found to be in practice and the Portuguese historians have noted that the principles of war were adhered to by the Hindu Kings in Kerala and elsewhere.

In the book, *History of Kerala,* by Padmanabha Menon, on the models of wars adopted in the distant Malabar in Southern Peninsular India, the author writes: 'And when they are in battle, and one army is distant from the other by two ranges of cross-bow, the King says to the Brahman, "Go to the camp of the enemy, and tell the King to let 100 of his Naeri, soldiers, come and I will go with a 100 of mine" and thus both go to the middle of the space and begin to fight in this manner. Altho' [sic] they fight for 3 days, they always give two direct blows on the head and one on the legs. And when 4 or 6 on either side are killed, the Brahmans immediately go to the armies on both sides and say, "Nur Mauezarhanno". The King answers "Matile", that is "Do you wish for any more?" The Brahman says, "No" and the adverse party does the same. And in this manner they fight one hundred against one hundred...."

Castenheda observes, 'when these kings are at war with each other, they often go into the field, and even join the fight in person upon occasion'. Sheik Zeen-ud-deen observes, 'In their wars, they have seldom had recourse to treachery; but fixing upon a certain day with their enemies to decide their quarrel by arms, they regard any treacherous departure from this engagement both as base and unworthy'.[49]

Menon continues, 'Whiteaway in his work, *The Rise of the Portuguese Power in India,* gives us the following account of the weapons of the Nayars, soldiers, and their methods of warfare. 'In arms and methods of warfare the Hindu of the extreme south, where Mohammedans had not yet penetrated, is behind his contemporary in Europe. Chiefly, perhaps, because they had then met no serious enemy, and had only fought with their own caste-fellows and co-religionists, war had become with a game governed by a series of elaborate rules, and to break one of these rules involved dishonour which was worse than death'.[50]

Whiteway adds: 'There was neither night fighting nor ambuscades. All the fighting was in the day time when the sun had well risen; the opposing camps were either pitched near each other, and both sides slept securely. At the sun rise, the soldiers of both armies mingled at the tank, put on their armour, at their rice, chewed their betel, gossiped, and chatted together. At the beat of the drum, either side drew apart and formed its ranks. It was creditable to be the first to beat the drum, and no attack was allowed until the other side had beaten theirs.'[51]

Whiteway goes on to say: 'The fighting was always in the open plain and they advanced – all stooping – very slow, now gaining ground, now losing, so that sometimes a whole day is spent in advance and retreats. When the drum beat sounded, both sides rose to their feet and fought no more for the day. The drum could only be beaten when both sides were halted, and it was a point of honour not to beat it unless some advantage could be claimed.'

'All the strategy was directed to capturing and defending the camp and scribes were in attendance to write down the different turns of the battle.'

'At times when the ranks on one side broke, the slaughter was very great, but after the drum sounded the two sides mingled together, and there was no bad blood even when a man killed his own brother. In certain cases, when a relative died or a vassal rebelled, the leader of the side that desired a suspension of hostilities, after the ranks were formed, advanced, stuck his javelin in the ground, leant his sword and shield against it and stood apart: the leader on the other side imitated him and truce ensued.'[52]

Obviously, the noble war models developed and consistently adopted by the Hindus were not mythological. They were imbued with the core of the Hindu civilisation and that was seen compulsively manifesting in the wars against even people whose war methods were barbaric and even when such noble war practices were found to be suicidal.

When the Aryan invasion-migration theory trotted out by the colonial theorists held forth, many writers including AL Basham, had credited the noble war rules prevalent in India to the Brahmins – read the Aryans. The implication was that since the Aryans, that is the Brahmins, who were believed to be from outside, were not originally Indians, India or Hinduism had no role in, nor credited for, evolving such noble war rules. The entire basis of the Aryan Invasion Theory is being questioned today.[53]

So, the earlier commentators of Hindu war ethics could be excused for not disputing or for assuming that the noble war rules were developed by the Brahmins. Even though it may be strictly out of place here, two questions about the Aryans/Brahmins as the source of noble war rules in India arises. First, how is it that the 'noble' Aryans who came from outside India, nowhere left traces of their nobility in war rules, in their original places or along the way? Second, how did the 'barbaric' Dravidians accept the noble laws of war? So ignoring the assumption that the Brahmins were the originators of the noble war rules – when in fact it was Manu, not a Brahmin, who was amongst the first to expound the noble war rules – the genius of entire Hindu civilisation should be credited with having expounded the noble rules of war. Thus, the commentaries of the earlier authors should be read with the caveat that they went by the assumptions of the time in which they were making their comment.

Invaders make Hindus abandon War Ethics

The Hindu civilisation which had evolved such noble war models was confronted by Islamic and colonial war lords with rules of war that had no morals or ethics, excepting victory, and in most cases victory for their religion or country, as the only target. The result was unprecedented defeats and finally the noble Hindu war rules yielded place to methods that were inevitable for survival. The latest recorded instance of how such noble war rules were given up by Hindus was recorded by the Portuguese.

Whiteway, in his work, *The Rise of the Portuguese Power in India*, after explaining how the wars were fought in Kerala on noble principles, says that confronted by the Portuguese war model, the noble war model was given up by the indigenous Kings. Whiteway says: 'This artificial system broke down very quickly under the stress of fighting against the Portuguese... Thus it had always been the custom of Zamorin to sound a trumpet that it took four men to lift to warn his enemy of an intended attack. In 1536 he nearly surprised the Portuguese by abandoning the custom suddenly.'[54]

Whiteway then goes on to say: 'None of the battles described by Portuguese historians – and they are numerous of them, each told in great detail – sound much more than magnified street brawls. The interest in this description of the methods of fighting in Southern India, transmitted to us by the Portuguese writers, is enhanced by the evidence that it affords, that these methods were introduced from Northern India by Brahamans, to mitigate the ferocity of the races whom they converted to the Hindu religion.

The earliest form in which they are found is the six rules agreed to by both sides in the great war of Bharata, celebrated in Mahabharata, which embody some of the most artificial of the customs. It may be as some have said, that these six rules were introduced into the poem by Brahmanical writers, at a later period, to give them an historical sanction in the eyes of the subsequent generations; but the same could hardly be said of their inclusion in the laws of Manu where also they were found. But whether this view be correct, that is, whether they actually governed the fight on the plains of Kurukshetra or not is of little importance; the fact is that these passages in the Portuguese write-ups give, that the Brahman carried with him in his civilising advance over India such influence that he could impose his humanising rules over savage races over which he establish his yoke; rules, too, which, although they have left their traces to the present day in the chivalrous tone of some Hindu races, notably Rajputs, laid those adopting them open to the attacks of outsiders, who could reap every advantage from the artificial system that bound their adversaries.'[55]

It needs no further discussion. If in the history of Hindus and of their culture and civilisation, such high ideals and noble war laws and principles could inspire, it is essentially because the Hindu religion – which is a commonwealth of diverse religions propitiating millions of Gods while believing that the Ultimate Reality is only One without a second – and its basic philosophical underpinning to develop such noble war methods. This is the contrast.

And in a world that was to be later dominated by the Abrahamic-Monotheistic faiths and the religion, culture and politics, they set out to universalise, the noble war models of Hindus became a disadvantage. It was this that forced great Hindu kings like Chhatrapati Shivaji, who built the Maratha Empire, to adopt guerilla warfare, which was not in tune with the noble war models of the Hindu civilisation as evident from the discussion above. They had to change their strategy and adopt *Kuta yudhha,* deceptive war, which is the very opposite of *Dharma yuddha* in the fight for survival.

An Illustration of Abrahamic War Ethics

It is necessary at this point to compare the theological and practical position of the Abrahamic, [Islamic and Christian] civilisations on the war ethics and religious rules regarding other faiths and peoples. The choice of these two strands of Abrahamic-Monotheistic civilisations as a contrast to the Hindu civilisation is a natural corollary because the Hindu civilisation confronted, struggled, fought and interfaced the Islamic and the trade-mixed colonial version of the Christian civilisation. The general impression that the Hindu civilisation lost was based on a superficial analysis of history.

The history of the world anywhere is the story of the victor. In Africa, it is said, 'in the struggle between the hunter and the lion, the hunter has written the history'.[56] But this is equally true of the history of all colonised states. Will Durant in his *The Story of Civilisations*, describes the Muslim invasion of India as 'probably the bloodiest story in history'.[57] Why did Islam invade India? It does not need a seer to answer this question. The reason for invasion was religious, not political, although religion provided the trigger and vigour for the political leadership to organise armies founded on faith. It is religion which transformed the game of war from the professional to the conscript, where the religious armies led by the Islamic and Christian faithful were not professional, but were founded on principles of conscription. So, the entire concept of warfare had changed with the introduction of religious beliefs to drive the moves and conquest by armies. It is Islam and Christianity which brought into wars the powerful element of acquiring lands and peoples in the name of God, that too, jealous Gods which explicitly would not and did not tolerate other Gods.

A mere comparison of the war ethics of the aggressive Abrahamic civilisations and the benevolent Hindu civilisation is adequate to bring out how and why the Hindu civilisation lost out, particularly, to the Islamic forces. It was largely because of the nobler war ethics followed by the Hindu civilisation consistent with its own philosophy of war and this proved to be a great disadvantage in handling the brutal and barbaric war methods employed by the Islamic invaders in India. The Quranic concepts clearly mandated war as one of the methods of spreading the Islamic religion and for the purpose the people of the defeated kingdoms could be compelled to accept Islam by different means. In contrast, the nobler Hindu war ethics clearly forbid the victor from imposing his faith or language or culture on the people of the vanquished kingdom. Further, the higher Hindu ethics command the victor to preserve the culture and faith of the people of the vanquished kingdom. A comparison of the Islamic Quranic concept of war with the Hindu Puranic concept of war expounded earlier will bring out the paradigm difference between the two. The Quranic warfare matches with the Hindu view of *Asura Vijaya*, namely the barbaric warfare.

The first of the five pillars of Islam is the profession of the faith: 'There is no God but Allah and Muhammad is his Prophet' upon which depends the membership of the community.[58] In this lie, the intolerant element in Islam, like in Christianity. Added to this intolerant ingredient is the structure of Islam as an organised Ummah, the community which is not just Islamic, but essentially Arabic in concept and form. Is not just the personal commitment to religion that makes one a Muslim, but his surrender to be part of the Ummah, the community of Islamic people.

The history of emergence of the Muslim Ummah is important. This is how a modern Muslim, in fact a military mind – a Pakistani Brigadier SK Mallik, understands the history of Muslim Ummah in Islam: 'The Muslim migration to Medina brought in its wake events and decisions of far-reaching significance and consequence for them. While in Mecca they had neither proclaimed an Ummahn or were they granted the permission to take recourse to war. In Medina, a divine revelation proclaimed them as "Ummah" and granted to them permission to take up arms against the oppressors. The permission was soon converted into divine command making war a religious obligation for the faithful. The mission assigned to the New State emphasised its moderation, balance, practicality and universality. "Thus we have made of you an Ummah justly balanced" declared the Book – Quran – "that ye might be witness over the nations, and the Apostle a witness over yourselves."

In a subsequent revelation, the Holy Quran ruled, "Ye are the best of peoples, evolved for mankind, enjoying what is right, forbidding what is wrong, and believing in Allah". These proclamations laid the foundations of the new political, social, economic and military philosophies of the new state and formed the basis of its policy.'[59]

In the preface to the same book – to which a foreword has been written by General Zia-ul Haq who led Pakistan for a whole decade and thoroughly Islamised the remaining un-Islamised remnants of Pakistan – Allah Baksh Brohi has written: 'It is true that in modern society the maintenance of international order and peace in the international community of mankind proceeds on the premises of sovereign equality of 'nation-states' whose number at present is 151. And this number is reached by taking notice of the territorial aspect of the structure of a modern nation-state. The idea of Ummah of Mohammad, the Prophet of Islam is incapable of being realised within the framework of territorial states, much less made an enduring basis of viewing the world as having polarised between the world of Islam and the world of war. Islam in my understanding does not subscribe to the concept of territorial state and it would be recalled that Iqbal in his lectures on 'The Reconstruction of Religious Thought in Islam' went as far as to suggest that, Muslim states to begin with, be treated as territorial states and that only as an interim measure since these are later on to be incorporated into a commonwealth of Muslim states. Each one of these states has first to acquire strength and stability before it is able to prepare the ground on which the unified state of Islam can be found on the historical scene.'[60]

Two things are evident in this approach. First, the Muslim Ummah is the real entity, the nation-state is not. Therefore, even the individual Muslim state is only a passing phase. One can imagine the legitimacy of the state and its laws in Islamic world in this approach. Second, the world will be polarised into two: the world of Islam and the world of War, that is, the world with which Islam will be at war. This book and preface were written in 1986. This is not an exceptional or extreme view. More well-known authorities understand this aspect of Islam precisely the same way.

Quran described the Muslim community as 'the best community produced for mankind' whose function is to 'enjoin the good' and 'forbid the evil'. 'Cooperation' and 'good advice' within the community are emphasised, and a person who deliberately tries to harm the interests of the community is to be given exemplary punishment. Opponents within the community are to be fought with armed force if persuasion does not work and deliberate trouble makers within the community are to be given exemplary punishment. So, Islam commends war within Islam also. As the mission for the community is to enjoin the good and to forbid the evil 'so that there is no mischief or corruption' on earth, 'the doctrine of *jihad*, in view of the constitution of the community as the power base, is the logical outcome'.[61] 'For the early community it was a religious concept. The object of jihad is not the conversion of individuals to Islam, but rather the gaining of control over the collective affairs of societies to run them in accordance with the principles of Islam.'[62]

This is diametrically the opposite of the position adumbrated in the Hindu texts on wars, which mandates the faith and tradition of the vanquished in the war should not be interfered with by the victor, rather should help to preserve it. What the Hindu civilisation prohibits is what the very intent and object jihad seeks to achieve! The Encyclopedia adds: 'Individual conversions may occur as a by-product of this process when power structure passes into the hands of the Muslim community. In strict Muslim doctrine conversions "by force" are forbidden, because after the revelation of the Quran "the good and the evil have become distinct" so that one may follow whichever one may prefer, Quran, and it is also strictly prohibited to wage wars for the sake of acquiring worldly glory, power and rule. With the establishment of Muslim empire, however, the doctrine of jihad was modified by the leaders of the community. Their main concern had become the consolidation of the empire and its administration and thus they interpreted in a defensive rather than in an expansive sense.'[63]

Muslim Invaders came with Quranic War Model

The developments within Islam had had their deep impact on non-Islamic world as Islam, like its other cousins in the Abrahamic world, not only laid down rules for its adherents, but also for the adherents of other faiths, as to how they would be handled by the Islamists. The main problem of the Abrahamic faiths is their world view which actually limits the world to their view. This means that each of the Abrahamic thoughts conflicts with the other in context of their world view, and they also conflict with the views of other faiths and cultures of the world. In this perspective, how the aggressive Islamic war commands against those whose faith was not acceptable to Islam, affected the Hindu civilisation which had high and noble war rules may be demonstrated by reference to an assorted collection of historic events, with authorities from where such facts were collected, as under:[64] Amir Timur or Tamerlane (1336-1405) the Turkmen Mongol conqueror wrote: 'My principal object in coming to Hindustan… has been to accomplish two things. The first was to wage war with the infidels, the enemies of the Mohammadan religion; and by this religious warfare to acquire some claim to reward in the life to come. The other was… that the army of Islam might gain something by plundering the wealth and valuables of the infidels: plunder in war is as lawful as their mothers' milk to Musalmans who war for their faith.'

While studying the legacy of Muslim rule in India, it has to be constantly borne in mind that the objectives of all Muslim invaders and rulers were the same as those mentioned above. Timur or Tamerlane himself defines them candidly and bluntly while others do so through their chroniclers. (Source: *The Legacy of Muslim Rule in India* by KS Lal).To start with he stormed the fort of Kator on the border of Kashmir. He ordered his soldiers 'to kill all the men, to make prisoners of women and children, and to plunder and lay waste all their property',Next, he 'directed towers to be built on the mountain of the skulls of those obstinate unbelievers'. Soon after, he laid siege to Bhatnir defended by Rajputs. They surrendered after some fight and were pardoned. But Islam did not bind Timur to keep his word given to the 'unbelievers'. His Tuzk-i-Timuri records: 'In a short space of time, all the people in the fort were put to the sword, and in the course of one hour the heads of 10,000 infidels were cut off. The sword of Islam was washed in the blood of the infidels, and all the goods and effects, the treasure and the grain, which for many a long year had been stored in the fort became the spoils of my soldiers. They set fire to the houses and reduced them to ashes, and they razed the buildings and the fort to the ground.'

By now Timur had captured 100,000 Hindus. As he prepared for battle against the Tughlaq army after crossing the Yamuna, his Amirs advised him 'that on the great day of battle these 100,000 prisoners could not be left with the baggage, and that it would be entirely opposed to the rules of war to set these idolaters and enemies of Islam at liberty'. Therefore, 'no other course remained but that of making them all food for the sword'. Tuzk-i-Timuri continues: 'I proclaimed throughout the camp that every man who had infidel prisoners should put them to death, and whoever neglected to do so should himself be executed and his property given to the informer. When this order became known to the ghazis of Islam, they drew their swords and put their prisoners to death.'(Source: *Kashmir – Islamic Atrocities in India*).

'Muslims invaders did record with glee their genocide of the Hindus, because they felt all along that they were doing their duty; that killing, plundering, enslaving and razing temples was the work of God, Mohammed. Indeed, whether it was Mahmud of Ghazni (997-1030), who was no barbarian, although a Turk, and patronised art and literature, would recite a verse of the Koran every night after having razed temples and killed his quota of unbelievers; or Firuz Shah Tughlak (1351-1388) who personally confirms that the destruction of pagan temples was done out of piety and writes: "On the day of a Hindu festival, I went there myself, ordered the executions of all the leaders and practitioners of this abomination; I destroyed their idols and temples and built mosques in their places.'"(Source: *Negationism and the Muslim Conquests* - by Francois Gautier).

Slaughter of the Hindus - Hindu Kush Mountains

Hindus, Sikhs and Buddhists have also suffered a terrible holocaust, probably without parallel in human history. Take the Hindu Kush for instance, which was probably one of the biggest genocides of Hindus. There is practically no serious research ever done about it and no mention in history books. Yet the name Hindu Kush appears many times in the writings of Muslim chroniclers in 1333 AD. Ibn Battutah, the medieval Berber traveller, said the name meant 'Hindu Killer', a meaning given by Afghan mountain dwellers. Unlike the Jewish holocaust, the exact toll of the Hindu genocide suggested by the name Hindu Kush is not available. 'However', writes Hindu Kush specialist Srinandan Vyas, 'the number is easily likely to be in millions'.

Afghanistan was a full part of the Hindu cradle till the year 1,000, and in political unity with India until Nadir Shah separated it in the 18th century. The mountain range in Eastern Afghanistan where the native Hindus were slaughtered, is still called the Hindu Kush which in Persian means 'Hindu Slaughter'. To note, to the Hindus, this mountain range was known as Paariyaatra Parvat. But when the last Hindu king of Kabul was killed, Muslims ruled this land and then called these mountains the Hindu Kush—'Slaughter of the Hindus'. It is significant that one of the very few place-names on earth that reminds us not of the victory of the winners but rather of the slaughter of the losers, concerns a genocide of Hindus by the Muslims. Few known historical figures can be used to justify this estimate. The *Encyclopedia Britannica* recalls that in December 1398 AD, Taimurlane (Tamerlane) ordered the execution of at least 50,000 captives before the battle for Delhi; likewise, the number of captives butchered by Taimurlane's army was about 100,000.

The *Britannica* again mentions that Mughal Emperor Akbar ordered the massacre of about 30,000 captured Rajput Hindus on 24 February 1568 AD, after the battle for Chittor, a number confirmed by Abul Fazl, Akbar's court historian. Afghan historian Khondamir notes that during one of the many repeated invasions on the city of Herat in western Afghanistan, which used to be part of the Hindu Shahiya kingdoms '1,500,000 residents perished'. 'Thus, it is evident that the mountain range was named as Hindu Kush as a reminder to the future Hindu generations of the slaughter and slavery of Hindus during the Moslem conquests'. (Source: *Where's India's Holocaust Museum?* – by Francois Gautier – rediff.com).

American Historian Abraham Valentine Williams Jackson (1862-1937) wrote: 'At Mahmud's blockade the defenders "fell to the earth like sparrows before the hawk". Immense stores of treasure and jewels, money and silver ingots, were laden upon camels, and a pavilion of silver and a canopy of Byzantine linen reared upon pillars of silver and gold were among the prizes of the Holy War. The booty was displayed in the court of the palace at Ghazni, "jewels and unbored pearls and rubies, shinning like sparks or iced wine, emeralds as it were sprigs of young myrtle, diamonds as big as pomegranates". The Eastern chronicles tell of seventy million silver dirhams, and hundreds of thousands of pounds weight of silver cups and vessels; and, with every allowance for exaggeration, the spoils must be colossal. All the world flocked to Ghazni to gaze upon the incredible wealth of India. Such rewards were incentives enough to carry on the pious work. Year after year Mahmud swept over the plains of Hindustan, capturing cities and castles, throwing down temples and idols, and earning his titles of "Victor" and "Idol-breaker", Ghazi and But-shikan.'

The zeal for Islam was the dominant characteristic of the tenth-century Turks, as of most new converts. The great missionary creed of Mohammed, which to the Arabs and Persians had become a familiar matter of routine, was a source of fiery inspiration to the untutored men of the steppes. To spread the faith by conquest doubled their natural zest for battle and endowed them with the devoted valour of martyrs: 'Mahmud of Ghazni was a staunch Moslem, and he vowed that every year he would wage a Holy War against the infidels of Hindustan.' The sack of Somnath had made Mahmud of Ghazni a champion of the faith in the eyes of every Moslem for nearly nine centuries, and the feat, signal enough in itself, has been embellished with fantastic legends. Mahmud died in 1030 A D and his tomb and two lofty minarets, stand to show Ghazni's life. On one of the minarets one may still read the resonant titles of the Idol-breaker, and on the marble tombstone an inscription entreats,

'God's mercy for the great Amir Mahmud.' Soon India was to witness something very similar in the repetition of his swift irresistible raids. For more than a century there was peace, at least, little war. Probably the Hindu troops and Hindu officials had to some extent Indianised them, and the last descendants of Mahmud made their home at Lahore without difficulty.

Mu'izz-ad-din, commonly known as Mohammad Ghori, led a series of campaigns in India which recalled the days of the Idol Breaker nearly two centuries earlier. For thirty years Mahmud had ravaged Hindustan from Indus to the Ganges; and for thirty years Mohammed Ghori harried the same country in the same way - full of religious zeal, and eager to send the 'groveling crow-faced Hindus to the fire of hell'. (Source: *History of India* by AV Williams Jackson, Volume 3 p. 17 – 28 and 52 – 54.)

This is adequate to show the contrast in war models and how, being noble proved to be a suicidal course for civilisations like the Hindu civilisation. This was precisely the experience of Amerindians when the Spanish exploration destroyed them and their culture in medieval times. How virtually a total homicide took place in the Americas is brought out in several works.[65]

Re-emergence of Barbarism after 1947

The history of barbarity against the Indian civilisation has not stopped with the advent of modern rules of war. Pakistan which was born out of Islamic theology still adopts the barbaric rules of war, which were employed centuries earlier by their Islamic forefathers against India. This is manifested in the acts of terror against India which Pakistan that was Islamised by the Zia UlHaq regime (1977-88) adopted against India. As Hussein Haqqani said: 'Zia ul-Haq is often identified as the person most responsible for turning Pakistan into a global centre for political Islam. Undoubtedly, Zia went farthest in defining Pakistan as an Islamic State and he nurtured the jihadist ideology.'[66] Pakistan redeveloped and re-weaponised Jihadi culture that was rooted in the political Islamist ideology that created it.[67] Deutsche Welle, the German Broadcaster, said in an analysis titled, *India's Partition and 70 Years of Proxy Jihad,* that 'The use of proxy jihadis in the Indian subcontinent is as old as India and Pakistan's independence from British rule. 70 years after partition, the jihadist network has become so huge that it threatens both states'.[68]

The invaders' barbaric rules of war was not limited to non-state actors promoted by Pakistan, but even the official army of the State of Pakistan adopted barbaric methods against the Indian army—like beheadings, mutilation of bodies and torture of Indian soldiers.

Here is an illustrative list of such barbarity inherent in the DNA of Pakistan given by the *India Today*:[69]

During the 1999 Kargil conflict Captain Saurabh Kalia was tortured by his Pakistani captors who later handed over his badly mutilated body to India.

(i) February 2000: Infamous Pakistani terrorist and al-Qaida member Ilyas Kashmiri had led a raid on the Indian Army's "Ashok Listening Post" in the Nowshera sector to kill seven Indian soldiers. Even then, Kashmiri had taken back to Pakistan the head of a 24-year-old Indian jawan, Bhausaheb Maruti Talekar of the 17 Maratha Light Infantry.

(ii) June 2008: A soldier of the 2/8 Gorkha Rifles lost his way and was captured by a Pakistani Border Action Team (BAT) in Kel sector. His body was found beheaded after a few days.

(iii) January 2013: One Indian soldier was beheaded and another killed by Pakistani troops who had crossed over into Indian territory in the Mendhar sector of Jammu and Kashmir.

(iv) October 28, 2016: A soldier was mutilated by a militant in Kupwaras Machil near the Line of Control while the army was engaged in cross-border firing with Pakistan's army. It continued even after 2016.

(vi) In 2017, Pakistan mutilated bodies of two Indian soldiers in Kashmir after Pakistan's Army Chief attacked India.[70]

Now the state of India has the capacity and authority to defend its subjects against barbarity and respond with surgical strike kind of aggressive response thanks to such barbarity becoming a global phenomenon and India having attained global stature to respond powerfully unlike in the past.

Conclusion

The answer to the question why the Indian civilisation was defeated by the invading forces can now be stated in one sentence—namely, what happened to the Roman Pagan religion at the hands of one of the Abrahamic faiths, political Christianity, is what happened to the Hindu civilisation at the hands of its other powerful cousin, political Islam. Just as 'Rome was not adapted to the treatment of a religion,[Christianity] that negated its religious foundations, and this inadequacy later influenced the breakdown of (Roman) paganism',[71] Hindu civilisation could not adequately understand a phenomenon like political Islamic theology which negated the foundations of other religions including Hinduism. This faulty understanding of the religious fire power of Islamic invaders who observed no rule in the wars waged and were barbaric in their methods and attacks led to the defeat of Hindu kingdoms which treated the invading political Islamic ideology like one of the Hindu philosophic branches. This was as much an intellectual failure of the religious scholars of India who could not understand the exclusivity of the Abrahamic religions in general and Islam in particular, as it was a failure of the Hindu kings who could not put their acts together, but confronted the invading forces, divided among themselves. Even many like Jayachand allied with the invaders against their own—not knowing that the invaders were not just political in their intent, but they had theological goals in their minds. Not just at the time of Prithviraj Chauhan, but even at the time of Maharana Pratap this realisation did not come about. It took a century after Rana Pratap, and a Chhatrapati Shivaji to understand the paradigm difference between Hindu philosophy which accepted all faiths and Islam whose theology negated all faiths other than itself. Forthwith the war rules changed. The way Shivaji handled Afzal Khan, as compared to how Prithviraj Chauhan handled Mohammed Ghori, brought out the change in the rules of war—which came a bit too late in history.

References

1 Ingrid Detter, 'The Nature of the Laws of War: The Historical Background', Chapter 5, in *The Law of War,* second edition, ISBN 0 521 78256 2.

2 *Encyclopaedia Britannica*, 'Warfare, Laws of', 15th Edition, Macropaedia Vol 19, p. 538

3 Ibid, pp. 538-39.

4 A L Basham, *The Wonder That was India,* Rupa&Co., Calcutta, 1981, p. 125

5 Balshastri Hardas, *Glimpses of The Vedic Nation,* rendered into English by S.S. Apte. Publishers: Sri Kamakoti Publishing House, 4, Francis Joseph Street, Madras-1 copies available with BG Paul & Co., Publishers, Abhyankar Road, Sitabuldi, Nagpur.

6 Ibid, pp 602-03.

7 Ibid, p 604.

8 Pandurang Vaman Kane, *The History of Dharma Shastra* (Ancient Indian and Medieval Religious and Civil Law), Government Oriental Series Class B No 6, Bandarkar Oriental Research Institute, Pune, 1973, Vol III, second edition, p 69.

9 Ibid p 70.

10 Ibid Vol II, Part II, p 1238.

11 Ibid, Vol III, p 69.

12 Ibid, Vol III, pp 70-71.

13 *The Penguin Dictionary of Religions*, p 135.

14 http://www.bbc.co.uk/religion/religions/hinduism/hinduethics/war.shtml accessed August 7, 2007.

15 The History of Dharmasastras Supra, Vol III, p 209.

16 Ibid, p 209.

17 Ibid, pp 209-210.

18 Ibid 210.

19 Ibid pp 210-211.

20 VR Rmachandra Dhikshitar, *War in Ancient India,* Cosmo Publications, ISBN: 8170208947, pp. 67-75.

21 The History of Dharma Sastra Supra, Vol III, p 72.

22 *Ancient Indian Tradition and Mythology*, translated and annotated by Ganesh Vasudeo Tagare and edited by Prof. J.L. Shastri, Vol 22, Motilal Banarsidas (Delhi, Varanasi, Patna) India, Vol 28 p 614.

23 *The History of Dharma Sashtra* Supra, Vol III, p 72.

24 https://www.speakingtree.in/allslides/unknown-facts-about-shivaji.

25 Jeffrey G. Snodgrass, *Casting Kings: Bards and Indian Modernity*, Oxford University Press, 2006,ISBN:0198041403, 9780198041405.

26 A L Basham, *The Wonder That Was India*, Supra, pp 8-9.

27 Eric Hobsbawm, *Nations and Nationalism since 1780 Programme, Myth, Reality*, Cambridge University Press, UK,1992, pp.14-18, ISBN 0-521-43961-2.

28 Dr Pandurang Vaman Kane, No. 8, p 64.

29 Ibid, Vol III, pp 65-67.

30 Ibid, Vol III, p 67.

31 Ibid, Vol III, p 67.

32 Ancient Indian Tradition and Mythology,translated and annotated by Ganesh VasudeoTagare and edited by Prof. J.L. Shastri, Vol 22, Motilal Banarsidas (Delhi, Varanasi, Patna) India, part I p lxxxi.

33 Ibid, Vol III, supra, p 68.

34 Ibid, 126.

35 *Encyclolpaedia Britannica*,15th Edition, Macropaedia Vol 15, Supra, p 538.

36 Basham, *The Wonder That Was India*, Supra, 124.

37 *The History of Dharmasastra*, Supra, Vol I, Part I, p 231..

38 Ibid, pp 174-75.

39 Ibid.

40 Henry Kissinger, *Diplomacy*, Supra, pp 56-57.

41 *The History of Dharma Sastra*, Vol III, Supra, p 68.

42 Ibid, Vol III, p 68.

43 Basham, *The Wonder That Was India*, Supra, p. 124.

44 Ibid, p 124.

45 Ibid, p 125.

46 Ibid, p 125.

47 Ibid, p 125.

48 Ibid, p 125.

49 KP Padmanabha Menon, *History of Kerala*, Lurier Books Ltd/AES, December 1, 1996,p. 397, ISBN-10: 8120601653 and ISBN-13: 978-812061659.

50 Ibid, pp 398-99.

51 Ibid, p 399.

52 Ibid, p 400.

53 For example,'Update on Aryan Invasion Debate' by Kondraad Elst, ISBN 81-86471-77-4; BBC Religion & Ethics - Hinduism: Aryan Invasion Theory http://www.bbc.co.uk/religion/religions/hinduism/history/history_4.shtml accessed August 14, 2007.

54 *History of Kerala*, Supra, p 400.

55 Ibid, pp 400-401..

56 Address by Professor Kader Asmal, MP, Minister of Education, SA. 'Keeping memory alive, shaping our future: The ten-year celebration of freedom', Centre for the Book, Cape Town, March 31, 2004, available at http://www.info.gov.za/speeches/2004/04040109461001.htm,accessed August 13, 2007..

57 http://www.frontline.org.za/new nd_of_islam.htm,accessed August 12, 2007.

58 *Encyclopaedia Britannica,* Supra, acropaedia, 15th edition, Vol 9, p. 918.

59 Brigadier S. K. Mallik, *The Quranic Concept of War,* Himalayan Books, New Delhi,pp. 11-12.

60 Ibid, p xx.

61 *Enclopaedia of Britannica*, Supra, Macropaedia Vol 9, p 914, marginal heading 'The Concept of a Community of the Faithful'.

62 Ibid, p 914.

63 Ibid, p 914.

64 http://www.jihadwatch.org/archives/009243.php accessed August 14, 2007.

65 Russell Thornton, *American Indian Holocaust and Survival: A Population History Since 1492,* University of Oklahoma P.

66 Haqqani, Husain, *Pakistan: Between Mosque and Military,* Carnegie Endowment for International Peace, Washington, 2005, p 131, ISBN 0-87003-214-3,accessed May 23, 2010.

67 Our Jihad Addiction, Husain Haqqani Director for South and Central Asia Hudson Institute https://www.hudson.org/research/10945-our-jihad-addictionaccessed April 17, 2018.

68 http://www.dw.com/en/indias-partition-and-70-years-of-proxy-jihad/a-40083688

69 https://www.indiatoday.in/india/delhi/story/body-of-jawan-mutilated-machil-sector-pakistan-ceasefire-violation-349183-2016-10-29accessed April 17, 2018.

70 http://www.financialexpress.com/india-news/pakistan-kills-two-indian-soldiers-in-kashmir-heres-what-pak-army-chief-general-qamar-bajwa-said-at-loc-a-day-before/649073/.

71 Haqqani, Husain, No. 66. *Encyclopaeida Britannica*, 19th edition, Vol. 4, p 492.

Internal Security: Essential Component of India's National Security

CD Sahay

In India, the concept of National Security has been evolving since the time of Chanakya. Since the World War II , the concept has been gradually expanding beyond the classical position of ensuring the survival of the State through the use of economic, military and political power and the exercise of diplomacy. It now encompasses a much broader range of issues including even issues like, Demographic security, Disaster security, Energy security, Resource security, Geostrategic security, Informational security, Food security, Health security, Ethnic security, Environmental security, Cyber security, Genomic security etc.

Internal Security has lately come to acquire an important position in any discussion on designing an effective architecture of National Security. In India, the terrorism related incidents, largely perpetrated from across our borders, have posed the greatest threat and challenge to our internal security for well over three and a half decades now. Initially, these were mostly dealt with as Law and Order problems. This approach has changed in the recent years, leading to the evolution of a more effective, professional and robust counter-terror policy. The new approach also includes our response to some of the other internal destabilising developments like Left Wing Extremism and Insurgency in the Northeast.

In this paper, some of the important aspects of the current internal security scenarios and how our security establishments have been responding to these, adequacy of the measures in place and what more need to be done.

Concept of National Security

ANY DISCUSSION on the concept of National Security and statecraft in India must necessarily begin with the principles enunciated by Kautilya (350-283 BC) in the *Arthashastra* where he said, '*the king shall always endeavor to augment his own power through the possession of a prosperous treasury and a strong army which is the strength of sovereignty*'.[1] He included the concepts of territorial integrity, impregnable defences, economic prosperity, strong military and dependable allies as some of the important pillars to maintain state's strength and security.

However, the concept of National Security as we know it today, developed mostly in the United States of America after World War II and was generally described as the requirement to maintain the survival of the state through the use of economic, military and political power and the exercise of diplomacy. Initially focusing primarily on military might, it now encompasses a broad range of issues that directly or otherwise, impinge on the military or economic security of the nation and the values espoused by the national society.

Prabhakaran Paleri, a US based Indian origin academician, lists a larger number of elements in his book, *National Security: Imperatives And Challenges* (2008), by including Military security, Economic security, Resource security, Border Security, Demographic security, Disaster security, Energy security, Geostrategic security, Informational security, Food security, Health security, Ethnic security, Environmental security, Cyber security, Genomic security and the list keeps ever expanding.[2] In a more contemporary context, India's National Security Council Secretariat (NSCS), in a study carried out in 2002, took a more holistic view of National Security by including even other issues like good governance, health, water management, environment, technology or even the economy, in addition to the conventional topics such as 'insurgencies and law and order, terrorism, foreign policy etc'.[3]

Whatever definition one goes by, it is quite clear that to ensure comprehensive national security, States take recourse to a variety of measures such as using diplomacy to rally allies and isolate threats; marshalling economic power to facilitate or compel cooperation; maintaining effective armed forces; implementing civil defense and emergency preparedness measures (including anti-terrorism legislation); ensuring the resilience and redundancy of critical infrastructure; using intelligence services to detect and defeat or avoid threats and espionage and to protect classified information; using counterintelligence services or secret police to protect the nation from internal threats.[4] Accordingly, nation states need to possess economic security, energy security, environmental security etc. In today's context, security threats to a nation involve not only conventional foes such as other nation-states but also non-state actors, trans-border violent groups, narcotic cartels, multinational corporations and non-governmental organisations; some authorities also include natural disasters and events causing severe environmental damage in this category.[5]

Challenges to National Security in the Indian Context

In the Indian context, one thing that clearly emerges is that internal and external security considerations are inseparable from each other.[6] Therefore, any meaningful discussion on India's internal security objectives and concerns would necessarily involve considerable overlap between threats to national security emanating from both external sources and internal instabilities.

Security experts believe that till recently, the Indian state continued to accord high priority to securing its territorial integrity against its two principal military adversaries, namely Pakistan and China. To this end, India's national security concerns primarily remained focused on military security. This approach was possibly in sync with the general perception that national security involved physical survival of the State; its territorial integrity, survival of its population and its political independence. This was also understandable in view of the repeated acts of war inflicted on the country by Pakistan and the Chinese aggression of 1962. However, over the decades, the other forms of externally-sponsored threat like trans-border terrorism emanating from Pakistan, affecting not only the states of Punjab earlier and Jammu & Kashmir (J&K) now, but even the hinterland; activities of international terror groups like the Al Qaeda and the Islamic State, IS, Daesh or ISIS; terror funding, narcotics trade through both the eastern and western borders, human trafficking, illegal immigration, cyber-attacks to name just a few, have emerged as areas of major concerns for India.

Add to these the problems posed by the activities of separatists and ethnic groups operating in our north-eastern States and those of Left-Wing Extremism (LWE) in a number of States in the east and central regions and the picture that emerges is nightmarish. It is of critical importance here to note that all these developments have a direct bearing on our internal security situation and need to be factored in designing the overall internal security architecture.

Internal Security Challenges and Concerns

Having not accorded due priority to internal security issues in the initial years, the policy approach of treating most of these issues as Law and Order (L&O) matters, led to a situation in which virtually all symptoms of serious internal threats to the state as in the north east or J&K and even the Maoist movement that started in the mid-1960s, were largely dealt with as such, with the lead role taken by the State police forces, aided by the Central Armed Police Forces (CAPFs). It is only in the past few decades that due seriousness has been accorded to issues that can be called 'non-military threats to the state through non-military means'. In addition, security experts and policy planners are also getting seriously engaged in developing an inclusive approach to bring in some of the other indirectly related issues such as justice, freedom, secularism, plural democratic values, federal polity, economic wellbeing of the citizen, development with equity and such other ideas into the overall debate on internal security.

Indeed, there could be many such issues that may directly or indirectly contribute to the degradation of national security environment in the urban and rural areas. Some of these that additionally come to mind are political instability on account of fractured polity, growing criminal-political nexus, ineffective and inefficient civil administration, perceived exploitation of the deprived sections of the population by the strong emerging private sector etc. that could have the undesired and unintended impact on the national security scenario.

Ironically, the very process of development and growth essential for India's emergence as a strong force in the region and beyond, might indirectly impact its internal security with the urban centres facing huge growth in population, with large number of youths migrating from rural areas in search of better opportunities and driven by great ambitions and expectations. Would there be a corresponding rise in the number of jobs available for them? Even though there would be expanded opportunities, there would still be a significant disparity between expectations and availability of these young people. Apart from lack of adequate employment opportunities, there may not even be enough educational facilities for these migrating youths. These would necessarily impact not only on the L&O situation but could even drive a segment of the frustrated youth to activities seriously prejudicial to the security of the state.

Another dimension of the growth story could be widening levels of internal and regional disparity between different States of the country that could contribute to the creation of an unhealthy social order totally not conducive to the ultimate vision objective of a happy and contended nation. It may be pertinent to mention here that the phenomenon of LWE, in its initial years and perhaps to an extent even now, has been on account of extreme poverty, lack of opportunities, exploitation and deprivation, and the benefits of development not reaching these sections of the community.

Main Components of Internal Security Threats

The main components of India's national security challenges can therefore be ascribed to ensuring state security, human security, countering external and internal threats, dealing with traditional and non-traditional threats and threats of specialised nature such as drug trafficking, illegal migration, small arm proliferation, counterfeit currency, cyber threats etc.

In this paper it is proposed to deal with these primarily in the context of the ever growing arch of:

- Terrorism;
- Security concerns in J&K;
- Security challenges in the North-East;
- Left Wing Extremism;
- New Challenges.

Additionally, attempt will also be made to briefly touch upon:

- Revamping India's Intelligence Apparatus and other related institutions; and,
- Efficacy of India's response to internal security challenges.

What we do not intend to cover in this paper are L&O and crime situation which though, to an extent, relate to the internal security scenario, are being dealt with by the State police machinery in the normal course of their responsibilities.

Terrorism

A report on National Security and Terrorism compiled in 2008 by a Federation of Indian Chamber of Commerce and Industries (FICCI) Task Force had noted that, 'the biggest external threat (to India's security) emanates from (the) ongoing cross-border jihadi terrorism, supported by Inter-Services Intelligence (ISI) and Pakistan-based Islamic fundamentalist organisations such as Lashkar-e-Taiba (LeT) and Jaish-e-Mohammad (JeM) who, in turn, are inextricably linked to international jihadi groups like the Taliban and Al Qaeda'.[7] The report went on to add that in the geographical reality of South Asia, 'India continues to reel under an intense onslaught of externally designed jihadi terrorism…more brazen, sophisticated and surprising capabilities of terrorism than anything that the country had ever known'.

Undisputedly, Pak-sponsored terrorism as part of proxy war, remains the most serious security challenge in the country. Pakistan's abiding strategic policy of using terrorism as an important tool of state policy has serious consequences for India. The first impact of this policy promoted, sustained and executed by the ISI was witnessed in Punjab, where the pro-Khalistan movement was provided all support including funds, training, sanctuary to the leaders and the wherewithal. From 1989 onwards, this operational technique was effectively replicated by the ISI in the State of J&K with careful fine-tuning in the light of the experiences gained by the ISI in the Afghan jihad.

As part of this policy, one saw the Jammu and Kashmir Liberation Front (JKLF) in the lead role initially in J&K, followed by the Hizb-ul-Mujahideen (HuM), Harkat-ul-Ansar (in its various incarnations) and finally the Lashkar-e-Taiba (LeT) and the Jaish-e-Mohammed (JeM), post its creation in early 2000. The other smaller groups also remained active but only as bit-players. LeT, because of its very strong commitment to hard core Islamic ideology, intensive ISI patronage, extensive network not only within Pakistan but even beyond, and its ability to extend its area of operation in India well beyond the borders of J&K, has remained the most potent, favoured and dangerous vehicle for export of terrorism to India; and is expected to continue to play this role in the future as well.

Apart from using its own modules in the major Indian town and cities with local facilitators, the LeT has also been using the network and resources of Indian groups like the Student's Islamic Movement of India (SIMI) and the Indian Mujahideen (IM). The IM, it may be mentioned, was also sponsored by the Pak ISI to shift the blame for terror incidents on Indian elements rather than on Pak entities like the LeT and JeM. David Coleman Headley confirmed this to the FBI.[8]

The JeM which was earlier known as Harkat-ul-Ansar and by various other names, was formally floated in early 2000, within a couple of months of the release of its leaders Maulana Masood Azhar in the IC-814 hijacking incident. The ISI which had moved Masood Azhar from Kandahar to Pakistan ensured funds and trained manpower for the JeM to start its terrorist attacks in India. The most notable of these was the attack on the Indian Parliament on 13 December 2001. The JeM, however, came under international focus leading to it being declared as a Foreign Terrorist Organisation[1] (FTO) by the US along with LeT on 26 December 2001.[9]

The overall security situation in the country gets further vitiated if one were to include the incidents of terror perpetrated by the ethno-terror groups operating in the north-eastern States; the LWE groups' activities in some of the central and neighbouring States and in more recent times, the terror

1 The organisation must engage in terrorist activity, as defined in section 212 (a)(3)(B) of the INA (8 U.S.C. § 1182(a)(3)(B)),* or terrorism, as defined in section 140(d)(2) of the Foreign Relations Authorization Act, Fiscal Years 1988 and 1989 (22 U.S.C. § 2656f(d)(2)),** or retain the capability and intent to engage in terrorist activity or terrorism.

modules actively backed or raised by the extreme radical Islamist groups like Al Qaeda and the IS. The net result of this comprehensively planned strategy of the ISI to keep India on the boil and destabilised has been the spread of Pak-sponsored terrorist actions and activities of other insurgent in different parts of the country over the years as can be seen in the Table 1. Obviously, these have contributed to the overall internal security scenario in the country.

Table 1: Terror Attacks from 2001-2017

Year	Terror incidents in J&K	Insurgency incidents in N East	LWE	Others	Total
2001	4522	1335	1465	NA	7322
2002	4038	1312	1597	NA	6947
2003	3401	1332	1533	NA	6266
2004	2565	1234	1608	NA	5407
2005	1990	1332	1509	NA	4831
2006	1667	1366	1565	NA	4598
2007	887	1489	1591	NA	3967
2008	708	1561	2258	NA	4527
2009	499	1297	2210	NA	4006
2010	488	773	2213	NA	3474
2011	340	627	1760	NA	2727
2012	220	1025	1415	NA	2660
2013	170	732	1136	NA	2038
2014	222	824	1091	NA	2137
2015	208	574	1089	1	1872
2016	322	484	1048	1	1855
2017	342	308	908	0	1558
2018 (February 24, 108)	49	50	122	0	221
Total	**2268**	**17655**	**26118**		**66413**

Source – Ministry of Home Affairs, Government of India

Security Concerns in the J&K

The situation in J&K continues to be a matter of serious concern. While recovering from a sense of acute betrayal in 2016 (Pathankot and Uri attacks) by Pakistan to the various positive overtures and initiatives taken by the National Democratic Alliance (NDA) Government, there still was a faint ray of hope that, with concerted efforts at repairs, the much-needed mend could take place in the year 2017. However, that was not to be. The year 2016 had ended with the post-Uri 'Surgical Strike' that stunned the militants and their principal backers alike. Local mischief-mongers, instigators of stone-pelting and others ducked for cover while search started for a new strategy to keep the 'pot boiling'. The end of the year 2016 announcement on demonetisation and measures to choke the flow of funds to the militants and the separatists, confirmed government's intentions to break the backbone of militancy.[10]

The year 2017 also did not witness any major improvement in security parameters. Militant violence, infiltration through the IB and LoC and cross-border ceasefire violations remained high. The demonetisation drive had profound impact not only on the flow counterfeit currency coming from across the border for financing of terrorism related incidents inside J&K, but also affected the incident of daily protests and stone pelting in the disturbed districts due to non-availability of cash. The major development for the Indian Security Forces was the neutralisation of 213 militants including some prominent Hizbul Mujahidin and Jaish commanders, thanks to pinpointed intelligence and coordinated efforts of Intelligence agencies and forces of the Central and the State governments.

On other security parameters, available data reveals increase in the number of terror-related incidents and higher level of militant activism in J&K. A total of 342 terror-related incidents were recorded as compared to 322 in 2016, the year Hizbul Mujahideen Commander Burhan Wani was killed in an encounter, leading to unrest in the Valley. The year 2017 also saw a much higher number (54) of civilians being killed in the valley as compared to 15 in 2016, primarily due to the rising level of public mobilisation to protest at encounter sites. However, during the year 2017, Indian Security Forces through targeted intelligence-driven coordinated action, eliminated 213 terrorists.[11]

There was a significant rise in the ceasefire violation in 2017, both along the Line of Control (LoC, guarded by the Army) and the International Boundary (IB, guarded by the BSF), and the trend for the current year is seriously disturbing as can be seen in Table 2 which also indicates the position on the major parameters of Pak-sponsored terrorism in J&K.

The year 2017 also witnessed an aggressive and relentless campaign against the top secessionist leaders to choke the flow of funds that has been critical to their activities. National Investigating Agency (NIA) on 30th May, 2017, registered cases, seized over 950 incriminating documents and more than 600 electronic devices and chargesheeted important leaders including Hafiz Muhammad Saeed, Syed Salahuddin, Aftab Ahmad Shah r/o Srinagar, Nayeem Ahmad Khan, Chairman, National Front, Farooq Ahmad Dar, Chairman of JKLF (R), Mohammad Akbar Khanday, Spokesperson/Media Advisor of All Parties Hurriyat Conference (Geelani faction) and others.[12]

Following Prime Minister Modi's Independence Day address on 15th August 2017 when, with reference to J&K, he said that the problem of Kashmir can only be solved, '*na goli se na gali se, baat banegi galle lagne se*',[13] (not by bullets, nor by threats,

Table 2: Terror-related Incidents

Infiltration across IB and LoC					
Year	**2013**	**2014**	**2015**	**2016**	**2017**
Infiltration Attempts	277	222	121	371	406
Net Estimated Infiltration	97	65	33	119	123

Casualties of Civilians and Security Personnel due to Ceasefire Violations						
Year	**Civilians**		**Army Personnel**		**BSF Personnel**	
	Killed	**Injured**	**Killed**	**Injured**	**Killed**	**Injured**
2014	14	101	1	11	2	17
2015	16	71	6	17	4	9
2016	13	83	8	74	5	25
2017	12	79	15	58	4	14
2018 (February 28,2018)	12	59	06	18	4	22
Total	**67**	**393**	**36**	**178**	**19**	**87**

Terror-related Casualties

Year	No of terrorist violence incidents	Civilians killed in Terror strike	SF Personnel Killed	Terrorist Killed
2010	488	47	69	232
2011	340	31	33	100
2012	220	15	15	72
2013	170	15	53	67
2014	222	28	47	110
2015	208	17	39	108
2016	322	15	82	150
2017	342	54	80	213
2018 (March 04, 2018)	60	02	15	17
Total	2218	222	412	1041

No of Ceasefire Violations			
Years	**Along the LoC in J&K**	**Along the IB**	**Total**
2014	153	430	**583**
2015	152	253	**405**
2016	228	221	**449**
2017	860	111	**971**
2018	432 (February 28) 2018)	201(February 28) 2018)	**633**
Total	**795**	**927**	**3041**

Source – Ministry of Home Affairs, Government of India

resolution would be found only through consultations). Home Minister Rajnath Singh paid a series of visits to the State and held wide ranging consultations. To follow up these initiatives, the government, appointed Dineshwar Sharma, former chief of Intelligence Bureau, as Special Representative for Kashmir to engage with all the stakeholders in J&K,[14] a move that was welcomed by State Chief Minister Mehbooba Mufti, though, as expected the Joint Resistance Camp comprising of three separatist organisations – Syed Ali Shah Geelani-led the hard line, Mirwaiz Umar Farooq led the moderate factions of the Hurriyat Conference and Yaseen Malik's JKLF – rejected the dialogue offer as a mere rhetoric and wastage of time.[15]

Despite these, the prospects for early restoration of peace in the State do not appear bright, primarily because the entire terror apparatus operating in the State is managed and controlled by the Pakistani Deep State, which only tinkers with the tactics but refuses to change its strategic approach of using terror as a tool of its policy towards India. Therefore, the security situation is likely to remain as grim in the near future as in 2016 and 2017.

Security Challenges in the North East

Another area of continuing concern for the internal security apparatus is the situation in some of the North-Eastern States. Table 3 depicts the change in pattern of violence in the recent years. The most intensely affected States continue to be Assam and Manipur, accounting for bulk of the incidents of violence.

An analysis of the above indicates a major improvement the overall security situation in the North Eastern States. The number of terror incidents have come down from a high of 1,561 in 2008 to 308 last year. Similarly, there have been reduction under the other parameters as well with 995 extremists arrested in 2017, 57 extremists killed, 130 surrendered etc. While the improving security environment in Manipur is an encouraging development, the State continues to witness periodic disruption in the supply of essential commodities on account of the blockade of NH-39 and NH-53 by the United Naga Council and the all-Naga Student Association of Manipur. Manipuris are extremely concerned on this account and the government needs to take effective measures against repetitions of this in the future.

Encouraged by the overall improvement in the security situation marked by around 85 per cent decline in insurgency-related incidents compared to the peak level about two decades ago, the government has decided to withdraw the Armed Forces Special Powers Act (AFSPA) totally from Meghalaya as well as parts of Arunachal Pradesh with effect from 31 March 2018. The AFSPA was revoked in Tripura in May 2015. AFSPA, however, continues to be in operation in Arunachal Pradesh, in three Districts covered by eight police station jurisdictions, Assam, Nagaland and Manipur, except the Imphal Municipal Area.[16]

Table 3: Status of Extremism in North Eastern States

Year	Incidents	Extremists Arrested	Extremists Killed	Arms Recovered	SFs Killed	Civilians killed	Extremists surrendered in North East	Persons Kidnapped
2001	1335	NA	572	NA	175	600	NA	NA
2002	1312	1070	571	610	147	454	350	413
2003	1332	1014	523	442	90	494	669	NA
2004	1234	846	404	316	110	414	1284	NA
2005	1332	NA	405	NA	70	393	555	NA
2006	1366	NA	395	NA	76	309	1430	NA
2007	1489	1837	514	NA	79	498	524	NA
2008	1561	2566	640	NA	46	466	1112	NA
2009	1297	2162	571	NA	42	264	1109	NA
2010	773	2213	247	408	20	94	846	NA
2011	627	2141	114	1354	32	70	1122	NA
2012	1025	2145	222	1856	14	97	1195	329
2013	732	1712	138	1596	18	107	640	307
2014	824	1934	181	1255	20	212	965	369
2015	574	1900	149	897	46	46	143	267
2016	484	1202	87	698	17	48	267	168
2017	308	995	57	432	12	37	130	102
Total	**17605**	**23737**	**5790**	**9864**	**1014**	**4603**	**12341**	**1955**

Source – Ministry of Home Affairs, Government of India

Notwithstanding the above, the problems are too deep rooted to be wished away in a rush and the government, both at the Centre and more importantly at the State levels, will have to be focused on a development-driven programme to ensure lasting peace in the region. Subir Bhaumik, BBC's East India Correspondent and a known South Asian affairs observer, in his book, *Troubled Periphery: Crisis of India's North East,* described the North East as the '*problem child since the very inception of the Indian republic. It has also been South Asia's most enduring theatre of separatist guerrilla war, a region where armed action has usually been the first, rather than the last, option of political protest*'.[17]

The North-Eastern States have over 5,000 kilometres boundary with five countries, Nepal, China, Bhutan, Myanmar and Bangladesh. No other States/region in India abuts so many other countries. Therefore, as noted journalist Varghese justifiably argues, '*the entire North East must be treated in all strategic respects as a single, unified entity, a federation within a federation*'. '*They cannot prosper without regional integration. This alone will ensure cohesion, overall development, coordination and economies of scale.*'[18]

The North Eastern States have also been facing a serious problem of 'foreigners'. This has always been a very sensitive issue and has to be treated with a great deal of care. While varying estimates are made by different groups, the fact remains that the number of illegal migrants in the different States could be very high, particularly if the base for calculation is taken as 1947. This, however, could be highly unrealistic an approach. There is a degree of agreement amongst experts that most of them could be described as 'economic' migrants who came from Bangladesh in search of livelihood. Many of them have been in

India for decades and it is generally agreed that they cannot be deported except through due process which may be redefined if necessary. As per available information, 330 Pakistani and 1,770 Bangladeshi nationals have been repatriated during the last three years.[19]

The government is already working on this complex issue. In Assam, the National Register of Citizens (NRC) is being updated under the supervision of the Supreme Court of India. The first list with 1971 as the cut-off date was published on 31 December 2017 and was required to be finalised by 31 May 2018. Efforts need to continue to find an acceptable and workable solution to this problem.

Left Wing Extremism

In April 2008, the then Prime Minister, Manmohan Singh had described LWE as '*India's biggest internal security challenge ever*'. In fact, given the political philosophy of the Maoists, the methods employed by them in their political and military campaign that draw straight from the *Red Book* of revolution, it would be naïve to continue to treat this as a mere security challenge. LWE, if allowed to go unchecked, may ultimately pose a serious threat to our democratic polity, the state structure and indeed the very essence of everything that the Indian state as we know, stands for.

Recognising the seriousness of the LWE movement, PM Modi, very early in his tenure, while chairing a high-level review on tribal welfare, said: '*There is a need for the development of strategies to stop the spread of left wing extremism and it should be the key role to be played by the Government.*' He urged the stakeholders to identify growth centres within tribal areas and ensure proper development of education, health and sports facilities in the country. '*One of the key objectives should be to work towards technology penetration – for instance, electricity and mobile phone reach – in the tribal areas. Another important objective should be to link relatively undeveloped tribal areas with developed areas through good infrastructure*', Modi said during the review meet.[20]

The government has in recent times, followed a consistent policy of intelligence-driven kinetic operations coupled with targeted developmental activities in the affected areas. Besides, there was positive impact of the November 2016 demonitisation as it seriously diminished availability of cash with the extremists to carry on their armed campaign.

Table 4 clearly brings out the sharp decline in LWE violence as compared to the figures in 2010.

An analysis of the figures above suggests an all-round improvement in the security situation in the LW-affected areas. For example, it may be seen that the number of LWE-related incidents have gone down significantly from 2,213 in 2010 to 908 in 2017; number of SF personnel killed from 285 to 75; civilian causalities 720 down to 188 during the same period. Besides, the surrender of extremists has gone up from 265 in 2010 to 685 in 2017; attacks on police parties and establishments are down from 230 in 2010 to 84 last year. According to government statistics, the States of Chhattisgarh (373), Jharkhand (251), Bihar (99), Odisha (81) and Maharashtra (69) continued to witness significant LWE terror incidents in 2017. However, there are some areas of continuing concern, primarily in land mine incidents and injuries (177 in 2010 &153 in 2017); though it must be added that the Security Forces are maintaining the pressure through sustained encounters (272 in 2010 & 234 in 2017) and arrest of LWE activists which was 2,916 in 2010 & 1,887 in 2017.

Table 4: Status of Left Wing Extremism

Year	2010	2011	2012	2013	2014	2015	2016	2017	2018 (Feb 2018)
No of LWE Incidents	2213	1760	1415	1136	1091	1089	1048	908	151
No of Deaths	1005	611	415	397	310	230	278	263	26
No of SF Personnel Killed	285	142	114	115	88	59	65	75	11
No of Civilians Killed	720	469	301	282	222	171	213	188	15
No of SF Personnel injured in landmine blast	NA	177	189	170	183	159	145	153	39
No of Encounters with Police 272	272	223	216	218	221	247	330	234	49
No of Attacks on Police	230	131	135	143	155	118	111	84	23
LWE Cadre killed in encounter	172	99	74	100	63	89	222	136	24
LWE Cadre Arrested	2916	2030	1901	1397	1696	1668	1840	1888	318
Number of LWE cadres surrendered in country	265	394	445	282	676	570	1442	685	58
No of Arms snatched by LWE cadre from CAPF Personnel	256	67	55	89	58	18	03	34	04
No of Arms Recovered	642	636	591	628	548	724	800	591	121
No of Arms Traiing Camps held	94	84	53	27	34	18	20	19	0
No of Jan Adalats held	75	97	62	63	54	41	21	21	1

Compiled from Parliament Q&A – tabled by Ministry of Home Affairs, Government of India

The tempo of intelligence-based coordinated kinetic action against ranking members of the movement and their over ground civil support structures must be maintained. Besides, the forces must also follow the prescribed SOP in their field movements and operations. Above all, it is of paramount importance that developmental activities are pursued in right earnest and the CAPFs operating in the area are provided with the required equipment, intelligence support, training and periodic breaks.

New Challenges

In the opening paragraphs of this paper, while discussing Paleri's formulation on national security, reference was made to the new emerging challenges to National Security by including areas such as Economic Security, Resource Security, Border Security, Demographic Security, Disaster Security, Energy Security, Geo-strategic Security, Informational Security, Food Security, Health Security, Ethnic Security, Environmental Security, Cyber Security, Genomic Security etc. It was also mentioned above that India's National Security Council Secretariat (NSCS), in the Indian context, further expanded the scope of study by including even issues like good governance, health, water management, environment, technology as factors relevant to the debate on ensuring National Security. And the list could be still expanded by including issues like demographic shifts, natural disaster, agitations, flash mobs, role of social media, cybercrime etc.

The question before the planners of our security architecture is whether we have established institutions geared to effectively deal with these new and emerging challenges and if so, are these robust enough? It is not within the scope of this paper to deal with all these issues in detail, yet it needs to be mentioned that the government is alive to these challenges and has initiated steps to address them. But it is largely a work in progress. In some areas like Disaster Management, public health, cyber security, environmental security and good governance etc. considerable progress has already been achieved.

Government's Policies to Address Internal Security Concerns

Needless to say that the internal security challenges facing the country are daunting. The question is whether our internal security architecture is strong and widespread to deal with them effectively or at least adequately. The answer perhaps is in the negative, not so much due to the enormity of the problems as on account of the long period of neglect, structural complexities and, of course, the absence of deep commitment.

The problem begins with our federal structure of governance under which maintenance of L&O is the primary responsibility of the State governments which have their own priorities. One tends to get the impression that, strengthening the policing system as the first line of responders to the security challenges, does not figure high on their list. Rural and urban policing in the States suffer from multiplicity of shortcomings, be it the lack of adequate manpower including the quality of personnel, training including technical skills to deal with changing nature of crimes and security tasks, communications support, equipment, working conditions, housing, welfare measures etc. etc. Interestingly, these issues are not new; they have been there for decades despite continuous pumping of Central assistance every year.

Another issue that has remained unresolved relates to

Police Reforms as advocated by Prakash Singh, IPS (Retd), a lone and relentless campaigner who, despite the full backing of the Supreme Court, rightly feels frustrated with the attitude of the State governments in stalling the process of reforms. This is a classic case where the governments and the citizen alike; publicly express support for a modern, efficient, impartial, responsible and responsive police force and yet no political party in power or in opposition has done anything to empower the police force and the police administration at any level.

Role of the Central Government

Within these structural constraints, there is much that the Central and State governments can do to improve the delivery on maintenance of internal security. In fact, the Central government has come to acquire the role of the main driver of policies relating to maintenances of internal security, certainly largely disproportionate to its constitutional obligations in a federal structure. Accordingly, government's policies would fall in two inter-related parts, i.e. those in the domain of the State governments and those in which the Central government has to play the lead role. Some of the issues at the policy and conceptual levels are listed below.

Absence of National Security Doctrine

Despite facing serious internal security challenges emanating from a variety of sources, India has not yet evolved a comprehensive Internal Security Doctrine. In its editorial commentary post-Pathankot attack, *The Hindu* wrote, 'The challenge thrown up by the terrorist attack on the Pathankot air force base is to evolve India's national security doctrine to include its response to non-state actors… India needs a firm strategy to deal with terrorist threats that are now the prime challenge to the state. Political consensus must be evolved, in a publicly transparent manner, to reflect the complex challenge facing the country, detail its thresholds and interests that would be protected at any cost and response calibration *vis-à-vis* armed aggression. The doctrine must be accompanied by a national security strategy that spells out the command and control structures for meeting eventualities such as terror strikes'.[21]

As stated earlier, the main reason for this lapse is that India has for long looked at internal security challenges in different parts of the country in an episodic manner and tried to deal with them largely as L&O issues. Writing in the *Indian Express* (10 July 2017) noted security expert Prakash Singh said, 'Successive governments have not cared to codify the country's internal security doctrine and the present government has also ignored this vital area and taken ad hoc decisions on crucial matters. The US and UK revise their national security doctrines every year and place them in the public domain. We have done nothing of the sort, despite the fact that our internal security problems are far more complex'.[22]

This issue needs serious consideration. If the exercise were to start now, we may perhaps get a National Security Doctrine in about 2 to 3 years' time after extensive debate at the level of experts and in the public domain. Never too late to start a good deed!

Terrorism, Terror Financing, Investigation, Legislations

The Government of India (GoI) did enact the Unlawful Activities (Prevention) Act (UAPA) in 1967 which is still valid and in use. It was given additional bite through two amendments in 2008, incorporating definition of terror and in 2013 incorporating economic and financial offences therein.

Following the assassination of PM Indira Gandhi, the GoI went in for the now infamous Terrorists and Disruptive Activities (Prevention) Act 1987 (TADA). This was, however, allowed to lapse in 1995 due to serious complaints of political misuse of its provisions. TADA did, however, give us a definition of terrorism for the first time. After the lapse of TADA, in the wake of the attack on the Parliament, the government came up with Prevention of Terrorism Act, 2002 (POTA). But soon, in 2004, this too was repealed on grounds similar to that of TADA.

So, currently the only Central law available for dealing with terror-related incidents is the UAPA with its two amendments as mentioned earlier. However, the State of Maharashtra came up with its own legislation: the Maharashtra Control of Organised Crime Act, 1999 (MCOCA). Two other States, Chhatisgarh and Karnataka, have also come up with their own legislations. What is still missing is a comprehensive anti-terror legislation with all-India applicability and containing the required special provisions of admissibility of evidence, provisions of arrest and bail etc. which lead to long delays. This needs to be taken up in earnest.

In the area of dealing with terror financing, the Central government has done commendable work over the last decade and half by enacting the Prevention of Money Laundering Act, 2002 which was repeatedly amended in 2005, 2009, 2012 and 2017. Two other legislations to regulate flow of illegal fund are Foreign Exchange Management Act (FEMA) 1999 and the Foreign Contribution (regulation) Act, 2010 (FCRA). Besides, Financial Intelligence Unit-India (FIU-IND) was set up in November 2004 as the central national agency responsible for receiving, processing, analysing and disseminating information relating to suspect financial transactions.

It may also be mentioned here that one of the major challenges being faced in India in the investigation and prosecution of terror cases is the inordinate delay in completion of the entire process. The reasons could be many and are well known. Primarily, this happens on account of absence of a single omnibus legislation, delays caused by procedural ambiguities, laws of bail and appeal, transfer of investigating officers etc. For example, the Bombay Serial Blast case of March 1993 could finally be decided after 22 years in 2015. Similarly, the accused in the Parliament attack case of December 2001 was finally hanged in 2013 after 12 years and Ajmal Kasab, who perpetrated the Mumbai Terror attack in Nov 2008, was hanged in 2012. These should amply justify the urgent need for a serious rethink on reforming the entire judicial system relating to investigation and prosecution of terrorism cases.

In a significant move, after the Mumbai Blast in 2008, the government decided to set up the now famous NIA to deal with all cases of terrorism. This has made a remarkable difference in the speed and quality of investigation into terror cases. NIA has so far investigated 166 cases since its inception and of the 35 cases already tried in the NIA special courts, a remarkably high number of convictions have been obtained in 33 cases.[23] The 95 per cent conviction rate achieved by the NIA shows its meticulous skills of investigations.[24] The NIA needs to be strengthened and given the required professional manpower etc. to emerge as a world class investigative agency in dealing with terror cases. Any attempt to turn it into another '*Caged Parrot*', must be shunned. The other significant action post-26/11 was the establishment of NSG hubs at different convenient locations around the country to ensure quick response to any serious situation.

What else does the Government need to do?

The role of the Central government is all encompassing; not restricted only to enactment of enabling legislations but also to establishment of comprehensive national security architectures to meet the existing and evolving challenges.

It is also expected to play a leading role in enforcing the rule of law in a fair and equitable manner; creating and maintaining a conducive socio-political environment of peace and amity; working towards timely resolution of issues that endanger internal disorder; establishing mechanism for redressal of grievances; putting in place a robust network of security forces starting with a modern, mobile and effective para military forces; establishing an efficient and effective intelligence apparatus at the federal and State levels; effectively handling all investigating procedures and ensuring the required judicial system for quick and effective dispensation of justice etc. The list could be endless but these are some of the essential elements constituting a responsible and responsive system of governance.

At this stage, one can safely say that the Central government has largely done its share of work and is in the process of doing more to meet its obligations. One would like to believe that most of these requirements have been or are being addressed. What is now left is for the government to enact special legislations providing for a modified version of the Evidence Act on admissibility of evidence, a CrPC variant on procedures to be followed for speedy trail, special provisions for Bail and Appeals etc. What also needs to be done is to aggressively push through its ambitious programme of modernisation of the State Police and CAPFs, requiring heavy investment of central funds, easy and timely provision of special equipment and above all, specialised training of thousands of police and CPMF personnel in dealing with insurgencies, militancy and subversive activities of anti-national elements. It may be mentioned here that the Central government had allocated Rs 1,500 cr in the 2014-15 budget but this has gradually come down to 769 cr in the 2017-18 budget with current utilisation at only Rs 451.66 cr. [25]

Another important aspect of dealing with internal disorder is the requirement of the State to establish an effective *National Counter Terrorism Centre* (NCTC). Soon after the Mumbai Blast, an attempt was made but had to be dropped in view of serious opposition from a number of State governments. There was justifiable apprehension that some elements of the proposed legislation were in conflict with the delicate balance of federalism as constitutionally established. Central and State governments need to evolve the necessary political consensus on these vital issues, sooner the better. Governments must also develop a bi-partisan approach on defining and clearly articulating its policy on national security.

Role of the State Governments

The local police being the first responder, both in terms of action on the ground and in legal aspects, remains the weakest link. Initially all serious crimes impacting internal security are dealt with by the local police under the provisions of the normal laws like Indian Penal Code (IPC), Explosives Act, Arms Act etc. and investigated under the omnibus procedures prescribed under the CrPC and the Evidence Act. Some cases were handled by the State CID and a few went to the CBI. To say the least, this was highly unprofessional and suffered the attendant limitations.

One of the most debated points in our internal security debates over the years has been the role played by the State governments as clearly some of the critical aspects of ensuring internal security fall within the purview of the State government's charter of responsibilities. The general perception has been that perhaps they have not done enough and that they could and should have done much more. For example, the State police forces are woefully short of manpower. What is worse is that even that has not been fully subscribed. The sanctioned strength is well below internationally prescribed yardstick. According to the latest report placed before the Parliament in response to a question, the all India figure of civil police vacancy stands at a staggering figure of 443,524. At present 1,545,771 police personnel are in position against 1,989,295 posts sanctioned by the government (GoI, 2018). Some of the major defaulters in this context are the States of UP with 214,335 vacancies followed by WB (38,580) Bihar (24,484), Gujarat (30,795), Jharkhand (25,927) and so on. Surprisingly, even the IPS cadre carries 938 vacancies against their sanctioned strength of 4,843 nationally! These need to be filled up in quick time.

The District Civil and Armed Police, as the first line of response, are apparently good enough only for meeting normal L&O duties. It must, however, be admitted, when adequately provided for and empowered, as in Punjab, J&K and even in LWE-infected areas, they have acquitted themselves admirably, rising to the occasion to meet difficult challenges.

Revamping Intelligence Apparatus

Revamping India's intelligence apparatus and mechanism for dissemination of processed and actionable intelligence is a specialised subject requiring separate study and debate.

Undeniably, many of the potentially developing internal security situations could be nipped in the bud with timely, accurate and actionable intelligence. One can cite scores of instances from personal experience in support of this perception. Yet, this also highlights one of the major inadequacies in our internal security management approach.

Intelligence is an area in which the local police has been generally found deficient. It is strongly believed that no one can have better access to real time actionable intelligence that can nip the trouble in the bud, than the local police and the local intelligence branch. Perhaps, this inadequacy has been the result of the over dependence of the State governments on the central agencies to play the lead role in this area and virtually spoon-feed the state agencies. This needs to be corrected, sooner the better. Greater accountability in the working of the State Special Branches is called for. Here also, it must be admitted that wherever they have done so, the results have been remarkable as had been witnessed earlier in Punjab and currently in J&K. It is understood that the local agencies have also done extremely well in generating actionable intelligence in the North East and the LWE-infected areas.

In 2008, the Government of India had, alongside the NCTC, envisaged the establishment of a National Intelligence Grid (NATGRID), a central agency to have an integrated intelligence grid that will link and store sensitive information for counter-terror investigations. It was established to bolster India's counter-terrorism capabilities by combining 21 sensitive databases on various domains including banks, credit cards, cell-phone usage, immigration records etc. Unlike the proposed NCTC and the NIA which are central organisations, NATGRID is essentially a tool that enables security agencies to locate and obtain relevant information on terror suspects from pooled data of various organisations and services in the country. It will help identify, capture and prosecute terrorists and help pre-empt terrorist plots.[26] The project needs to be expedited.

It is encouraging to note that according to the Annual report of MHA, 2017-18, '*Multi Agency Centre has established connectivity between the National Capital, 25 Central Member Agencies and all the State Capitals. In the State Capitals, this network links the Subsidiary Multi Agency Centre (SMAC), State Police Special Branches and Offices of all the Central and other Counter Terror Agencies. The network is also being extended to District Police Headquarters wherever found feasible. At present total of 429 SMAC Nodes and 251 District Police Offices are connected to the MAC/SMAC Network*'.[27]

People's Expectations - are these Being Met?

While the desirables have been listed out, it needs to be reiterated that even within the constraints and inadequacies the expectation of the State, the society and the common citizen is that their security concerns be effectively addressed under a well-defined National Security Policy. They expect the security forces to deliver, and these deliverables are not difficult to enumerate. In simple terms, the people expect the security forces to enforce the rule of law, be fair and impartial in their actions, maintain peace and stability, deal effectively with the trouble makers while, at the same time, conforming to the requirement of observing human rights.

Are these expectations being met? The general perception is otherwise. Virtually every instance involving internal security issues, is accompanied by major public and media outcry of perceived excesses by the security forces either in terms of disproportionate use of force, absence of humane approach, inadequate understanding of the causes leading to the event, unsympathetic post-event management among others. Security experts have even been raising the question, with some justification, as to whether the deployed forces have the basic training to deal with different types of internal security challenges or are they simply following the normal crowd control procedures in every instance? One of the frequent refrains in these debates has been of the forces adopting a '*trigger-happy*' approach. Another oft-repeated allegation is political interference in internal security management. Maintenance of internal security is a vital component of national security. It is a huge national challenge that requires national debate and national response. It is imperative that the existing systems under the national security architecture be strengthened and updated and the deficiencies addressed with a view to '*Securing India*'.

References

1 Shama sastry, R. (1915). *Kautilya's Arthashastra.* Bangalore, Karnataka, India: Government Press. Retrieved March 23, 2018, from https://csboa.com/eBooks/Arthashastra_of_Chanakya_-_English.pdf

2 Paleri, P. (2008). *National Security: Imperatives and Challenges.* New Delhi: Tata Mcgrawhill. Retrieved March 12, 2018.

3 Chandra , S. (2015, June 26). National Security: Concept, Measurement and Management. *Strategic Analysis, 39*(4), 337-359.

4 International Business Publication. (2015). *Global National Security and Intelligence Agencies Handbook Volume 1 Strategic Information and Important Contacts.* Washington DC, United States of India: International Business Publication. Retrieved 2018.

5 Chaturvedi, A. K. (2014). *Nuclear Energy in India's Energy Security Matrix: An Appraisal.* New Delhi, India: Vij Books India Pvt Ltd.

6 Government of India. 2000. *Report of the Group of Ministers on National Security.* Review , New Delhi: Government of India, 2. Accessed March 12, 2018. www.vifindia.org/sites/default/files/GoM%20Report%20on%20National%20Security.pdf

7 FICCI . (2008). *Task Force Report on National Security and Terrorism.* New Delhi: Federation of Indian Chamber of Commerce and Industries. Retrieved September 12, 2017, from http://rajeev.in/task_force_report_on_national_security_&_terrorism.pdf

8 Government of India, N. M. (2011). *Interrogation report of David Colman Headly.* Retrieved December 12, 2017, from https://www.investigativeproject.org/: https://www.investigativeproject.org/documents/case_docs/1602.pdf

9 US Department of State, B. (2001, December 26). *Foreign Terrorist Organizations.* Retrieved December 26, 2017, from Designated Foreign Terrorist Organizations: https://www.state.gov/j/ct/rls/other/des/123085.htm

10 Government of India, M. (2017, February 7). *Demonetisation of old 500 and 1000 Rupee Notes.* Retrieved September 23, 2017, from pib.nic.in: http://pib.nic.in/newsite/mbErel.aspx?relid=158183

11 Government of India, M. (2018). *Annual Report 2017-18.* Ministry of Home Affairs. New Delhi: Government of India. Retrieved April 20, 2018, from https://mha.gov.in/sites/default/files/MINISTRY%20OF%20HOME%20AFFAIR%20AR%202017-18%20FOR%20WEB.pdf

12 Government of India, N. M. (2017, May 30). *Case Detail - Funding to separatist organisation in J&K.* Retrieved May 02, 2018, from www.nia.gov.in: http://www.nia.gov.in/case-detail.htm?169

13 Express Web Desk. (2017, August 15). Na goli se, na gaali se: Embrace Kashmir, says PM Narendra Modi in Independence Day speech. *The Indian Express.* Retrieved January 23, 2018, from http://indianexpress.com/article/india/na-goli-se-na-gaali-se-embrace-kashmir-says-pm-narendra-modi-in-independence-day-speech-4797241/

14 Government of India, M. (2017, October 23). *Centre appoints Shri Dineshwar Sharma as its Representative in J&K.* Retrieved January 23, 2018, from pib.nic.in: http://pib.nic.in/newsite/PrintRelease.aspx?relid=171866

15 Dulat, A. S. (2017, November 06). Unsettling the status quo in Jammu and Kashmir. *The Hindu.* Retrieved December 12, 2017, from

http://www.thehindu.com/opinion/op-ed/unsettling-the-status-quo/article19993615.ece

16 Jain, B. (2018, April 24). AFSPA removed from Meghalaya after 27 years. *The Times of India.* Retrieved April 26, 2018, from https://timesofindia.indiatimes.com/india/afspa-removed-from-meghalaya-after-27-years-assam-too-may-reduce-afspa-area/articleshow/63887983.cms

17 Bhaumik, S. (2009). *Troubled Periphery: The Crisis of India's North East* (1 ed.). New Delhi, India: Sage Publication.

18 Verghese, B. G. (2013, May). *India's Eastern Gateway.* Retrieved May 01, 2018, from http://www.bgverghese.com/EasternGateway.htm

19 Government of India, M. (2018, March 20). *Illegal Immigrants* . Retrieved from https://pib.nic.in/: http://pib.nic.in/newsite/PrintRelease.aspx?relid=177727

20 Government of India, M. (2015, January 15). *PM chairs review meeting on tribal welfare, describes the tribal communities of India as a great force for national development.* Retrieved January 12, 2018, from pib.nic.in: http://pib.nic.in/newsite/PrintRelease.aspx?relid=114817

21 The Hindu Editorial Team. (2016, January 5). Opinion -Time for a national security doctrine. *The Hindu.* Retrieved December 12, 2017, from http://www.thehindu.com/opinion/editorial/Time-for-a-national-security-doctrine/article13980984.ece

22 Singh, P. (2017, July 10). Internal insecurity. *The Indian Express.* Retrieved January 12, 2018, from http://indianexpress.com/article/opinion/columns/india-internal-threats-kashmir-issue-naxalities-protest-against-government-internal-insecurity-4743274/

23 Government of India, M. (2017, October 08). *Union Home Minister to inaugurate NIA Hqrs Office Complex on 10th October* . Retrieved from https://pib.nic.in: http://pib.nic.in/newsite/PrintRelease.aspx?relid=171489

24 IANS. (2018. January 24). Our conviction rate is 95%: NIA DG. *The Times of India.* Retrieved April 23, 2018, from http://www.business-standard.com/article/news-ians/our-conviction-rate-is-95-nia-dg-118012401487_1.html

25 Ibid 11.

26 Ibid 11.

27 Ibid 11.

National Aspirations and Military Spending

Anil Chopra

In the current world order, military instrument is a significant ingredient of projecting, perceived and actual power and greatly impact international dynamics and relations between nations. It is also greatly relevant to national prestige and influence, and is a ubiquitous factor in diplomacy, international negotiations, and bargaining positions on the global stage. No amount of soft or sharp power can substitute for possessing the capability which allows a viable military option when required.

India's military spending, as a percentage of both its GDP (and of annual government outlays), has been steadily falling in recent years Can India's greater aspirations be met without significant conventional military power? Can the ends of economic and comprehensive security be realised without adequate spending on traditional military forces? Will nuclear capability by itself be enough? Can the soft voice of deft and superior diplomacy carry heft without being backed by the proverbial, usable "big stick"?

Reduced Military Spending

INDIA'S MILITARY spending, as a percentage of both its GDP and of annual government outlays, has been steadily falling in recent years, from a high of 2.35 in 2009-10 to 1.58 for the current year, the lowest figure in over five decades. For a country which is emerging on the global stage as a nation of some consequence, this is an unfortunate development.

In the current Westphalian world order, the 'conventional' military instrument is a significant ingredient of projected, perceived and actual power, since it is usable, and has been observed to impact international dynamics in both geo-political and geo-economic spheres. It is also greatly relevant to national prestige and influence, and is a major omnipresent, albeit understated, factor in diplomacy, rule-making, commercial and trade negotiations, and sundry bargaining positions on the global canvas.

A refusal to accept this reality and consider the military as only germane to infrequent and unlikely fighting of wars, will almost surely result in delaying or even negating India's rise in a world which acknowledges and values hard power, and has little time for those bereft of it. No amount of soft or sharp power can substitute for possessing the capability which allows a viable military option when required. 'The strong do what they can, and the weak suffer what they must', holds as true today, as in the time of Thucydides.

India is indeed increasingly perceived as an economic, demographic, maritime and nuclear power, with much greater potential even in the near-term. It has a large, apolitical and professional military, with considerable combat experience; and a balanced, three-dimensional, blue-water, actively-deployed Navy, which has attracted the attention of friends and foes alike. It's nuclear and space capabilities are also acknowledged as worthy of a regional, if not a great power in the making.

However, it also has an underdeveloped defence industrial base, a less than ideal military R&D structure, note-worthy operational gaps in equipment and ordnance, unresolved organisational issues and less-than-ideal civil-military relations. Moreover, the force-levels of its armed forces have remained stagnant, or even declined in some areas. Modernisation programmes face many hurdles, resulting in precious time and attendant cost over-runs, and in operational voids.

The inability of the Indian 'system' to find the political, financial and procedural fusion to induct critically and urgently required military platforms and equipment, in the required time-frames, is a telling commentary on national will and strategic foresight. This would doubtless have been observed in many quarters, both malignant and benign, as would have been the detrimental consequences of inadequate funding for maintenance, repair and training—in effect, for both military preparedness and operational readiness.

Consequently, in informed circles, the jury is still out as to whether India can be regarded as a significant military power. Does this even matter in a globalised world obsessed with technology and economics? Many in India's polity think not. In simplistic terms, *there is a growing belief that in an age of 'comprehensive' security, nuclear deterrence, and global economic and cyber linkages—conventional military power and threats are increasingly irrelevant, and monies can be better spent elsewhere—* on more positive national aspirations, so to speak.

What are these aspirations? Ever since Independence, there has been an absence of officially published white papers and similar documents by successive governments in India. Some would argue this is but a reflection of incoherent thinking at the admittedly complex grand-strategic level, which requires synthesis of diverse and often contradictory objectives. The lack of an articulated strategy is however explained away as an attribute of a superior 'grand-strategy of ambiguity'.

Be that as it may, under the circumstances of officially published documents, broad proclamations of national aspirations and interests by elected representatives and officials have to suffice. These generally highlight the 'security, prosperity and well-being of the people', in addition to 'eradication of poverty and illiteracy' as a core national interest; 'sovereignty and strategic autonomy' as another; and not the least, for India to find its 'rightful place in the comity of nations'.

These aspirations naturallv translate into a quest for donning the mantle of a regional/Asian power through development and economic growth, enhanced trade and influence, and putting in place the required infrastructure for logistics and connectivity. Besides, many in the Indian intelligentsia also see the country as a 'net security provider' in the Indian Ocean Region – and given its population, size and economy, a significant player on the world stage, with permanent membership of the United Nations Security Council.

The moot question, therefore, is whether India's greater aspirations can be met without being a significant conventional military power? Is a strong regular military of any advantage on the international stage? Can the ends of economic and comprehensive security be realised without adequate spending on traditional military forces? Will nuclear capability by itself be enough? Can nuclear weapons ever be used to garner negotiating advantage in everyday global issues, or is their bluff easily called? Can economic and soft power be a substitute for raw military force in routine international affairs? Can the soft voice of deft and superior diplomacy carry heft without being backed by the proverbial, usable 'big stick'?

In sum, can India's aspirations and interests be met through suitable alignments, intelligence inputs, diplomacy and guarding the borders, be backed by economic and nuclear power? Given India's declining conventional military strength and budget, answering these questions, or at least considering them, would be prudent.

Whilst there is no gainsaying that 'gross national power' is clearly far more than just military capability, and 'comprehensive security' is indeed a larger concept than being able to address possible military action by adversaries, *the general discourse prevalent in the Indian strategic community is increasingly and alarmingly dismissive about the criticality, and even the centrality, of conventional military power* in the prevailing international security-power matrix.

The pursuit of all national aspirations demands that external actors not be allowed to disturb the peace. Do we have adequate deterrence and dissuasion? Can the real and present conventional and sub-conventional danger posed by being simultaneously confronted with two major adversarial neighbours, acting in concert with one another, be met with current levels of military expenditure, especially in a scenario where the nation lacks a developed defence industrial base?

One uses the phrase 'military' expenditure rather than 'defence' spending, because the defence budget, now itself at a historic low, sustains many ancillary and auxiliary organisations and pursuits, and does not necessarily give an accurate picture of the substantially lesser funds available to the fighting forces for modernisation and procurement on one hand, and day-to-day operating costs on the other.

The present level of military expenditure appears to suggest that India can disregard any serious full-scale military threat, and the harsh realities of our 'tough' neighbourhood. Before examining linkages between military spending and national aspirations, it might be appropriate to first examine the probability or otherwise, of non-nuclear conflict between states in contemporary times, which many appear to have discarded as a possibility. It would also be helpful if we desist from applying the geopolitical templates of Europe and the Americas to our part of the planet, although great power rivalry between developed nations is making a reappearance on the global stage.

Conventional Conflict and Traditional Security

The contemporary world order, despite globalisation and economic inter-dependence, continues to be cast in the essentially anarchic Westphalian mould, where might is still demonstrably right, as any number of examples in the recent past, from the South China Sea and the Crimea, to Syria and Iraq can vouch for.

There are, however, many within both India's polity and its strategic community, who do sincerely believe that the spending on the conventional military is adequate, and that the nation has other pressing non-traditional security, developmental and social demands which can only be met by limiting expenditure on the armed forces, the traditional instrument of hard power. This school of conviction is of the opinion that significant conventional conflict is well-nigh impossible between nuclear powers, that the usage of conventional force can at best result in skirmishes which can be addressed by border guarding mechanisms, and that anything more serious than a spat would be limited by appropriate actions of the international community.

This body of opinion further underscores its arguments by articulating that the economic linkages of nations that trade with each other in a globalised economy would also inhibit 'war' in the traditional sense. Last, but not least, there is the belief that the destructive power of modern conventional weapons is so great, and the effects so horrific, that even the most crazed regime would not embark on military adventures of any great consequence. In sum, this opinion believes that conventional war on a large scale is passé.

Is war really passé? History records that wars have been fought for any number of reasons – territorial, religious, ideological, sectarian, for living space, for natural resources, for vendetta, for imagined or real slight, for sheer domination and influence, and so on. Some even argue that violence and conflict are endemic to the human species, inherent in its very DNA, a premise readily accepted in popular cultural extrapolations into the future, which often paint a scenario of Star Wars! A struggle for supremacy, or for defending a way of life, has been a constant feature of the human condition. The end of the Cold War has regrettably not heralded the 'end of history', and new conflicts and alignments rage anew. The US National Security Strategy released in 2017 and its National Defence Strategy 2018, highlight the traditional military threats from China and Russia, and the world seems poised, once again, for possible great power conflict.

It would be unrealistic to imagine that the motivations for conventional armed conflict are likely to disappear, either due to the scale of possible destruction or because of a nuclear overhang. The only means of securing peace, given human propensity for using force, is through balance of power and deterrence mechanisms. This requires military force. In fact, the roles and functions of the military in peacetime and crises are critical in keeping the peace through the time-tested principles of deterrence and credible rapid response capability.

Should deterrence fail, and war be thrust upon a nation, it needs to be highlighted that *the defence of the realm requires a great deal of offensive action*. Enemies are not defeated by holding operations on the ground, fences, border guards, air defence, and protecting coastlines, but rather by proactive manoeuvre warfare on land, sea and in the air. Forget victory, even successful defence requires strategies, tactics and plans which involve sending the armed forces into enemy territory and into harm's way, even at the cost of massive enemy retaliation and heavy casualties. Military operations can only succeed through bold planning, good leadership, a great amount of training and modern weapons and equipment. All this requires money—not only in the capital budget, but under revenue heads.

The alternative, of course, is to outsource security through military alliances and pacts, as we have seen in Europe, and also in the case of Japan after the World War II. However, as George Washington famously warned his countrymen, 'entangling' alliances dilute a nation's strategic autonomy and flexibility, and there is never any certainty that allies, despite a convergence of interests, would indeed enter into armed conflict on behalf of another, when the push comes to a shove.

Nations and civilisations who have predicated their grand strategy on the assumption of sustained peace have in the past, paid heavily for what is essentially wishful thinking. Let there be no doubt that there is plenty of space beneath the nuclear threshold for successful conventional, sub-conventional and hybrid conflict. *If conventional deterrence were to fail, geographies can indeed be significantly altered, and what is of more concern, 'strategic humiliation' can be inflicted,* even if one were to hypothetically accept a short-war scenario. In fact, as technology drives us towards artificial intelligence, robots and unmanned platforms, the propensity for outbreak of conventional war is only likely to increase.

Nations, especially those at India's stage of development, with its prospects for a bright future, *can ill afford to be humiliated or suffer a set back through a military reversal,* stemming from a loss of deterrence due to inadequate conventional military wherewithal or operational readiness, in itself brought about by inadequate defence funding. It would be rather difficult to enhance national prestige and influence and aspire for regional leadership in the wake of military misfortune. Nations, like humans, are contemptuous of losers.

Let us, however, reject the notion that a conventional hybrid war is a possibility, and subscribe to the conviction that deterrence can be achieved by large numbers of para-military personnel at the borders, with moderate military capability and air power in reserve, in the rear. It would be evident that even if this essentially defensive arrangement – in tandem with nuclear capability – can ward off threats and war, it would be of little utility in pursuing India's interests and aspirations across the region and the globe.

Military Power and National Influence

Even a cursory historical examination of the interplay between nations would force us to acknowledge that military power lies at the heart of any world order—be it old or new, Pax Romana, Britannica, or Americana, unipolar, bipolar or multipolar. This is particularly true of the Westphalian system we now live in, wherein there are no designated enforcers of prevailing international law or acceptable behaviour. Certainly, the UN Security Council (UNSC) and a plethora of economic sanctions have not been able to prevent nations and other groupings from resorting to violence, and assertive use of force to protect and further national interests. Direct military action, unilateral, or in concert with allies, or through willing coalitions, and even through proxies, is indeed the order of the day, and continues to alter geopolitical realities and boundaries, constantly impacting geo-economics.

The last three decades since the Cold War have witnessed huge military build-up across regions and nations, and military capacity building has become a major objective across the globe. Even small and impoverished states are seen to be acquiring potent weapon systems and platforms, including precision guided munitions, and submarines. Balance of power imperatives weigh heavily on all nations. There can be no better example of aspirational linkage to military spending than that observed in the case of the People's Republic of China. Beijing's admittedly great and rapid economic gains since the 1980s had the world both admiring and applauding, but there was little talk of it being a major power, let alone a great power. Neither had its nuclear arsenal since the 1960's conferred it the great power status. It was only after its recent acquisition of considerable conventional and expeditionary military power that a shaken world has taken note of China's challenge to the *status quo* and acknowledged its bid for great power status. Beijing's maritime thrust since 2008 has reinforced this perception.

Economic power by itself can never provide adequate influence and weight in international affairs. This can best be illustrated by the post-war fortunes of Germany and Japan. Despite being the second and third largest economies of the world, both nations remain at the fringes of the world's core power structures and arrangements. Even if their present lack of military power is due to their defeat in World War II, the fact remains that they are in no position to demand a seat at the high table, or greatly influence rule-making and standard-setting in the globalised geo-economic architecture.

Why is this so, when conventional wisdom appears to discount a major conflict among most nations. This is because deep down, all nations, even the most pacifist and peace-loving of them, realise that in international affairs, despite humanity's best efforts, force is the ultimate arbiter, and often necessary when talks and parleys fail to address differences and discord. Militaries have then to act to meet the threat of force, or to protect and further far-flung interests.

In addition, history reveals that trade follows flag, or flag follows trade. On the global canvas, economic and military fortunes of nations are intertwined. This was not only true in the age of colonisation but is clearly evident in the policies of diverse nations, from China to France, even today. Military deployment and presence in areas of economic interest are a *sine qua non* in global competition. All matters of geo-economic endeavour - trade, investments, markets and resource mining benefit from the latent stability and security provided by deployable conventional forces.

Be it in interpersonal or corporate or political affairs, the projection of incipient power is standard operating procedure on the part of whosoever possesses it. Nowhere is this more apparent than in the military arena. Power projection is a legitimate military role in peace and crisis to achieve ones ends without the actual use of force. Military visibility and presence serves to influence, coax and cajole both opponents and allies. Clearly, any nation with usable, expeditionary capability has a tremendous advantage in the Westphalian order.

In this regard the attributes of the oceanic domain, and of navies, are particularly noteworthy. The seventy per cent of the Earth's surface which is covered by water is indeed the last great commons of mankind on the planet and provides legitimate access to all manner of sea-farers including those in warships. This freedom of navigation enshrined in the concept of Mare Librium, or freedom of the seas from ownership by any power, allows strong navies immense utility as instruments of state power in peace and crisis. Using their inherent access, mobility, flexibility, versatility, reach and persistence, warships can be used to convey a variety of messages and diplomatic signalling. They can appear over the horizon to threaten or reassure, and just as easily disappear into the blue without the stigma of retreat. Fully self-sufficient in logistics and armament, they can be hurled into action at a moment's notice, be it for combat or disaster relief.

In sum, conventional military power matters greatly, and is of consequence for far more than just for war-fighting. If this was not the case, the world's nations would not be spending billions of dollars to maintain conventional military machines, and certainly nuclear powers would not need to do so. It may be noted that it is the foremost nuclear powers, including

United States, Russia and China who are spending the most on the conventional military forces.

It, of course, needs no highlighting that the conventional military forces of the world are increasingly used in non-military fashion, principally for international humanitarian and disaster relief, for non-combatant evacuation operations, for regional search and rescue, for UN peace-keeping operations, and for international constabulary functions such as the anti-piracy initiative off the Horn of Africa.

Guns versus Butter

Whilst exploring the links between aspirations and military expenditure, it would be appropriate to accept that economic strength is at the fountainhead of all types of hard power, and a considerable part of soft power too. Clearly, none of India's aspirations can be met without strong economy, and military power does indeed also stem from it. Modern militaries are a frightfully expensive business, and only nations with relativity deep pockets can afford to be major military powers.

History is certainly replete with examples of how excessive military spending by nations, beyond their sustainable economic capacity, can deplete national coffers of the means required to progress in other aspects of national endeavour, such as internal stability, economic growth and development, and the upliftment of the economically and socially disadvantaged, leading in extreme cases to national collapse, as witnessed in the recent past in the case of the Soviet Union. However, history is also replete with many examples of how prosperous nations squandered their wealth, their reputation, their influence and even their very freedom, by not possessing the means to deter rivals and defend themselves on the fields of battle or of geopolitical contest. Such was the case of France, whose relative military weakness, and consequent appeasement of Hitler did little to prevent Germany from occupying it in World War II.

Besides suffering the dishonour and ignominy of defeat, being vanquished or even humiliated militarily also results in a huge loss of national confidence and self-esteem. The effects of such a blow to the national psyche lasts over many generations and centuries, and often alters the very character of a people for the worse. Tales of individual valour cannot erase the harsh realities of defeat in war. A history of military reverses can hardly command respect in the international arena, and also serves to make a nation effete. Resolve is replaced by caution, assertiveness by appeasement, and an offensive spirit by an overtly defensive one. Defence is reduced to fences and walls, and sentries and guards become the face of national defence. Survival at all costs replaces adherence to principles, and pride and honour are consigned as irrelevant to the objective. National character suffers.

There are, of course, any number of empirical studies which underline the contribution of military spending towards economic development in terms of energising local economies, driving infrastructure and connectivities, giving impetus to job creation, enhancing technical skills and so on. This aspect is often overlooked by those who see all defence appropriations as being wasteful, and a drain on the exchequer. Moreover, as highlighted above, the absence of a robust, deployable military force results in major intangible opportunity costs, in terms of political influence and economic advantage, be it in the immediate neighbourhood, or further afield. This is not just a question of loss, but of potential danger, as geopolitical rivals gain footholds in vital contested areas.

Clearly then, mature nations have to find a realistic balance between 'guns and butter'. This debate is not of one between economic development and military wherewithal, but a debate on how much, given the threats and interests prevailing, needs to be spent on the nation's military. It would be evident that this figure cannot be arrived at in isolation of the geopolitical environment, or by executive diktat. It will necessarily depend, *inter alia*, on the threat perception, vital interests which need to be protected or furthered, instability in the neighbourhood, the military capabilities of possible adversaries, and any alliances from where direct military support may be forthcoming. It will also have to take into account the indigenous availability of 'credible' weapons, sensors and military equipment, and the compulsions to import material.

India's Strategic Compulsions and Imperatives

Newly independent at the dawn of the Cold War and partitioned at birth, India was extra-ordinarily diverse in every way, desperately underdeveloped, immediately faced with multiple internal crises, and had to contend with severe food scarcity. Though facing a hostile Pakistan let, stay, it certainly had more on its plate than just military concerns. Economic development and upliftment of the poor was seen then, as now, as a more pressing and noble endeavour, which it doubtless is. The possibility of a military attack seemed far-fetched and provided justifiable reason to neglect the military in the early years. Inadequate attention was paid to military preparedness, operational readiness and balance of military power. This regrettably led to humiliation and loss of territory on the northern borders. The blame game, and search for scapegoats, thereafter scarred the national psyche even more.

It would therefore be an useful exercise to broadly highlight a few of India's strategic compulsions, threats and interests, so as to dwell on whether the contemporary environment requires a well-equipped and robust military with the attendant expenditure, or whether these can be addressed through non-military means.

Both China and Pakistan have territorial claims on Indian territory across long borders, which they have kept alive through prolonged conflict, which are ongoing wars in all but name. Clearly, conventional deterrence through overwhelming superiority has possibly been lost, and the conflict rages below the nuclear threshold, with sub-conventional, hybrid characteristics. In the absence of alternatives, any military solution would have to be conventional. Moreover, the possibility of the much pilloried 'two-front' conflict cannot be dismissed off-hand, especially if the Axis is emboldened by increasing US isolationism, and Russian ambivalence.

Far from its continental threats to the north, China's maritime challenge to India has materialised over the last decade, through a combination of the deployment of the rapidly strengthening PLA Navy in the Indian Ocean, the sustained acquisition of a network of Chinese military and commercial facilities and relationships along its sea lines of communication, which extend from the Chinese mainland to Port Sudan.

The sea lines run through several major maritime choke points such as the Strait of Mandeb, the Strait of Malacca, the Strait of Hormuz, and the Lombok Strait as well as other strategic maritime centers in Somalia and the Maldives, Pakistan, Sri Lanka, Bangladesh, Myanmar around India and loosely characterised as a 'string of pearls', if not bases, and of course, the Belt and Road Initiative, as it seeks resources, energy and markets in Africa and in West and South Asia. India can ignore these developments in its strategic neighbourhood at its peril, or conversely, seize the opportunity in terms of Chinese vulnerabilities in the Indian Ocean Region (IOR) to modify Beijing's behaviour elsewhere.

India's own energy lifeline from West Asia demands security for the sheer scale of dependence on shipped crude. As in China's case, even a large number of pipelines cannot substitute for the train of vulnerable tankers that feed the Indian economy, and indeed its very social order. Disruption of the vital sea-lanes in the North-west Indian Ocean could be catastrophic for India. Only conventional military means can protect them. This goes for all Sea Lines of Communications (SLOC), as Indian trade increases, and India seeks to invest in the promising markets of Africa and Central Asia.

Terrorism, be it from land, sea, air, cyber or space, is far from defeated and needs to be annihilated wherever it be located. There is little to be gained by awareness of terrorist outfits, camps and cells, if one lacks the means to neutralise the same. Attempts to strangle finances, or arrest of a few culprits, do not serve to eradicate the menace. Whilst all manner of other avenues must certainly be brought to bear in the war on terror, the possession of conventional military means to address the threat cannot be lost sight of, even if for deterrence.

The contours of a new Great Game can now be discerned, with a Eurasian Russia-China Axis seemingly intent on challenging the US-led post-Cold War globalised order. In this realignment, India faces considerable challenges, as it takes stock of its long standing Russian liaison, both from its new-found US affinity as well as from increasing convergence of Moscow with Beijing and even Islamabad. A strong military would enable India to ride out the impending storm.

India does not yet possess security of weapon and ammunition supplies. It is the world's largest importer of armaments, but is not assured of timely provision of spares, repairs, overhauls, upgrades and replacement of obsolescent equipment. The indigenous defence industrial base, almost completely in the public sector, has not yet been able to deliver cutting edge weapons and platforms to the armed forces. This not only results in greater acquisition and maintenance costs, but is a strategic challenge of immense proportions. More money needs to be spent on military research and development, as well as catalysing the emergence of vibrant private defence corporations.

Due to its centrality in the IOR, and its size, population, economy and military potential, India is the only country which can bring stability to this vast underdeveloped conflict-prone region. This would require substantial investment in the military instrument. A failure to do so would be tantamount to abdication of its manifest responsibilities and would lead to loss of prestige and influence in its backyard, or vital strategic neighbourhood, if you will.

Distinctive Features of Military Expenditure

The Tyranny of Technology

No sector has seen more technological progress, or is more prone to technology disruption than the military industrial complex producing military weapons, equipment and platforms. The pace of technological change has increased so rapidly over the last few decades that much equipment becomes obsolete shortly after induction, and sometimes even before it is commissioned. Technological research, designs, development and performance benchmarks are set by a handful of prime integrators—a dozen or so large and competitive US and European corporations, utilising science, expertise and innovation from around the world. The funds required to undertake blue-sky research are humongous and the defence industry, be it publicly or privately owned, requires enormous government subsidy and support. It is a hugely expensive game, and increasingly beyond the reach of all but the richest and largest economies.

Capable militaries are an expensive business, and no nation wanting to possess such forces can escape sustained large spending, be it to import, or to indigenously develop and produce armaments.

Defence Inflation

Defence equipment defies an almost universal rule that any item of every-day technology becomes cheaper and more plentiful with passage of time. This contradiction stems from the fact that defence equipment has to be as close to the state-of-art, cutting edge as possible, to be competitive and victorious against potential adversaries. This can only be achieved by ever increasing costs.

For more than a century, defence equipment costs have increased at a year-on-year rate of 7 to 8 per cent on account of advancing technology alone. Inflation and varying exchange rates (for large importers) ensure that the increase is much higher in practice. Successive generations of any specific weapon or platform, typically twenty years apart, will usually witness a price rise of over 400 per cent. Defence inflation is thus inherently considerably higher than general inflation.

The expenditure only increases after acquisition and induction. As a rule of thumb, life-cycle costs of military hardware are two to four times the acquisition cost. Life-cycles can range from as low as seven years to over four decades. Any amount spent in capital expenditure will thus inevitably increase the revenue expenditure by many orders of magnitude. When obsolescent, ageing and overexploited equipment is sustained beyond the designed life, the financial burden for maintenance and repair goes up even more. This also affects standardisation and inventory costs.

The argument that despite a fall in the defence budget as a percentage of GDP, there has been a constant rise in military spending in rupee terms due to the sharp increases in GDP growth itself, falls flat on its face when viewed in the backdrop of galloping costs of modern military hardware. To make matters worse, a substantial amount of already modest defence budgets are 'surrendered' due to 'inability to spend', a classic phrase of double-speak. In any case, rupee increases in the defence budget have barely kept pace with even general inflation, and purchasing power has remained static, resulting in over two-thirds of the Army's equipment being obsolescent or obsolete.

Manpower Costs

It is quite disconcerting to observe the cacophony of voices bemoaning the expenditure on military personnel in terms of manpower costs, in comparison to money spent for modernisation and capital acquisition, almost as if this were wastage. Whilst there is always room for streamlining personnel, it must be remembered that at least until robots and unmanned platforms replace the soldier, manpower is the army's fighting capital. The army, unlike the navy and air force, fights with men more than it does with platforms, especially in difficult terrain such as in the mountains and jungles. It is these 'boots' that are indeed required on such a ground which adds meat to its arsenal.

There is however scope for paring unskilled and bloated manpower from a host of ancillary organisations functioning under the 'defence' umbrella and paid from the defence budget. A manpower audit must be comprehensive, and not just target the uniformed combat and combat support elements of the military establishment alone.

Due to inadequate understanding of the manpower-intensive support required for high-tech systems, there is much uninformed comment on the 'teeth-to-tail' ratios. Essentially, this is a yardstick from the age of industrial warfare beginning with the World War I. The more complex and more technological a weapon system or platform is, the more manpower support it requires to maintain and operate. Whilst technology can reduce the number of personnel at the front-end, it often increases the numbers required for operational support. For example, and ironically, 'Unmanned' Aerial Vehicles (UAVs) require more 'men' on the ground including the pilots and controllers to exploit their round-the-clock capability, than what older manned reconnaissance aircraft would have required. As a non-military example, it bears highlighting that the US National Aeronautics and Space Administration (NASA) required a 'tail' of over 100,000 people to put the 'teeth' in the form of two astronauts on the Moon!

Armchair pundits, with little knowledge of ground realities, especially in the Indian 'two-and-a-half front' context, decry the size of the Army without suggesting alternatives, whilst vaguely commenting on teeth-to-tail ratios.

Capital vs Revenue

Another fallacy which has gained ground is that you can increase funding for capital expenditure, and thereby increase force levels and thus modernise the system, by simply reducing revenue expenditure, and 'improving' and 'rebalancing' the budget and the capital to revenue ratio, like a zero-sum game. This is akin to suggesting that you can increase your automobile holdings from three cars that you may possess, to five cars, by buying two new higher performance and more expensive cars from the money budgeted for operating and maintaining the three cars that you have!

Let there be no mistake. The revenue budget is as critical if not more than the capital budget, since it provides the monies for all ongoing operations, all training and exercises, all maintenance and repairs and all establishment costs, including fuel, ratios, electric power etc. There is little point adding to weapon and equipment inventory if one cannot maintain it due lack of spares and facilities, or if your men are inadequately trained, and if the entire military machine is turning hollow, shoddy and ultimately ineffective.

The Defence Industrial Base

For the purposes of this paper, it is suffice to say that unless India puts in place a vibrant and capable Defence Industrial Base – DIB – in the private sector and breaks the ideological preference for public ownership, the country will have to pay more for both equipment and spares, besides being dependent on the source of supply, be it on another nation or foreign corporations. India simply has to grow and evolve competitive global corporations of its own. The methodology to do this must be realistic, and lessons learnt from the historical experiences of major powers. Though attempts have been made, and are ongoing, success has thus far eluded the Indian 'system', riddled as it is with vested interests, determined to preserve the status quo.

Most importantly, no defence industrial base can come about if there is inadequate money in the defence budgets, and no assured commitment for funding the five and fifteen-year long-term acquisition plans. Without adequate capital resources, it would not be possible for the defence ministry to place orders in sufficient quantity for extended periods, so as to make large enterprises viable. The alternative is to continue to absorb the losses of the Defence Public Sector Undertakings (DPSU) and keep them afloat by injection of funds, both using taxpayer's money, and granting them contracts by 'nomination'. Whilst this may work for the interests of the political economy, it is unlikely to decrease our dependence on foreign arms.

In a globalised world, which is increasingly creating wealth and power through technology, we must take cognisance of Intellectual Property Rights (IPR), and not delude ourselves in regard to 'complete' transfer of military technology, from those who have spent money, time and effort developing the same. This holds true irrespective of the size of the market. The fruits of brainpower are more valuable than mere cash, and we certainly have the intellectual capacity for a good harvest, but not yet the organisational acumen. Moreover, given the paucity of funding, Indian enterprise is likely to be restricted to Micro, Small and Medium Enterprises (MSME) who can be the cogs in the global supply chains of prime contractors and defence majors situated in more discerning shores.

The Procurement Process

The Defence Procurement Procedure, like the Defence Industrial Base (DIB), is a work in progress. Presently it takes too long, and decision-making is still mostly sequential rather than collegial. Suffice to say, there is merit in removing the process and procedure of military acquisition from the ambit of the Ministry of Defence, through the institution of an independent procurement executive. This may bring focus, urgency, procedural simplicity and accountability to this undoubtedly difficult task. Moreover, even the decisions of the apex level Raksha Mantri-chaired Defence Acquisition Council, are hostage to approval of the Finance Ministry, despite working within the stipulated budget. Long-term plans of the military and even the Ministry of Defence (MoD) are never officially approved by the Ministry of Finance (MoF). Though one can justify finance being the ultimate arbiter, the system needs to modify the present virtual stranglehold the MoF enjoys over matters military.

Political will needs also to be found to create a roll-over mechanism for monies appropriated by Parliament for capital defence expenditure. At present, it is all too easy for a cash-strapped MoF, fighting fiscal deficits, to re-appropriate literally thousands of crores back into its kitty from the defence budget. Expenditure can be stalled through a host of queries and procedural bottle-necks, and desperately required military modernisation and acquisition funds, returned back into the virtual black-hole called the consolidated fund of the Government of India!

Conclusion

The instability of the under-developed and conflict prone region demands that India plays a stabilising role in it, even if only for its own security and economic growth. Nuclear weapons, soft power and diplomacy cannot alone, or together, substitute for a powerful, highly trained, rapidly deployable, well led, proactive and committed military in facilitating a stable environment. India needs to spend more on its conventional military forces, if it truly aspires to become a prosperous and influential power, at least within its immediate strategic neighbourhood. India can, and should be able to afford appropriating between 3 to 3.5 per cent of its GDP on the regular military, especially given the clear and present danger, which if undeterred could pour cold water on all other national aspirations.

A failure to do so would also result in significant opportunity costs, in terms of lost economic advantage, be it for commerce, trade, investments, markets, resource mining and energy security. A cavalier attitude towards the serious business of military capacity, capability, preparedness and readiness could result in a catastrophic humiliation, which would set India back in terms of international stature, self-confidence, and derail economic and developmental objectives.

The Government has recently taken a step forward in establishing a high-powered multi-disciplinary body to address this very challenge of appropriate military spending. The Defence Planning Committee, under the chairmanship of the National Security Advisor, and with the military chiefs, the Defence Secretary, the Foreign Secretary and the Secretary (Expenditure) as members, has both the mandate and the power to expeditiously correct the downward spiral in defence spending.

The current levels of military spending are not in consonance with India's rising international profile, and is weakening its capacity to deter and dissuade rivals intent on bleeding it through a thousand hybrid cuts. Asking the Chiefs to 'prioritise' is neither here nor there. It will result only in a lot of money being spent to no worthwhile end, and even less capability to address the real challenges, while failing to avail of the many opportunities at this point in our nation's history.

Should the monies available not be in consonance with the quantum of funds required to sustain a military which can quantitatively and qualitatively address India's various threats, interests and aspirations, it would only be prudent for New Delhi to cut its coat according to its cloth, by scaling down its regional and global ambitions.

India's Higher Defence Organisation

Role, Responsibility and Re-structure

Gautam Banerjee

If you don't have a strategy, you're part of someone else's strategy
—Alvin Toffler

Over the past three decades, India's Higher Defence Organisation (HDO) has remained stagnated in relation to the modern tenets of political management of national defence. The obsolescence is so pronounced that the concerns of our national defence get addressed by short-term political, bureaucratic and military expediencies, and sometimes by neighbourhood aggression rather than an institutionalised system of profound and fiscally sustainable defence policy-making. Of late, however, there are signs of stirring of the Indian state's strategic conscience.

This Paper is focused on the 'Role' that India's HDO is ordained to play in India's future management of national defence, and its central plank, the nation's military security. Inference of broad parameters of a responsive and contemporised 'Structure' for India's HDO that is in tune with strategic commitments and capabilities, must be an expected fallout of that discussion. Comprehensive analysis of the subject matter entails that it is rooted at the conceptual nuances that govern the cause of a nation's military security. The discussion then follows up with an evaluation of India's past and present HDO as well as its lien upon the non-combat but equally salient civilian defence sector. Lastly, inferring from such considerations, the paper goes on to suggest the broad parameter of a restructured HDO that is destined to answer the call of an emergent India.

The Issue

THE INDIAN strategic community has long held the opinion that ever since the Independence, India's apex organisational structure for national defence – or the Higher Defence Organisation (HDO) – has been way short of the requisite level of effectiveness. To wit, the nomenclature of HDO here refers to India's apex-level defence policy-making body that comprises the political authority, defence bureaucracy and military professionals.

Indeed, there is profound disconcert over a stark fact that over the past three decades, India's HDO has stagnated to such a state that the concerns of our national defence get addressed by the inclinations of few political, bureaucratic and military incumbents of the high bench, and sometimes by neighbourhood aggression, rather than an institutionalised system of defence policy. That has indeed been a case with roles and anti-roles played by the HDOs of most of the past governments.

In this context, the purpose of this paper is to examine the 'Role' that India's HDO is ordained to play in future management of national defence. It is also expected that such discussion would offer suggestions of a more responsive structure for India's HDO which is in tune with national aspirations and capabilities.

The subject matter is discussed under the following parts:

a. Part 1: Concept of National Security, Military Security and HDO.
b. Part 2: India's Past and Present HDO.
c. Part 3: Features of Re-structured HDO.

National Security, Military Security & HDO

The Concept of National Security

Political theory defines *national security* to be a summation of three aspects:

a. One, *social* or *political security* that provides for the fundamental rights of the citizens while preserving internal stability and rule of law;
b. Two, *economic security* that promotes the citizen's wellbeing; and,
c. Three, *military security* that prevents adversarial powers from impinging upon the nation's sovereign rights to pursue its interests.

Nation-states devise their security architecture in a manner which accommodate all the three above listed elements of *national security*.

Concept of Military Security

Unlike constitutionally enforceable laws to settle disputes within, when it comes to external issues, the principle of sovereignty comes in the way of contending parties from forcing compliance upon each other. Extra-territorial disputes have therefore to be settled through accommodation of mutual political, diplomatic and economic concerns. But many times, when reason and better sense fail to find such mutual accommodation, then application of military power remains the only recourse to force the intransigent to respect one's national interests. In actual terms, such recourse to military power could:

a. Either be aimed at *deterring* or *defending* one's vital interests against arrogation;
b. Or, to secure the nation's rights and interests when there is left no option but to *sally out* to make the intransigent see reason.

In the Indian context, the ambit of *military security* remains defined by the fact that India does not subscribe to the policy of application of military power in securing her national objectives; she depends on her defence forces just to keep military aggressors away. India's case therefore responds to the first case above, wherein military recourse becomes unavoidable only when there is left no peaceful means to protect own interests against aggressive impositions.

India's Lien on Military Security

India is situated between two ideologically expansionist powers operating in collusion from either flank. Indeed, China and Pakistan are but habitually revisionist powers who stake on that affliction as key to their progress. Then, on the southern flank, is the Indian Ocean where China, alluring smaller neighbourhood nations with economic enticements to serve her purpose, cannot wait to extend her hegemonic control. Neither of the adversaries show scant inclination towards even-handed neighbourly relations and international norms of behaviour. The nexus is so compelling that in spite of fundamental cultural differences, the two have opted to forge a master-vassal relationship, describing it as 'all-weather, high-and-deep, etc. etc.' friendship. In consequence, since Independence, India has had to be drawn into five wars, two 'police actions' and four near-wars. Thus, in spite of Indian's accommodative foreign policies, her military security cannot but remain under strain into the foreseeable future. After all, even if two are required to engage in fight, one is enough to start it.

The malediction, however, does not end here. Many parts of the country are sold to anti-national inclinations – indigenous as well as externally sponsored – to inflict insurgency and mayhem upon huge tracts of the Indian landmass where the state's writ runs but in exception. In this instance too, if situations deteriorate beyond a point, exercise of military power becomes the ultimate recourse to preserve the nation's integrity. Activation of military power to control as many as six insurgencies over nearly the entire post-Independence period, and numerous deployments on internal security duties are the testimonies of that necessity.

No doubt, leverage of military security is essential in dealing with such challenges to India's sovereign rights, foreign relationships and domestic governance. It is that imperative which causes a developing nation like India to commit to substantial defence expenditure to maintain a level of 'minimalist' military capability. But then, allocating funds is just one end of the process of higher defence management; the system must lead to nurturing of a competent military organisation that is founded upon a robust defence infrastructure, and guided by a sound process of defence policy-making. Furthermore, when the nation's military security requirements have to be met within a limited fiscal affordability, the challenge upon the nation's HDO to manage that kind of intensely complex obligation becomes even more demanding. That indeed is India's case.

Role of Higher Defence Organisation

That brings us to the role that the HDO is destined to play in any nation's security architecture. Briefly put, the universally adopted role of HDO is to respond to the following charter of responsibilities:

a. Promulgation of an appropriate *political directive* in tune with the national goals.
b. Providing guidance in formulation of appropriate *military strategies* to meet the said political directive.
c. Framing policies to marshal the nation's overall resources to provide for the needed gamut of *war-wherewithal* to the military forces.

Construct of HDO

Points to note here is that defining a political directive for the military institution to follow is a process of reconciling nationalistic priorities, scientific and industrial competences and fiscal capacity. It is therefore a political process, to be shaped by the nation's elected political leadership in consultation with various state entities, professional bodies, the electorate and the military leadership, with the bureaucracy articulating the process into action. But when it comes to application of military power which requires professionalism of an extraordinary kind that must be a purely military responsibility. Therefore, HDO must be an amalgamation of political and military participation and served by dedicated bureaucracy. Indeed, this is how HDOs are structured in advanced countries, even if the forms may vary.

Having defined the fundamentals of HDO, we may now turn to see as to how our HDO stands challenged by the concerns of India's *military security*. To infer the right perspective, we have to begin at the beginning, that is, from the time of Independence.

India's Past and Present HDO

HDO in the post-Independence Era

As the British left, they structured a mechanism for the management of national defence in independent India. That mechanism consisted of a 'Defence Committee of the Cabinet' for promulgation of political directions at the apex level, while a 'Defence Minister's Committee' with Service Chiefs and Defence Secretary as its members attended to the routine policy issues at the Ministry level. Then there was a Tri-Service 'Chiefs of Staff's Committee' to respond to inter-services matters. Integrated approach to defence management was fostered through the committees for 'Joint Intelligence', 'Joint Planning' and 'Joint Training'. Besides, there was the 'Defence Coordination and Implementation Committee' chaired by the Defence Secretary to synergise defence research, development, finance, production and acquisitions.

Remarkably, with their institutional membership of the Defence Minister's and other Joint Committees, the Service Headquarters had been integral part of the ministerial as well as tri-service policy-making system, and so exercised adequate jurisdiction over all departments and appendages of the Ministry of Defence – viz, defence production, Finance, Defence Estates etc. A legacy of World War II military leadership, this was the inter-service integrated system that thwarted Pakistan's aggression in Kashmir.

During the 1950s, an era of peace-rhetoric gained ground among the Indian leadership and the prominence of higher defence management got gradually diluted. Defence forces were mandated just to check Pakistan's occasional, limited armed forays, till, as it was believed, that new-born adversary came to terms with itself. The institution of Commander-in-Chief was apportioned among three Services' Chiefs of Staff which, in practice, virtually disfranchised the military leadership from apex policy-making bodies. The Cabinet and the Defence Minister's Committees ceased, more or less, to function. Soon enough, the Service Headquarters, in their myopic aplomb, disowned the Joint Committees and the authority of the Chiefs of Staff Committee, thus rendering these as mere embellishments and little more. The most telling effect of all these changes was the loss of the military's lien upon the nation's joint intelligence set up and other defence establishments at-large.

Having been assigned to the status of 'Attached Offices', the Service Headquarters were hereafter marginalised from the apex level defence policy-making process. The Defence Ministry, headed by constituency-minded politicians and manned by bureaucrats coming from any and all departments, sought to view Services related issues just as any other, and found it expedient to defer to pseudo-experts to justify their narrative, and to disregard the unmistakable signs of approaching military debility.

Post-1962 Revival and post-1991 Relapse

The sanctity of the HDO was revived after the 1962 debacle and the process of higher defence management proceeded well for some time. Indeed, for the next 25 years, substantial political dividends – 1965 and 1971 Wars, various insurgencies, interventions in Sri Lanka and Maldives, and above all, nearly three decades of effective deterrence against Pakistan's and China's aggressiveness were earned from that investment. That spring period, however, ended in 1991 when Indian economy fell into distress. The military institution was again marked to bear the brunt of that economic adversity, and soon enough, it debilitated into a 'hollowed' behemoth of little operational capability other than keeping insurgencies in check. And that encouraged Pakistan, finding its proxy war at the verge of total defeat, to venture into Kargil, and then attack our Parliament.

Meanwhile, the rest of the defence establishment – procurement, research, industry, estates and bureaucracy – was, in a misplaced notion of 'civilian control', gradually released of accountability to their sole cause of existence – the military institution. Various defence establishments were allowed to turn autonomous, and much to the exclusion of professional military lien, began to enjoy the licence to dictate their charters of objectives and time-lines. Deep systemic aberrations – like defence scientists self-certifying war-worthiness of their product and defence accounts deciding on necessities of weapons and equipment – thus found host in India's system of defence management.

Decline of Defence Preparedness, 1990s and After

In the years following 1991 and till recently, the military institution was gradually consigned to impoverishment in terms of its inventory of weapons, ammunition and equipment. Even military training had to be curtailed, much to the dilution of traditional élan of the forces. With defence preparedness being consigned to the government's lowest priority, departments of defence, defence finance and defence production became intent on denying, rather than preserving if not improving, what operational capability, with what meagre funds allocated, the Services hoped to maintain. All this while India's HDO, besides rhetorical eulogy, did little to address the mounting debilities of the military institution. Defence expenditure turned into something to be scrupulously avoided and slack in the nation's defence preparedness became a matter of stoic acceptance. It was the innate culture of unflinching loyalty to the constitutional mandate, regardless of all odds, that kept the military institution standing as best as it could. It did not let poverty come in way of dealing with the proxy war, Kargil intrusion, Operation Parakram, etc., the deficiencies being made up by leadership, gallantry and blood.

The Present System: Political Direction

Promulgation of the appropriate political mandate for the nation's military institution to organise accordingly and support it with allocation of adequate structural and fiscal provisions, flows out of the *apex body of the HDO, the 'Cabinet Committee for Security'* (CCS). It is a committee of decision-making politicians having the counsel of competent national security professionals. Indeed, in past occasions, our political leadership has shown strategic maturity in handling the 1965 and 1971 Wars, the Sri Lanka, Kargil and 2001-02 'Parakram' Operations, and the process of nuclear weaponisation, hindsight debates notwithstanding.

Organisation for Grand Strategy: National Security Council

To advise and guide the nation's political rulers, there is a formally constituted body to formulate the nation's grand strategy or the 'National Security Strategy'. This body is the 'National Security Council' (NSC), having its dedicated Secretariat. Headed by the 'National Security Advisor' (NSA) and assisted by consultative bodies in the form of the 'National Security Advisory Board' (NSAB) and the 'Strategy Policy Group' (SPG), the NSC undertakes grand strategic advisory functions for the CCS. National level intelligence functions are attended to by the 'Intelligence Coordinating Group', which is responsible for tasking and coordination among various intelligence agencies like the Intelligence Bureau (IB), Research and Analysis Wing (RAW), National Technical Research Organisation (NTRO) and Defence Intelligence Agency (DIA). Further support also comes from the Technical Coordination Group (TCG) and the National Information Board (NIB), each having their satellite expert groups.

Management of the nuclear force is undertaken by the 'National Command Authority' (NCA) and its dedicated 'Strategy Programme Staff'. The NCA is made up of a 'Political Council' and an 'Executive Council' to administer the intended nuclear posture, the former composed similar to the CCS and the latter having the NSA, Service Chiefs, Commander-in-Chief of Strategic Forces Command and the heads of the Defence Research & Development Organisation (DRDO) and Department of Atomic Energy (DAE) as its members.

Policy Making and Superintendence: Ministry of Defence

Universally, strategically conscious nations have their Ministries (or Departments) of Defence to translate the nation's political mandate – or the 'National Security Strategy' – into an efficient mechanism for national defence. This is the *functional level of HDO*, where regular policy promulgations

– like 'defence reviews, 'guidelines', 'white papers' etc.—are undertaken for the military leadership as well as the defence bureaucracy to take up the cudgels of focused implementation. Such promulgations prepare the military leadership to find right balance of organisational architecture, force-composition, equipment profile and professionally trained and motivated personnel in conformity with the political mandate. Similarly, the Ministerial HDO orient the rest of the non-combat defence sector to be truly responsive to the requirements of the military forces. Needless to state, formal participation of military professionals in all such functions is mandatory.

In India, the Ministry of Defence (MoD), manned by a generalist bureaucracy and headed by a Defence Minister or Raksha Mantri (RM) attends to that responsibility. Curiously, neither qualify to the possession of the necessary strategic expertise and experience of military functions, nor have they been inclined to appreciate the benefits of integrated military participation in policy-making. Notably, few years ago, the Service Headquarters were 'integrated' into the MoD, but that has turned out to be a subterfuge – attitudes have not changed. In theory thus, the CCS, MoD and rest of the security apparatus have the option of inviting professional military advise, but in matters of national defence, such advice, 'invited' from 'visiting' participants, cannot be expected to do justice to the complex cause. Absence of formal military participation at the policy-making level reflects in optimal harness of the nation's intelligence, technological and industrial assets, as indeed it has happened all along.

As a result of this anomaly, the MoD, at its best, merely attends to the staff work associated with projections made by the Services on various capital, revenue and personnel management schemes. At its worst, the MoD invokes the process of scrutiny and audit to divert or dilute professionally adjudged projections on the pretext of 'cost saving' to the exchequer. Having found provisions for what it considers to be 'adequate' wherewithal for the military forces to fulfil the given political mandate, the MoD then stands by, more like an observer-at-large than the custodian of national defence – the last role is left for the military professional to exert upon. Gross mismatch between government's specified inventory of weapons, ammunition and spares against insufficient funding to maintain such holdings is one example of that disorder.

Executive Management: Services Headquarters and Directorates General

Lastly, at the third tier of defence management, there are the three Services on the one hand and the various civilian domains of the defence sector – DRDO, Defence Estates, Ordnance Factories, Defence Public Sector Units (PSU), etc. on the other. Autonomous more or less, these perform their charter under such self-centrality that departmental aspirations and expediencies assume priority over broader causes of military security. Incomprehensive force-structuring, procurements and budgeting by the Services Headquarters, and mixing military modernisation with indigenous development by the rest are the fallouts of that autonomy.

Inferences So Far

From the above discussion, it may be observed that the organisation for *national security* at the *political level of HDO* is somewhat adequately attended to, albeit sans integral military advice. Indeed, the option to seek military advise exists, and that option is usually adopted, but still the option being discretionary, this arrangement is but imperfect. That shortcoming can be easily made up by mandatory participation of military professional(s), in whatever form, in CCS and NSC confabulations. But more than that, there is a need to strengthen the role and functions of the NSC in matters of defence preparedness.

Next, we find that at the *MoD* and the *Service Headquarters levels*, policy making and superintendence over matters of national defence are attended to through an extemporised mechanism. Difficulties in promulgation of formal *political directive* or *National Security Strategy*, to optimise the process of national defence planning, is but a fallout of the that shortcoming. That, in turn, prevents the innovation of focused *military strategies* in terms of *military objectives*, *policies*, *force-structure* and *tactical procedures*.

Here, it would be in order to list certain adverse effects of inadequacies of the existing HDO:

Incongruities in Higher Defence Management

The degree of mis-alignment between India's envisioned level of *defence preparedness* and the actual accrual of *military capability* is exemplified by certain representative examples, as listed below:

a. The only nation of some stature that is obliged to maintain a massive military establishment and yet remains unable to institutionalise a joint force-structure, is India. Here, individual Services, and even self-assuming scientists, fiscal managers and bureaucrats articulate, with misplaced aplomb, their own versions of war doctrines, battle procedures and even the weapons that the forces must fight with. Thus propounded without the benefit of institutionalised harness of profound professional sense, the level of *military preparedness* that could be adequate to uphold the nation's military security gets adjudged by subjective, compartmentalised, shallow and opinionated considerations.

b. In similar vein, restructure and modernisation of the forces in tune with the contemporary calls for operational *jointness* is stalled to accommodate inter-arm and inter-services rivalries. In India's archaic system of defence management, there is no professionally competent authority designated to arbitrate among the competing Services, the bureaucracy and defence technologists. The matter of the institution of Chief of Defence Staff (CDS) remains stuck by professional obduracy and myopic attempts to render that institution into toothlessness.

c. By 'peacenik' policy adaptations in the 1950s and ever since, the Indian state has opted to sequester its significant scientific, technological and industrial capacity from producing indigenous *military hardware*, even the basic weapons and war-like equipment. Thus a 1.3 million military force, under relentless aggression from either flank, has to fight with imported weaponry – if and as affordable.

d. The state's inability to protect *defence procurements* from corrupt practices has led to the military forces being denied, over the last two decades plus, of the

> deserved wherewithal to engage in battle – individual arms, protective gear, artillery… just to list only some of the alarming deficiencies. Indeed, much to the contradiction with the pristine state-military covenant, the Indian military is not equipped with what best hardware the nation can afford.

Obviously, there is a need to strengthen the superintendence of responsibility, authority, accountability and integrated approach to the nation's *military security*. This need has been regularly pointed at by almost all Parliamentary Committees, and recently alluded to by the Minister of State for Defence in his presentation to the Prime Minister.

Contemporising the HDO

Defence policies that address the forestated anomalies and so reap the benefits of cost-efficient national defence, must be the need of the day. As stated, the first step in that direction would be to contemporise the existing HDO. That in turn will lead to effective system of promulgation, prioritisation and coordination of the nation's *military security* and its corollary: inter-services jointness, optimum modernisation of forces, accountability of the civilian domains of the defence sector and fiscal planning for effective and affordable national defence.

Presently, the political dispensation gives strong indications of mending the situation for the better. Propelled by angst against military hollowness and emboldening of inimical forces, the Government of the day has taken many concrete steps to resuscitate the military institution. But under severe neglect for over quarter of a century, it would be a long haul before the mandated level of India's defence preparedness is achieved.

Features of a Re-Structured HDO

Reality Check of National Defence

With the structures, practices and shortcomings of India's HDO discussed in the preceding parts, in this Part it is proposed to focus upon the key parameters of re-structuring the existing HDO. But to keep that focus, first a reality check of India's current management of national defence is necessary:

a. Even while maintaining one of the world's largest military force, India finds her adversaries just about partially deterred from undertaking overt military aggression, while finding ways to strike at her through other forms of warfare without any fear of retribution.

b. Only a part of India's military force-structure is maintained in the state of operational readiness, a reckonable proportion of it being consigned to the conditions of 'hollowness' and obsolescence. Consequently, a good part of the forces could be found to be wanting at the time of reckoning.

c. In the era of 21st Century multi-spectral (or hybrid) warfare, the Indian military forces find themselves constrained in jettisoning the 20th Century practices related to force-composition, weapon and equipment technology and scaling, as well as personnel management and training.

d. As a corollary, the Indian military leadership remains denied of the opportunities of developing innovative strategies and new tactical procedures. Such stagnation of conceptual and operational development, as history points out, is a disconcerting military affliction.

Mandate for the HDO

That brings us to the role that the India's HDO is destined to play in modernising the system of defence planning and preparedness free of the above listed incongruities. Accordingly, the mandate of the HDO may be summarised as follows:

a. As discussed above, the apex or *CCS level of the HDO* would be mandated to promulgate the 'political directive' or 'National Security Strategy' that is in tune with the 'national goals', and defined by the nation's technological, industrial and fiscal capacity to support such goals. This process would have to be processed at the *Integrated MoD level* and nurtured at the *NSC level of the HDO* through conjoined civil-military deliberations.

b. The apex level HDO's National Security Strategy would beacon the *military leadership* to devise appropriate *military strategies* to the attainment of specified political 'end-states'. Nation's 'military security' would thus be achieved through optimal force-application across the wider spectrum of war-waging if and when needed – within the resources affordable.

c. A truly integrated MoD, monitored at the NSC level, would complement the *military strategies* by provisioning requisite force-structure, sustenance of military preparedness, and initiation of periodic force-modernisation – all within the ambit of the nation's fiscal affordability.

d. Orienting the non-combat enterprises of the defence sector towards their military-specific purpose would be a crucial part of the charter of the MoD level of the HDO. This would entail enabling the nation's defence research and development, industry, estates, engineering services and logistic installations to the furtherance of the strategic doctrines and tactical concepts by which the military institution plans to meet its mandate.

e. Framing policies to marshal the nation's dual-use capacities in provisioning for the needed gamut of *war-wherewithal* to the military forces – in terms of right kind of men, military hardware and logistic back up – would be another charter for the MoD. It is also for the HDO to promote a robust civilian sector that can undertake base-area roles of transportation, supplies, power, communications and internal, rear area and cyber security to bolster national defence.

Key Terms of References

To foster the principles of 'integrated military management' and 'integrated military logistics' according to the modern tenets of warfare, the above-listed charter of responsibilities of a re-structured HDO has to be performed across a diverse spectrum over which modern operations of war are to be prosecuted. But in achieving that purpose, advancements in military sciences, long gestation for the defence manufacturing industries to deliver, and need for high fiscal commitments have to be the key factors. Next, to reap full benefits of 'defence dividend', understanding of the extra-ordinary cerebral make-up of the soldiery, and upholding the hoary covenant of *state-soldier relationship* are equally important responsibilities for the nation's HDO to shoulder.

To translate the above mandate at the war-fighting end, a re-structured HDO must accelerate the process of modern joint-services force-structuring and integration of war-waging capabilities. Notably, this part of HDO restructure need not be linked with the long-contentious issue of integrating tri-services theatre commands *per se* – that can wait till the contradictions are sorted out and time turns ripe. Similarly, to strengthen the roots of war capabilities by incentivising defence research and industry, promulgation of special dispensations for accelerated development of defence infrastructure – under the spirit of 'military necessity' – have to be intrinsic to that charter.

All that would require the HDO to depend upon a cadre of defence-dedicated bureaucracy and a military industrial technocracy. Obviously therefore, performance of such a diverse charter highlights the need to re-structure the existing HDO for it to be in tune with modern imperatives.

HDO in India's Security Architecture

Defence planners of advanced nations have, over many decades of trials and practice, learnt many lessons in their endeavour to optimally manage their national defence, and within its ambit, their mandate of *military security*. Taking cue and customising for Indian conditions, it emerges that the imperatives of new era multi-spectral warfare, military application of science and industry, and exercise of military lien over civil infrastructure are best attended to by the creation of two distinct streams of professional competences which confluence at the functional HDO (MoD) level. Obviously, either stream would incorporate certain elements of the other as necessary, and there would be flexibility of cross-movement at various levels.

Accordingly, irrespective of the nomenclatures used, we may structure our MoD-level HDO in two distinct streams.[1]

1 *India's National Defence: Defining Defence Reforms and Military Modernisation*, Lt Gen Gautam Banerjee, Pentagon Press, Delhi, 2017.

While the proposition would require to be worked out in great details, at this stage it would suffice to consider the broad parameters of restructuring India's HDO along following lines:

a. To recall the discussion, we have found that the apex body for management of *national security*, *national defence* and *military security* – the CCS and the NSC – may continue in the present form, with more formal participation of military professional advisors.
b. The MoD may be structured into two departments or wings, say, the *Department of Defence Forces* (DDF) and the *Department of Defence Establishment* (DDE). Each could be headed either by a political appointee or a senior professional, with the Defence Minister, assisted by a small secretariat, in overall control of defence policy-making.
c. The DDF, manned by Headquarters of the Chief of Defence Staff (CDS), would be responsible for operational management of the Defence Forces made up of the individual Services. Apart from the services headquarters and various single service regional (joint, in future) theatre commands functioning under the CDS, there would also be a joint logistic command to control, coordinate and optimise the functions of the existing service-specific logistic directorates.
d. The DDE would be manned by defence-dedicated cadres of professional bureaucrats and technocrats, with the Defence Secretary heading. The DDE would be responsible to control and manage the various domain-expert departments to organise defence procurements, research and development, estates, defence industries, etc. – in short, the entire constellation of non-combat

part of national defence endeavours. Obviously, this Department would also have specified posts for military professionals embedded, as necessary.

e. Notably, both the streams would have horizontal and vertical inter-connectivity as well as mobility at each level of their charters, thus making the process of defence management a composite whole.

It will be seen that the suggested HDO is in many ways similar to the universally adopted frameworks, and that much of it already exists in India's MoD. But even then, re-structure of the elements of national defence cannot be a one stop matter, it would require much time and flexibility to mature.

For example, as advanced nations have learnt, it is worthwhile to assign both the suggested Departments to be headed by politicians – Ministers of State, Deputy Ministers or political appointees – working under a senior Defence Minister. Finally however, it is the political will to overcome the short-term attractions of *status quo* and take up the cudgels of re-structuring according to the call of the times, which would count.

Mandate Extraordinary

Finally, there is a responsibility of extra-ordinary sensitivity. As every nation goes through the dilemma of 'bread-versus-bullet' and social security versus military security, the wise ones, with due forethought and hoary wisdom, manage to find the right balance among these contending requirements. They do so by:

a. One, tuning down their *politico-military goals* to be in compatibility with the *resources allocable for military preparedness* – as indeed Britain, France and Russia, among many others, have done; and,

b. Two, enjoining the professional wisdom of their military leadership to find *innovative strategies to defend the nation with what level of combat power the nation might be able to afford* – as do United Kingdom, Russia, Taiwan, Japan, Vietnam, even Pakistan, among many others.
c. Three, affording *extra-ordinary dispensations* to raise the level of indigenous defence technology and industry to modern standards. To do so, as advanced nations do at one time or the other, the latest being China, all barriers are to be bypassed regardless.

All that requires strong political will to emulate.

The Defence Planning Committee

Recently, The government has formed a new body named as the Defence Planning Committee (DPC) with its charter specified to the management of higher defence policy, strategy and plans, capability building, defence diplomacy, and defence industry. In order to monitor the nation's defence preparedness, the DPC would also oversee the formulation of the national military strategy and undertake periodic strategic defence reviews. The DPC is to be a permanent body headed by the National Security Advisor, and with the Chairman of the Chiefs of Staff Committee, other service chiefs, and defence, foreign, finance and expenditure secretaries as members. Formation of this body is indicative of the government's seriousness in comprehensive and integrated management of national defence.

Notably, this initiative is in line with the arguments preferred in Part 3 of this Paper. However, in the context of the nation's HDO, it is still short of being an institutionalised structure having the full range of competencies – it is still just a

Committee. In the event, the advantages of creating the DPC would accrue only if it is driven by a singular mission which overrides departmental priorities of its duel-hatted members. Real effectiveness of the DPC would also be in bridging the otherwise restrictive procedures that bureaucracy has inflicted upon itself over the decades. But ultimately, the nation's defence can only be managed well if it enjoys the due fiscal backing.

Conclusion

To sum up, India's huge fiscal commitment on defence remains anomalous on all three counts. To reiterate:

a. Mandate of defence remains incongruous with allocation of resources. The resultant 'hollowness' encourages the habitual adversaries. That is even when most of the world's militaries have moved up to devise new strategies and organisations for the prosecution of 21st Century warfare.
b. Military hierarchy, having to confine force-modernisation to occasional acquisition of a few current generation war-machines, remains stuck with obsolete operational procedures and archaic force-structures. Due dividends of defence expenditure is thus unrealised.

A New Horizon

Although some of the afore-stated weaknesses in India's existing system of defence management prevails today, visions of coming of a long overdue revamp of national defence seems to be on the horizon at last. This vision comes from the government pronouncements regarding redress of operational hollowness and modernisation of defence infrastructure. Arguably, being subjected to flagrantly aggressive behaviour from inimical neighbours, the nation's political class seem to be recovering from their weariness of military power, India's aspirations of establishing international relevance being a catalyst.

Re-structure of India's HDO is mandatory.

> No army of 50 years ago before the date selected would stand a dog's chance against the army existing at that date
>
> —JFC Fuller

India's Neighbourhood Outreach

Strengthening Peace and Prosperity

Kanwal Sibal

India has an obvious interest in maintaining good ties with its neighbours and has striven to do so within its constraints. Prime Minister Modi has given focused attention to our neighbourhood. But our outreach to them to strengthen peace, tranquillity and prosperity cannot be crowned with success automatically. Large countries with smaller neighbours always face problems because the latter feel insecure and explore ways to balance disparities in size and power by resisting a close embrace, exaggerating sovereignty concerns and bringing in external powers as a balancing strategy.

Pakistan, in particular, has vitiated the environment in the Indian subcontinent by its endemic hostility towards India and taking recourse to state sponsored terrorism. It has not allowed SAARC to unite the subcontinent around shared political,

> *economic and security interests. The China-Pakistan nexus has been most damaging to India's interests in its neighbourhood. With China's rise, its Belt and Road Initiative and policies of expanding its footprint in our neighbourhood, India's task of managing its neighbourhood has become even more challenging. Many in India argue that we have mismanaged our neighbourhood ties because of lack of generosity and unwillingness to make unilateral concessions. In diplomacy, the guiding principle has always been reciprocity and it is followed by the biggest and most powerful countries. While the give and take between big and small countries need not be equal or symmetrical, it cannot be one-sided either. If India should show sensitivity towards its neighbours, they too have to respect India's concerns and interests, which they frequently do not. None of India's pressing needs depend on ties with its neighbours, yet it is a bonus to have friendly neighbourhood ties.*

A Politically Boiling Neighbourhood

INDIA'S NEIGHBOURHOOD outreach requires clarity about how we define our neighbourhood. Do we have a strategic or a strictly geographical definition? Strategically, our neighbourhood would encompass the region from the Straits of Hormuz to the Straits of Malacca because developments there have a major impact on India's security. We have vital manpower, energy and financial interests towards the west, while, in the east, it is in the Andaman and Nicobar Islands above the Malacca Straits.

Geographically, Pakistan, Nepal, Bhutan, Bangladesh, Sri Lanka and Maldives, as members of SAARC constitute the core of our neighbourhood. Although Myanmar is a contiguous neighbour, it remains outside SAARC, but it is part of BIMSTEC and as a crucial link in our Act East policy and connectivity projects its profile as India's neighbour is rising.

Afghanistan is not a direct geographic neighbour today, but we can treat it as one as a SAARC member and, more importantly, because Pakistan is illegally occupying that part of Jammu and Kashmir (J&K) which is contiguous with Afghanistan.

With its occupation of Tibet, China has become our direct neighbour. It is occupying our territory in Ladakh and laying claim to more, especially in Arunachal Pradesh, China is entrenching itself increasingly in our neighbourhood and undermining our influence around. Through its policies it is disturbing peace and tranquillity in the region; and its economic projects too are not merely prosperity oriented as they are intended to advance Chinese geo-political interests in a disruptive manner.

India's Efforts in the Neighbourhood

India has always reached out to its neighbours with a view to strengthening peace, tranquillity and prosperity. We have major assistance programmes in Bhutan, Nepal, Sri Lanka, Maldives, Bangladesh, Afghanistan and Myanmar as well. We are giving duty free access to goods from our region. We have been supportive of our neighbours economically and have been time and again reaching out in times of crises. We cannot be accused of disturbing peace and tranquillity around us. If tensions exist and conflicts have occurred, it is because of claims on our territory and terrorism directed at us from the neighbourhood.

It can always be debated whether what we have done is enough in relation to our capacities and interests or the expectations of our neighbours. India's interests are not served by creating or neglecting problems in its neighbourhood. If the situation around us is unsatisfactory the reasons for that have to be put in perspective, properly analysed and better understood. When Prime Minister Modi took oath of office after winning the 2014 elections he made the imaginative move to invite all SAARC leaders, including the Pakistani Prime Minister, to attend his swearing-in ceremony. Unlike his predecessor, PM Modi has made frequent official bilateral visits to neighbouring countries to signal India's commitment to friendly and productive ties with them.

He resumed contacts with Pakistan to see if a veritable dialogue could be re-started by addressing the central issue of Pakistan-sponsored terrorism against India. He even made an unscheduled visit to Pakistan on the occasion of a marriage in the family of Nawaz Sharif in an attempt to break barriers. He visited Nepal on two occasions and it seemed that his message had succeeded in enthusing the Nepalis about India's goodwill towards the country. India's assistance to Nepal following the devastating earthquake was rapid and massive. He has visited Sri Lanka on more than one occasion, with reciprocal visits from the Sri Lankan leadership, with a view to imparting a new positive thrust to a relationship weighed down with past differences. He has settled outstanding territorial issues with Bangladesh and opened mutually beneficial economic and connectivity doors with that country, transforming the bilateral relationship in the process. With Afghanistan the level of understanding reached and the commitment made to the country's development has been remarkable given the difficult security situation there. The outreach to Myanmar has strengthened links with a country that is geo-politically critical for India's outreach to Southeast Asia. At the last BRICS summit at Goa in 2016, PM Modi invited all the BIMSTEC countries in another imaginative move. With China high level exchanges have been maintained, with more than one meeting with President Xi, both in India, China and elsewhere.

India can reach out, Neighbours must Respond Too

The end result of all these attempts at enhancing peace, tranquillity and prosperity in the region is a serious breakdown of the ceasefire in J&K, killing and displacement of the civil population on the border, surgical strikes by India across the LoC, harassment of diplomats and so on. Relations with Maldives have broken down, with President Yameen brazenly defying us and damaging our security interests. Nepal under Prime Minister Oli is openly playing the China card against us and is calling for a re-definition of bilateral ties. Sri Lanka has ceded ground to China in ways that are a source of strategic concern to us, indicating difficult days ahead with China's encouragement. The stand-off with China at Doklam revealed China's ploy to create divisions between India and Bhutan. The abusive and contemptuous nature of Chinese diplomacy towards us was exposed. Rather than analyse these developments objectively, all this has fuelled the entrenched perception amongst many experts, sections of the media and the political class that the government has failed to give shape to a coherent and successful neighbourhood policy.

Improving relations with neighbours is always a declared priority of any country's foreign policy (and this was reiterated when Prime Minister Modi took over) because it is believed that a stable neighbourhood strengthens a country's foreign policy posture, whereas an unstable one weakens it. The credibility of a country's regional and global posture is also adversely affected if it is embroiled in conflicts with neighbours. However, a simplistic view should not be taken of the complexities of India's relations with neighbours and our ability to manage them to the satisfaction of critics.

Big Countries always have Problems with Smaller Neighbours

In actual fact, big countries generally have problematic relations with smaller neighbours because the disparity in size and power creates insecurities in them. They fear loss of sovereignty and independence in decision-making, as well as of identity, particularly in the case of India's neighbours who share with us ethnic, linguistic, cultural, civilisational and religious commonalities. To avoid subservience and maintain their separate identity, they are sometimes prone to assert their independence for their own sake. Concerns about their domestic politics being manipulated and a client leadership put in place by the bigger neighbour, impedes a fuller relationship. Mutually beneficial economic ties are often sacrificed because of negative political thinking. Consequently, they look for ways to differentiate themselves and resist India's embrace. Wooing them more, as is advocated, could well increase resistance, depending on their internal politics, the balance between various factions and relations with third countries that court them. As ethnic groups straddle India's frontiers with others, this latent source of friction erupts at times. India is constantly accused of interference in the internal affairs of neighbours. While India cannot altogether stand aloof and has to play legitimate politics within diplomatic bounds to protect its interests, India's interference is exaggerated to serve domestic politics. Our smaller neighbours will seek the support of external powers as a counterweight.

Looking at other big powers and their relations with their neighbours, we must note that China, which has many more neighbours than India, has tense relations with most of them, barring Pakistan. The US has serious problems with its immediate neighbours such as Mexico or those further afield in Latin America. Cuba is a prime example of a big country, indeed the world's most powerful one, being unable to handle a tiny neighbour as it would wish. Russia too has problems in subjecting its smaller neighbours to its will. Its western neighbours have found security under the US/EU/NATO umbrella, while the eastern ones resist its full control.

Contrary to what is believed, big countries are not necessarily held back in their growth or power projection because of neighbourhood problems. Historically, Britain as well as France rose to global power status despite constant conflicts with their neighbours. China has tensions with almost all its neighbours, without its inexorable rise as a global power being affected. Turkey's regional status has grown despite friction with virtually all its neighbours. A stable neighbourhood may be helpful in pursuing foreign policy interests at regional or global levels, but is not a pre-requisite. There are other determining factors.

Reason's for India's Special Problems with Neighbours

Normally, the strong, historically deeply rooted civilisational, cultural, linguistic and ethnic bonds between India and its neighbours should have acted as building blocks of enduring people to people ties and brought the countries of the subcontinent closer. However, India's overwhelming civilisational influence makes the neighbouring countries feel insecure in their separate identities. As identity is a core constituent of a sense of nationhood, these countries foster it by consciously asserting their separate identity.

The ethnic links, such as those of the Madhesis in the Terai in southern Nepal and the Sri Lankan Tamils with the Tamils in Tamil Nadu, instead of being a human link between India and these countries, as is the case with the Indian diaspora abroad and their country of origin, is a source of tension. These sections of the population are not as yet fully integrated and suffer from dichotomies and handicaps. They are either suspected for their extra-territorial loyalties or are seen as instruments of Indian influence, or the sympathy and support they receive from groups in India create distrust in bilateral relations.

International Relations based on Reciprocity Not Unilateral Concessions

Therefore, we need to analyse relations with neighbours without sentimentality and without recourse to platitudes about a bigger country having a moral imperative to show generosity and tolerance towards smaller neighbours and follow the commandment, 'Love thy neighbour as thyself'. However, love has never figured as a component of diplomacy. Smaller countries often have unrealistic expectations, as they believe that the bigger country should be generous and not demand reciprocity, and as there is no internationally accepted measure of what constitutes generosity, generous acts are quickly forgotten, the problem of unmet expectations endures.

Options for Smaller Countries Dealing with Big Neighbours

While in theory the need to have a peaceful, stable, friendly and prosperous neighbourhood may appear self-evident, it cannot always be ensured. It can be built through partnerships, not unilaterally. Concessions can be made but there has to be some degree of reciprocity. The burden of establishing good relations cannot fall only on the bigger country. The smaller countries, as we have seen, are not always right in their demands or policy choices. A country cannot seek extra consideration simply because it is smaller. Unreasonable or unfriendly conduct cannot always be excused on the ground that the fears, vulnerabilities and even the paranoia of smaller countries need to be sympathetically understood. The role of third parties who seek to carve out areas of influence beyond their borders as part of their regional or global ambitions cannot be ignored. Countries cannot always act in their neighbourhood as they please simply because of unequal power equations, as smaller countries will invite an external actor to counter a perceived regional hegemon, or external powers themselves, for balance of power considerations, or policies of containment, may intrude into the region and manipulate their local partners for larger strategic purposes.

Domestic Criticism of India's Failure to Manage Neighbours

Sections of Indian public opinion are prone to criticise New Delhi for its failure to stabilise our neighbourhood, arguing that India as the biggest country has the primary responsibility for managing the regional environment. Often India is criticised for not being sufficiently generous towards its neighbours, of not making unilateral concessions, especially on the economic side, when as a huge economy it can easily absorb the sacrifice expected of it. India is called upon to attach neighbouring economies to itself in a mutually beneficial, inter-dependant manner so that the scope for adversarial politics is reduced.

India's Capacity to Shape Neighbourhood Exaggerated

India's capacity to order its neighbourhood in a manner most congenial to its interests is exaggerated. Chastened by its costly intervention in Sri Lanka in 1987, for instance, India chose to stand aside and let extra-regional powers handle the peace process with the Tamils over many years and opted out of any central role in influencing developments that led eventually to LTTE's defeat and decimation. It is still not in a position to ensure an equitable settlement of the Tamil question. India's intervention in the Maldives in 1988 at the request of its government was more successful, but India is unable to control the current developments there even though they are very damaging to its national interest.

The Terrorism Issue

Our inability to control our environment is demonstrated by the fact that India, despite its size and power, is, ironically, the country most targeted by terrorism from its own neighbourhood. This greatly hinders India's efforts to strengthen peace, tranquillity and prosperity in the region. Although terrorism is now considered a global threat and the view that it should be fought collectively by the international community has gained ground, India is still largely left to deal with this menace from Pakistan on its own. Under Trump's administration Pakistan has come under greater pressure from the US to eliminate terrorism, with India's concerns getting more recognition. The US pressure, however, has not compelled Pakistan to break its links with the Haqqani group or cease supporting the Taliban, not to mention its continued abetment of terrorism in J&K. The reluctance of the US to seriously issue sanctions on Pakistan gives it no real incentive to cease using terrorism as an instrument of state policy towards both India and Afghanistan. Pakistan has not taken any serious step in the last ten years to conduct trials against those responsible for the Mumbai terrorist attack or investigate and punish those responsible for the one at Pathankot. Hafiz Saeed continues to spew jihadi venom against India and Jaish-e-Mohamed is still abetting terrorist acts in J&K, even though both have been designated as international terrorists by the UN Security Council. India has to take into account Pakistan's nuclear capacity in any attempt to force it to abandon the instrument of terrorism as a foreign policy option.

Within the SAARC region, apart from the recognition by the Afghan Government of Pakistan's sponsorship of terror, the other countries maintain a muted position on the issue. Each of them, barring Bhutan and now Bangladesh under Sheikh Hasina, have an interest in maintaining good ties with Pakistan for a mixture of motives that include political leverage against India, defence support or Islamic links, as in the case of Maldives. Pakistan, of course, has always had interest in undermining India's leadership role in South Asia. SAARC conventions on combating terrorism have little meaning given Pakistan's complicity with terrorist groups.

Limits of the Gujral Doctrine

The debate about unilateral concessions versus reciprocity exists in the context of international negotiations between the developed and developing countries on trade or climate change issues and so on, where the principle of differential treatment is conceded, though this is being resisted and diluted now by countries such as the US. At the purely bilateral level, this debate surfaces in the context of the subcontinent in particular. In international relations, a big country has no less responsibility than a small one to legitimately maximise its own interests. India has tried a policy of unilateral concessions, but without much result.

Former Prime Minister IK Gujral wanted to craft an approach that would modify India's image from a regional hegemon to one of an accommodating neighbour acting generously, without expectations of reciprocity. In September 1996, as foreign minister, Gujral outlined five basic principles that would govern the neighbourhood policy of the United Front government. First, with Nepal, Bangladesh, the Maldives and Sri Lanka, India will not ask for reciprocity but give all that it can in good faith and trust. Second, no South Asian country will allow its territory to be used against the interest of another country of the region. Third, none will interfere in the internal affairs of another. Fourth, all South Asian countries must respect one another's territorial integrity and sovereignty. And fifth, they will settle all their disputes through peaceful bilateral negotiations. Four of these principles, however, are standard ones governing international relations. The first principle did constitute a major break with conventional diplomatic thinking. Bhutan was excluded from the list because the principle of non-reciprocity is embedded in our relations with Thimphu. Pakistan violates, till today, four of the five principles of the Gujral Doctrine.

The Gujral Doctrine was a product of that incessant search by our political class for the best way to manage our neighbourhood. If non-reciprocity is no longer part of our governmental discourse, even though lobbies continue to propose unilateral concessions to our neighbours, including Pakistan, it highlights the complex challenge of finding the right mix of policies that would preserve the essential interests of all.

Enlarging areas of understanding, reducing points of conflict, fortifying mutual trust and confidence, building rapport at the leadership level and earning people's goodwill are obvious policy goals. But these are very difficult to achieve practically because huge disparities in size and power, nationalist sentiments, identity issues, religious forces and the role of external powers complicate India's search for balanced equations.

India's Difficult Choices

If India is tough with its smaller neighbours, it opens itself to accusations of hegemony. If it is indulgent, it presents a picture of weakness and indecisiveness that encourages a disregard of its own sensitivities and interests. There is no magic formula for an optimal mix of self-assertion and accommodation that can be applied with success. That India has the power to shape its immediate environment with supposedly more enlightened polices and that the principal blame is on us if we have neighbourhood problems are questionable assumptions. Actually, we need to be less romantic about the rewards of generosity, less guilty about our supposed failings and more self-confident about our capacity to rise even with the burden of our neighbourhood.

It is ultimately a question of pragmatism. If making a concession in one area can yield a return in another area, it should be made. In any case, reciprocity need not be confined to balanced exchanges in specified areas. If Nepal, for instance, had been more sensitive to India's security interests, India could be even more generous in areas of Nepal's economic interest. Nepal has for years blocked any progress in implementing joint water resources projects, with the result that India's energy security plans now exclude Nepal. If Bangladesh, as is the case now, has become more cooperative in dealing with anti-Indian insurgents present on its territory, India has reciprocated with greater generosity in economic exchanges and financial assistance.

Failure of the SAARC Option

Rather than look at such issues within the framework of bilateral relations between India and its neighbours, they could be addressed within the framework of SAARC. The problem of unilateralism or reciprocity is side-stepped once the SAARC countries as a whole agree on terms of trade and economic exchanges. Unfortunately, Pakistan has right from the start worked to limit progress within SAARC so that its own policy of linking trade exchanges with India to a resolution of the Kashmir problem did not get undermined. It refuses to accord India MFN treatment even now. Indeed, because of Pakistan's obstructive policies, economic integration in the SAARC area is poor. With Afghanistan joining SAARC, common sense would have dictated that Pakistan accord transit rights through its territory to facilitate Afghanistan's trade with India as part of the process of stabilising Afghanistan and giving its people economic opportunities so that they can, amongst other benefits, expand their legitimate economy so that the size of the illegitimate drug-based economy is also reduced for regional benefit.

Neighbours Invite External Powers to Balance India

From the viewpoint of India's South Asian neighbours, realpolitik would demand that they try to balance India's weight by bringing into play external powers. This with the objective of giving themselves greater margin of manoeuvre vis-a-vis India, extorting more concessions from it than would be the case otherwise, not to mention making themselves more eligible for economic and military assistance from powers wanting to checkmate India's rise or imposing costs on India for not following policies congenial to their interests.

Pakistan's Endemic Hostility thwarts India's Outreach

Two of India's neighbours were part of historical India, with separation occurring in bloodshed, hate and religious hostility. This legacy of partition survives in Pakistan's case and fuels its unremitting animosity towards us, of which terrorism and Kashmir is an expression. Despite the passage of 70 years and transformational changes in international relations, Pakistan's animus towards India has not ended. It is exceptional in its use of terrorism as an instrument of state policy. General Musharraf publicly avowed most recently his admiration for Hafiz Saeed and the value he placed on the use of terrorist groups to keep the Indian army in J&K under pressure. Pakistan refuses to normalise trade relations with India. It has obstructed regional cooperation to prevent India from drawing strength from it in dealings with other regional groups or important individual partners. An increasingly dysfunctional state like Pakistan effectively run by generals and increasingly wracked by religious extremism and terrorism cannot make peace with India. No amount of dialogue will change this reality. The flip-flops of successive Indian governments in their Pakistan policy, including the initial outreach by PM Modi to his Pakistani counterpart and his tough posture towards Islamabad subsequently, denote the intractable nature of our Pakistan problem, not merely our inconsistency.

Pakistan has, of course, in its obsessive pursuit of 'parity' with India and a pathological refusal to accept any status of inferiority vis-a-vis it, has been most instrumental in facilitating the entry of outside powers in the subcontinent. Today China is Pakistan's biggest defence supplier. The US too has not stopped supplying arms to Pakistan as part of its policy to obtain the cooperation of the country's military to help combat the insurgency in Afghanistan. With the US increasingly cognisant of Pakistan's duplicity on the terrorism front, tensions in US-Pakistan relations are palpable. The US is now openly supporting a stronger Indian political and economic role in Afghanistan, as well as in military training. India was the first country with which Afghanistan signed a Strategic Partnership Agreement. In Nepal, Bangladesh and Sri Lanka, Indian and the US policies have converged far more than was the case in the past, with the result that the governments of these countries are no longer able to leverage India-US differences as before to counter the Indian weight.

China's Adversarial Role in India's Neighbourhood

China, with its increased political, economic and military weight, continues its policies to counter India's "hegemonic" policies towards its neighbours. It continues to deepen its strategic relations with Pakistan, with continuing nuclear cooperation, major road and power projects in POK as part of the China-Pakistan Economic Corridor, and the development of the port of Gwadar as a potential military base. Pakistan has been a useful pawn in its hands to thwart India's ambitions, and keep it boxed in South Asia. By making Pakistan nuclear and giving it the weapon delivery capability, China has neutralised India strategically within South Asia itself. Pakistan has been given the means to continue its politics of confronting India without India being able to retaliate militarily even though it enjoys conventional military superiority. By building up a countervailing military power in India's neighbourhood, China has used Pakistan to prevent India from exerting its leadership role even within South Asia. The depth of its strategic commitment to Pakistan is demonstrated by the fact that it is opposing India's NSG membership and preventing Masood Azhar being designated as an international terrorist by the UN Security Council. China is adopting double standards on terrorism.

But it is not Pakistan alone that uses the China card against us. Nepal has done this traditionally and continues to do so to supposedly escape India's total domination. It has long resisted water resource cooperation with India that is so clearly in the interest of both countries, and now has given China big openings in this sector. The attitude of the Nepalese ruling class towards India is fickle. Modi's two earlier visits to Nepal enthused the Nepalese but the disruption of oil supplies because of turmoil in the Terai, arising from constitutional issues, created a deep anti-Indian backlash. The fundamental attitudes of Nepal's hill elite towards India are deeply embedded, for which China provides cover. With the election of Prime Minister Oli we can anticipate difficult days ahead as he is determined to play the China card against us. His recent visit to India, successful as it might have been in some respects, may not produce a lasting effect. In Nepal, China is becoming more assertive in demanding equal treatment with India. With the Maoists now a powerful political force in Nepal and given their ideological inclination to draw Nepal closer to China, coupled with their periodic rantings calculated to inflame public opinion against India, the political terrain has become more favourable for

China to expand and deepen its presence and influence in Nepal. This can only make India's task in handling Nepal more difficult. Nepal supports China's Belt and Road Initiative (BRI) and is backing connectivity projects with China in full awareness of India's security concerns. Actually, virtually all our neighbours support China's OBOR/BRI project and its entry into SAARC despite India's position. China even says, it will run a Bullet Train up to India's Bengal border through Bangladesh.

China's position in Bangladesh is entrenched. Even the friendly government of Sheikh Hasina would see that it is in its interest to maintain close ties with China for the many benefits it can derive from that, including giving India an incentive to woo Bangladesh more. China has earned the gratitude of the Sri Lankan government by supplying it arms that helped in defeating the LTTE militariiy. Sri Lanka, along with Myanmar, Bangladesh and Maldives, are, in India's eyes, targets for the naval ambitions of China in the Indian Ocean area to protect its vital lines of communication through these waters. The so-called maritime silk road strategy involving construction of new port facilities in these countries may have commercial goals in view in the short-term but has military goals in the longer-term perspective. To promote these objectives, China is bound to step up further its engagement with these countries, especially with increasing material means at its disposal, posing further challenges to India's equities in its neighbourhood. China is now intervening in Afghanistan politically in facilitating the reconciliation with the Taliban.

China has, of course, every right to take dispositions in the Indian Ocean area to protect its trade and energy flows. The countries with which China is cooperating are independent, sovereign countries and have economic and investment plans of their own to which China with its vast financial resources can contribute. Ultimately, for India's neighbours, it is a question of political judgment how far they should be cognisant of India's concerns and how to balance sometimes different pulls so that they do not become platforms for tensions because of the divergent interests of external partners.

Prospects

One can broadly conclude that India will not be able to shape its immediate environment optimally for itself in the foreseeable future. Unless Pakistan is ready to genuinely end its politics of confrontation with India, an integral part of which is the over-assertion of its Islamic identity, its propagation of the jihadi mentality, its nurturing of extremist religious groups involved in terrorism, and the political domination of the military in the governance of the country, the SAARC region will remain under stress.

India cannot afford to be indifferent to developments in Nepal because of its common border with Tibet in the north and the open border with India. At the same time, India cannot be seen as openly interfering in Nepal's internal affairs. Anti-Indian elements in Nepal are ever ready to pick up and exaggerate any perceived interference with a view to distorting public perceptions of India's policy.

The prospects for a border settlement with China remain distant. China has, on the contrary, added to the existing tensions by making aggressive claims on Arunachal Pradesh. India has been compelled to begin upgrading its military infrastructure in the north in the face of mounting Chinese intransigence on the border. With Chinese actions in the

East China Sea and South China Sea, India has to be even more on the alert. After the set-back it received at Doklam, it is possible that China may stage another incident in an area where it is better positioned to recover from that repulse. It must be said though that both sides have managed to prevent their differences from erupting into military confrontation. No bullet has actually been fired on the India-China border since 1967. India continues to engage China where it can, in the RIC, BRICS and SCO forums, apart from bilaterally as it does not seek a conflict with it. On the economic side, China has become India's biggest trade partner in goods, which is remarkable, given the differences between the two countries.

With the Sheikh Hasina government in power India's relations with Bangladesh have improved remarkably. Bangladesh has eliminated safe havens to anti-India insurgents and is willing to accord transit facilities for India through its territory to the northeast. A solution has to be found, however, to the problem of illegal Bangladeshi migration into India. Our borders with Bangladesh remain porous and the illegal influx of Rohingyas from Myanmar through its territory has added to the problem.

Sri Lanka is, in Beijing's planning, the hub of China's Maritime Silk Road project. Its submarines have already surfaced at the Colombo port. Sri Lanka is aware that it has walked into a debt trap with Chinese financed projects but, besides lacking the political will to rebuff China, it calculates that an anxious India will be induced to offer more projects to it to its gain. Sri Lanka balks at signing a Comprehensive Economic Partnership Agreement (CEPA) with India but is negotiating a Free Trade Agreement (FTA) with China. As a neighbouring country we cannot ignore what is happening in Sri Lanka, if developments here have a political impact in India. On the one hand, India must not intervene in Sri Lanka's internal affairs; on the other, if they impact on India's internal affairs, a case for a dialogue opens up with a view to helping find constructive solutions.

India cannot prevent Myanmar from developing close links with its neighbour China, including connectivity links through its territory to the Bay of Bengal. How far it should move in that direction and lose its capacity to manoeuvre is for the Myanmarese government to decide. So long as India-China relations are not normalised, India will always have concerns about strategic encirclement.

India's hitherto cordial relations with the Maldives have nose-dived. Maldives has destroyed any semblance of constitutional rule in the country and is openly disregarding India's concerns and sensitivities. It is aggressively playing the China card against us. Maldives has leased several islands on long term lease to China. It has signed a FTA with China in murky circumstances and supports the BRI, ignoring India's concerns. It is now seeking to undermine the security relationship with India.

Afghanistan presents potential problems of a grave nature. If the extremist religious forces ultimately win there, the strategic space for these obscurantist elements will expand enormously, with the risk of a seriously adverse fall-out in the region. A triumphant radical Islamic ideology can be destabilising for the religiously composite societies of South Asia. Pressure on India from these forces would grow.

Bhutan has been the only real success story in terms of India's relations with its neighbours. Bhutan has border differences with China. It has kept its distance from Pakistan and the great powers as well, giving them little scope for interfering in its relations with India. This underscores the point that good relations between India and its neighbours depend not only on wise policies on our side, but, equally, the pursuit of wise policies by our partners. The ruling classes in our neighbours have to take enlightened decisions on optimal relations with India. The burden is not on India alone. Bhutan provides an excellent example of a country that has preserved its unique personality and independence while maintaining close ties with India in self-interest without the need for external balancing that undermines India's security and other interests.

Conclusion

To conclude, it is not that India alone is mismanaging its relations with neighbours, equally, our neighbours, because of their own choices and enticed by China as well, are mishandling their ties with India. They know India's limitations in imposing its will on sovereign countries in today's world. Reciprocity is the governing principle of diplomacy. While a bigger country may not seek strict reciprocity, it cannot sacrifice its national interest simply because it must be generous. Our neighbours cultivate China at India's cost even though generosity is by no means the guiding principle of China's foreign policy. Rather, it is a display of power, meting out punishment and asserting sovereign rights unilaterally that are the hall marks of its increasingly nationalistic external conduct.

'Neighbourhood First' cannot be a particularly productive basis of external policy, especially at a time when the world's most powerful country is pursuing an 'America First' policy. India needs investments and access to technology. It needs to fulfil its defence needs through imports and 'Make in India' projects. It must secure its energy needs and defend its interests in international trade negotiations, besides seeking reform of the international financial and political institutions to obtain its rightful say in global governance. None of these pressing needs can be fulfilled by our neighbours. And so, while it is a bonus to have friendly neighbourhood ties, it is not a prerequisite for India's progress and the achievement of its aspirations.

Pakistan: Perilous Water Situation

Tilak Devasher

Pakistan squandering its water resources is finally catching up with it. During the last phase of the rabi season 2017-18, water shortage was estimated at 56 per cent and 47 per cent respectively in Punjab and Sindh. For the early kharif season, the shortage has been calculated at 30-40 per cent. This would adversely impact production of vital crops like rice, cotton and sugarcane. Apart from seasonal weather variations, the long-term causes for such shortages are inadequate storage, inefficient usage, diminishing ground water and increasing population. As its ground water dwindles, Pakistan is seeking regulation of ground water extraction on either side of the border. Another issue being raised is the provision of minimum environmental flows for the eastern rivers—Ravi, Sutlej, Beas to pre-empt India from fully harnessing their waters. Meanwhile, the gap between availability and demand for water in Pakistan is predicted to increase being almost equivalent to another Indus river by 2025. Where does Pakistan get another Indus river from?

The Worth of Water

BENJAMIN FRANKLIN, one of the founding fathers of the United States, famously remarked, way back in 1746, that when the well is dry we know the worth of water. Despite being a predominantly agricultural country, Pakistan has been squandering its water resources to such an extent that today it is faced with a serious water crisis.

Like India, Pakistan has two agricultural seasons: *rabi* (November-March) and *kharif* (April-October). Towards the end of the *rabi* season 2017-18, the Indus River System Authority (IRSA), the apex water regulator in Pakistan, revealed that water shortage from 1 October 2017 to 10 March 2018—that is the bulk of the *rabi* season—was 31 per cent in Punjab, 32 per cent in Sindh, 07 per cent in Balochistan and 21 per cent in Khyber Pakhtoonkhwa (KPK).[1] Resultantly, almost 400,000 acres of land could not be cultivated in Punjab. This shortage went up to 56 per cent and 47 per cent respectively in Punjab and Sindh in the final weeks of the *rabi* season.[2] In fact, for the last few years, there has been a consistent shortfall in the availability of surface water for *rabi*. According to the various Economic Surveys of Pakistan, during the *rabi* season in 2013–14 there was a shortfall of 10.7 per cent, in 2014–15 of 9.1 per cent, in 2015–16 of 20 per cent and of 25 per cent in 2016-17.[3] The serious water shortage in the *rabi* season has continued into the current *kharif* season. During 2017, the availability of water for *kharif* showed a decrease of 2 per cent over *kharif* 2016. However, the situation in *kharif* 2018 is very different.

In mid-March 2018, the IRSA announced that Punjab and Sindh would face 66 per cent and 54 per cent shortage of water, respectively in the early *kharif* season (01 April - 10 June) and 20 per cent later in the season (10 June onwards). Subsequently, due to rains in catchment areas, this shortage was revised to 30-40 per cent during the month of *kharif* season, starting 01 April while in the late *kharif* season water losses continued to be predicted at 20 per cent. One reason for the severe shortage predicted in April was due to unusual weather conditions. Despite the temperatures being above normal, there was below normal melting of snow in the catchment areas. This was possibly because there had been about 50 per cent less snowfall compared to earlier years. In early April, the water inflows were only 44,000 cusecs compared with inflows of 123,000 cusecs last year. According to the IRSA, 'Last year, Skardu temperature was 16.7 degree and discharge was 27,600 cusecs. Today, temperature is 20.6 degree but the discharge level is 17,000 cusecs'.[4]

According to the recently released Economic Survey of Pakistan 2017-18, there were severe water shortages during the monsoon, post monsoon and winter seasons. During the monsoon (July-September) 2017, actual rainfall was 22.8 per cent lower than normal; during the post-monsoon season (October- December) 2017, the actual rainfall remained 39.0 per cent below the normal and during the winter season (January-March) 2018, the actual rainfall was 56.7 per cent below the normal. Rainfall recorded during the monsoon, post monsoon and winter is given below.

Consequently, the four major rivers (Indus, Jhelum, Chenab and Kabul) received 23 per cent less water flows than the ten years' average during the early *rabi* season 2017-18. The

Rainfall* Recorded During 2017-18 (in Millimeters)			
	Monsoon Rainfall (Jul-Sep) 2017	**Post Monsoon Rainfall (Oct-Dec) 2017**	**Winter Rainfall (Jan-Mar) 2018**
Normal**	140.9	26.4	74.3
Actual	108.8	16.1	32.2
Shortage (-)/excess (+) in mm	- 32.1	-10.3	-42.1
% Shortage (-)/excess (+)	-22.8	- 39.0	-56.7
*: Area Weighted, **: Long Period Average (1961-2010)			

Source: Pak Meteorological Department[5]

rivers most seriously affected by this were the Jhelum that is at a 42-year low and Kabul that received 55 per cent less flows. Bulk of the water shortage for the late *rabi* and early *kharif* was due to decline in the flows of the Jhelum and Kabul. Accordingly, water availability has been calculated at 95 million-acre feet (MAF) for the *kharif* season compared to 107 MAF last year, while the average flow in the river system during past 10 years has been 112 MAF. This, according to observers, is one of the largest gaps in recent memory. While the IRSA has projected a 30-40 per cent water shortage for early *kharif*, ground reports, however, suggest that shortages have reached an alarming level of 60 per cent at a time when the *kharif* crops are being sown.

Another alarming fact for Pakistan is that the two main reservoirs – Tarbela and Mangla – reached dead levels during the *rabi* season, and therefore, were unlikely to carry forward any water quantities into the *kharif* season. The total storage in mid-March in the two reservoirs was estimated at only 0.105 MAF as against an installed capacity of about 15 MAF when constructed. In 2017, too, they were operating at dead levels since March 10. In 2018, according to data released by the IRSA at the time of writing, Tarbela was at its dead level of 1,386 feet, with inflows of 15,700 cusecs and outflows of 15,700 cusecs, having zero water storage. Water level at the Mangla Dam stood at 1,050 feet against its dead level of 1,040 feet, having a storage of 0.034 MAF. Inflows at Mangla were recorded at 11,700 cusecs against outflows of 12,900 cusecs.[6] If the water flow in Jhelum remains the same level as during the *rabi* season, the Mangla reservoir is unlikely to be fully replenished during *kharif*. This would have a cascading effect on the next *rabi* season.

Given the water shortages, not surprisingly, during 2017-18, acreage under wheat crop showed a decrease of 2.6 per cent compared to the corresponding period last year. Likewise, wheat production recorded a decline of 4.4 per cent over last year. The shortfall in production was, according to the Economic Survey 2017-18, due to decline in area sown and acute water shortages. Curiously, however, there was an increase of 7.8 per cent in the acreage under sugarcane in 2017-18 as also an increase of 7.4 per cent over the last year's production. Given the water shortage this would mean that there was heavy reliance on underground water exploitation further stressing the water table. The other problem with sugarcane is that the average water requirement is 1,800 millimetres (mm) that is more than the combined average water requirement of wheat (480 mm), maize (550 mm) and cotton (620 mm).[7] The question to be asked is whether Pakistan can really afford to expand the production of such 'thirsty crops'. The logical answer should be no, but so long as influential politicians like former Prime Minister Nawaz Sharif have a major stake in the lucrative sugar industry, things are not going to change.

Apart from the impact of climate change, several reasons

account for Pakistan's precarious water situation. The four critical ones are inadequate storage, inefficient water usage, diminishing ground water supplies and increasing population. The marked feature of Pakistan's water situation is that it is dependent only on the Indus river system and ground water for its needs. The Indus depends on glacial melts and rain for its flows. Resultantly, almost 75-80 per cent of its flows are in the summer and monsoon months from June-September and only 20-25 per cent during the rest of the year. However, the agricultural demand for water is 60 per cent in summer and 40 per cent in winter. Such a situation dictates the storage of adequate water in the surplus period for use during the water shortage period.[8]

Pakistan has been unable to so. Since its creation, it has built only three mega storage facilities – Mangla (1967-on the Jhelum), Tarbela (1976-on the Indus) and the Chashma Barrage (on the Indus). These storage facilities had total live storage capacity of 15.73 MAF when constructed. However, due to silting, the storage capacity of the three reservoirs. has been reduced to about 11.2 MAF. With the increase of the height of the Mangla Dam in 2009, the total storage capacity was enhanced to 14.15 MAF. However, it is estimated that the storage capacity of around 8.37 MAF is likely to be lost by 2025 due to silting. According to a study carried out by a Chinese consultant, de-silting of the Tarbela dam was neither viable economically nor technically. It could even damage the country's largest power house and reservoir. The study recommended that it would be more economical to build a new dam of the same size and capacity.[9]

Given that the average availability of surface water is about 145 MAF, Pakistan's capacity of storage is about 10 per cent or a thirty days supply. The international standard is of 120 days[10]. The consequence of insufficient storage capacity is that about 30 MAF of water flows into the sea. To put this in perspective, the entire flow of the Chenab is 27.1 MAF. Thus, water equivalent to more than the entire flow of the Chenab is going into the sea. While a certain amount of environmental flows are necessary, yet over 25 MAF of water is being actually wasted. In monetary terms this annual loss has been estimated at $21 billion.[11] According to specialists, Pakistan needs at least 200 small, medium and mega dams. Unfortunately, it only has 61, out of which only two are mega dams.

The second issue is of water utilisation that is among the worst in the world. Pakistan's water intensity rate, which is the amount of water in cubic meters used per unit of GDP, is the world's highest. This indicates that Pakistan's economy is the most water intensive and water dependent compared to other countries in the world. Against the world average of $8.6, Pakistan's one cubic meter of water contributes only 34 cents to its GDP.[12] Water usage in Pakistan's agriculture is also extremely inefficient. It is estimated that only about 36 per cent of the water reaches the fields with 64 per cent being lost in transmission.[13] As a result, Pakistan's crop productivity per unit of water is very low at 0.13 kilograms per cubic meter. What this means, is that 'Pakistan is using 97 per cent of its allocated water resources to support one of the lowest productivities in the world per unit of water'.[14]

The third issue is of dwindling ground water. Ground water has correctly been likened to nature's last resort when surface supplies are disrupted. However, in Pakistan's case there has ground water has been extracted indiscriminately. Consequently, the Indus basin aquifer is now the second most stressed (i.e. rapid depletion with little sign of recharge) in the world.[15] It is estimated that about 45 MAF of groundwater out of an estimated 55 MAF, is being withdrawn annually to supplement surface water through over a million tube wells, both private and public. Such incessant use of tube wells has led to lowering the ground water tables drastically. Such usage is also not maintainable as the gap between withdrawal and recharge is decreasing.

The fourth issue is the exponential growth of population. From a population of 32.5 million in 1951 Pakistan's population was estimated to have risen to 194.5 million in 2015 and as per the 2017 census is 207 million and growing at 2.4 per cent. Not surprisingly, Pakistan has had to grow more food to feed its population, which has meant bringing more land under cultivation and more consumption of water. When developed, the irrigation system in what in now Pakistan was designed for 64 per cent cropping intensity. The Canal and Drainage Act of 1873 legally mandates enough water delivery to sustain 64 per cent cropping intensities (a farmer sowing 100 per cent of his or her land twice a year would be equivalent to 200 per cent cropping intensity). Today real cropping intensities are between 150 and 200 per cent, to keep pace with population growth. Such cropping intensities can only be sustained by massive use of water. At the rate Pakistan's population is growing, it could well be over 350 million by 2050. It would not only be difficult for Pakistan to feed its population but would also create massive water scarcity problems that would defy solutions.

Being an arid country, water is a critical issue for Pakistan, where 60 per cent of the population is dependent on agriculture for its livelihood, especially in the dominant province of

Punjab. Agriculture contributes 20 per cent of the GDP and over 70 per cent of Pakistan's exports are agro-based. Not surprisingly, therefore, over 95 per cent of all water—surface and groundwater—is consumed in irrigation for agriculture. Severe consequences will follow if there is any reduction in water availability; it would not only cause drought in many parts of the country but will inexorably lead to violence and migration.

In fact, India needs to anticipate the potential large-scale exodus of 'water refugees' from the adjoining parts of Pakistan and brace itself for dealing with the problem. Taking a leaf from the Middle East, it was the influx of 600,000 Syrian refugees into Jordan that seriously affected the latter's ground water resources.

Consequences

Several consequences flow from this situation. First, water shortage in the early *kharif* period could lead to delayed sowing or even no sowing at all in some places. This would, in turn would impact the entire agricultural cycle.

Second, the yields from the current *kharif* crop could be affected adversely. The key *kharif* crops are rice, sugarcane, cotton and maize. Rice and cotton are critically important since rice exports bring in over $2 billion in foreign exchange and 60 per cent of cotton exports are dependent on the *kharif season.*

Third, quite possibly there would be no carryover water storage in *kharif* after many years and the entire irrigation would depend purely on river flows, i.e. glacial melts and rain. In case of a poor monsoon, the impact on agriculture can well be imagined.

Fourth, apart from food production, water shortage would lead to a drop in hydel-power generation causing load-shedding across the country. This will impact agriculture, commercial and residential units. The total hydel-power generation has dropped to 1,050 megawatts (MW) due to a cut in reduction in water releases from dams against the installed capacity of 7,000 MW. This would come at a time when Pakistan already faces power shortages due to a variety of reasons.

Fifth, surface water shortage would lead to increased use of tubewells for pumping groundwater, provided there is adequate electricity. Already the Indus aquifer is among the most stressed in the world. Increased pumping of ground water would further deplete one of the already most stressed aquifers, in the world, that of the Indus.

An ambitious programme has been laid out in the NWP that was approved by the Council of Common Interests (CCI) on April 24, 2018. It includes doubling Pakistan's water storage capacity to at least 28 MAF from existing 14 MAF, that is, increasing the water storage from the present 10 to 20 per cent of the total water flows. Plans also include reducing by 33 per cent, the water that is lost in conveyance and increasing water efficiency by at least 30 per cent with the gradual replacement and refurbishing of irrigation system. For this, an investment of Rs 2.891 trillion in the water sector has been projected including Rs 1.6 trillion for building the Diamer-Bhasha and Mohmand Munda Dams, Rs 800 billion for water conservation, Rs 150 billion for drainage, Rs 12 billion for flood control, Rs 300 billion for rehabilitation of barrages, head works and canals and Rs 29 billion for research purposes.[16]

The policy acknowledged that there was need to provide at least 10 per cent of the federal Public Sector Development Programme (PSDP) to the water sector, gradually increasing it to 20 per cent by 2030. The provinces, too, would have to correspondingly increase their expenditure on the water sector. However, the apathy of the Government is evidenced from two statements made to the National Assembly Standing Committee on Water Resources recently. One, with regard to current allocations for the water resources, the country would not be able to construct any big water reservoir during next 100 years. Two, there are currently 81 water-related projects under development but with the paltry allocations in the federal budget of 2017-18 of Pak Rs 36 billion, against the demand Rs 120 billion, it would take 14-32 years to complete them.[17] In fact, the NWP recognised that a total allocation of Rs 145 billion or 7 per cent of the combined federal and provincial development budgets for 2017-18 was inadequate to address the challenges.

Despite this, in the budget for 2018-19, only Rs 65 billion or 3.18 per cent of the PSDP has been allocated to the ministry of water resources as against their demand of Rs 203 billion.[18] Hence, the high-sounding projections made in the NWP are likely to remain only on paper. The Government seems to have abandoned water management and agricultural water needs to the monsoon, as farmers further deplete an already stressed aquifer. While successive Government are responsible for this situation, it is the Pakistan Muslim League-Nawaz (PML-N) Government that has been so obsessed with high visibility construction projects like the China Pakistan Economic Corridor (CPEC), the Orange Line and Metro that it has ignored the clear and present danger of water scarcity.

An interestingly element in the NWP is that it calls for trans-boundary cooperation in watershed management including the sharing and management of underground aquifers, as well as the sharing of real-time water-flow information, particularly in low-flood months. The point emphasised is that due to the aquifers being connected, there must be a system to regulate ground water extraction on either side to prevent unregulated extraction. The reason for this exposition is that satellite data has shown that the aquifer tilts towards India. Hence the apprehension that if India extracts too much water it would affect Pakistan's ground water availability. Not surprisingly, therefore, the formulation has been made that both countries need to work together for the management of their common underground water resource.[19] Undoubtedly, more will be heard about this issue in the future as Pakistan's own ground water resources dwindle.

Another issue being debated is that though the Indus Waters. Treaty provides a mechanism for river-sharing, hydropower development in India has the potential of threatening Pakistan's water security. In addition, it is felt that the treaty does not provide for minimum environmental flows for the eastern rivers—Ravi, Sutlej, Beas, that have been allocated to India—when they enter Pakistan. This adversely affects the waterbed environment and the population living downstream.[20] Clearly, as India gears itself up to fully harness the waters of the eastern rivers, Pakistan is apprehensive of the impact it will have on its total water resources. This is another issue that more will be heard about in the future.

Meanwhile, the overall gap between availability and demand of water is predicted to increase exponentially due to the surge in population and the impact of global warming. According to the IMF report, 'Is the Glass Half Empty or Half Full', while the total availability of water is unlikely to change from the present 191 MAF (surface and ground water) the water demand by 2025 is expected to be 274 MAF i.e.

a shortfall of 83 MAF.[21] To put this in perspective, the entire flow of the Indus is about 91 MAF. In effect, Pakistan would need another Indus river by 2025 if it does not make massive investments in its water infrastructure very quickly.

Since there are no signs of massive investments, where does Pakistan get another Indus river from?

Editor's Acknowledgement: Pakistan Water Crisis was also discussed by the author in his article titled 'Water Woes and Impact on Indo-Pak Relations', published in *Defense And Diplomacy*, Vol. 7 No. 2, January-March 2018.

Reference

1 Fawad Yousafzai, 'Decrease in Water Flow: Punjab to Face 66pc, Sindh 54pc Water Shortage,' *The Nation*, March 13, 2018, https://nation.com.pk/13-Mar-2018/punjab-to-face-66pc-sindh-54pc-water-shortage. Accessed April 1, 2018

2 'Severe Water Shortage Ahead, Kharif Crops Likely to Suffer', *Dawn*, March 22 2018, https://www.dawn.com/news/1396826/severe-water-shortage-ahead-kharif-crops-likely-to-suffer. Accessed April 1, 2018

3 Various Economic Surveys, Government of Pakistan.

4 Zafar Bhutta, 'Kharif Crops Likely to Suffer Due to Severe Water Shortage,' *The Express Tribune*, April 2, 2018, https://tribune.com.pk/story/1674899/1-kharif-crops-likely-suffer-due-severe-water-shortage/ Accessed April 5, 2018

5 *Economic Survey of Pakistan 2017-18*

6 'Severe Water Shortage Ahead, Kharif Crops Likely to Suffer', *Dawn*, March 22, 2018, https://www.dawn.com/news/1396826/severe-water-shortage-ahead-kharif-crops-likely-to-suffer. Accessed April 1, 2018

7 Muhammad Shafiq Haider, 'Why Pakistan Will Soon Become a Water Scarce Country,' *The Express Tribune* blogs, August 15, 2015, http://blogs.tribune.com.pk/story/28880/why-pakistan-will-soon-become-a-water-scarce-country/. Accessed April 1, 2018

8 Dr Zaigham Habib, 'Water Worries,' *The Friday Times*, April 24–30, 2015.

9 Javaid-ur-Rahman, 'Pakistan Wastes Water Worth Rs.25b Every Year: Wapda Chairman', *The Nation*, July 13, 2017, http://nation.com.pk/national/13-Jul-2017/pakistan-wastes-water-worth-Rs.25b-every-year-wapda-chairman. Accessed September 27, 2017

10 Simi Kamal, 'Pakistan's Water Challenges: Entitlement, Access, Efficiency, and Equity,' in Michael Kugelman and Robert M.Hathaway (eds), *Running on Empty: Pakistan's Water Crisis*, Washington DC: Woodrow Wilson International Center for ScholaRs., 2009, pp. 28–44. However, addressing a conference on 'Regulation of Hydraulic Structure for Flood Management' in June 2013, the Minister of Planning asserted that this had fallen to eighteen days due losing 4.6 MAF of live storage in the existing reservoiRs. because of sedimentation. 'Percapita Water Availability Alarming: Minister', *The News,* June 29, 2013,http://unesco.org.pk/ns/documents/2013/fms/pc_The-News.pdf Accessed September 27, 2017

11 'Wasting Water', *The News,* November 6, 2017, http://thenews.com.pk/print/242240-Wasting-water. Accessed February 1, 2018

12 'Per Capita Water Availability Alarming: Minister', op cit

13 Simi Kamal, op. cit

14 Simi Kamal, op. cit.

15 Syed Mohammad Ali, 'IMF's Advice for Our Water Woes', *Express Tribune*, July 10, 2015. https://tribune.com.pk/story/917872/imfs-advice-for-our-water-woes/. Accessed September 26, 2017

16 Khalid Mustafa, 'Pakistan to double its water storage capacity', *The News,* March 29, 2018 https://www.thenews.com.pk/print/298015-pakistan-to-double-its-water-storage-capacity Accessed April 1, 2018

17 Fawad Yousafzai, 'No Dam in 100 Years. with Current Allocations, MPs Told,' *The Nation*, March 1, 2018, https://nation.com.pk/01-Mar-2018/no-dam-in-100-yeaRs.-with-current-allocations-mps-told?show=preview?veRs.ion=amp?veRs.ion=amp?veRs.ion=amp. Accessed April 1, 2018

18 Ibid

19 Mohammad Hussain Khan, 'Will We be Able to Go Beyond the Rhetoric to Face the Water Challenges Ahead?' *Dawn*, January 1, 2018, https://www.dawn.com/news/1380112/will-we-be-able-to-go-beyond-the-rhetoric-to-face-the-water-challenges-ahead, Accessed February 1, 2018

20 Khaleeq Kiani, 'Pakistan to Work with Kabul, Delhi on Water Management' *Dawn*, May 3, 2017, https://www.dawn.com/news/1330768/pakistan-to-work-with-kabul-delhi-on-water-management. Accessed September 25, 2017

21 See the author's *Pakistan: Courting the Abyss*, Harper Collins, India, pp-207-227

Afghanistan in Transition

Increasing Role of India

Gautam Mukhopadhaya & Ravi Sawhney

Afghanistan is one of India's most important relationships historically, politically, culturally and strategically, from at least the times of Alexander, through the Mughals and the British, till today. Since the 'shocks' imparted by the Soviet intervention, the Pakistani grip on the Mujahideen, the end of the Cold War, and the Taliban, India has proactively rebuilt its relationship with, and regained its standing in, Afghanistan as a whole through the smart use of hard and soft power. Nevertheless, it remains a largely Pakistan-centric, security driven, development and trade relationship.

Deteriorating political and security conditions, emergent regional and geo-political developments, improvements in regional connectivity, and fresh political stirrings and elections in 2018-19, demand that India lift its game in Afghanistan with its geographic location and untapped economic potential as its strategic core through a greater commitment to Afghanistan's unity and security, an outward oriented, public-private, resource and people-centred investment partnership, and invigorated regional diplomacy. This paper outlines some ideas in this direction.

Strategic Importance

FEW COUNTRIES can be more important for India from a historical and strategic point of view, as Afghanistan. It has been the staging ground or a corridor for virtually every military campaign into India from Alexander to Babur until the advent of the Europeans by the sea route and has effectively defined India in its own imagination as a continental power at the expense of the maritime. It has been at the crossroads of trade, culture and religion between Europe, West, Central and South Asia, and the Arabian Sea, and a theatre in the 'Great Game' involving not just Imperial Russia and Britain, that has left a lasting legacy in the region in the form of the still contentious Durand Line between Pakistan and Afghanistan, but also virtually every aspiring power in the region and world including lately, China.

Afghanistan has been described as a 'graveyard of empires'. It became the last battlefield of the Cold War that brought about the collapse and dissolution of the Soviet Union*; then*, under the Taliban, a laboratory for religious extremism and fundamentalist Islam midwifed by Pakistan, the staging ground for 9/11 and more recently, the first, and still major frontier in the global war on terrorism. It was a witness to the demise of communism, the birth of radical Islam and is now a testing ground for liberal democracy in the face of Pakistan-sponsored terrorism using faith and religion. And, it is still a playground for Pakistan's obsessive search for strategic depth against India through the political use of Islam.

India-Afghanistan Relations

No other country, except Imperial Britain has had a larger impact on India or at least northern India, than Afghanistan. Separated since 1947 by Pakistan, it is easy these days to forget Afghanistan's intimate ties with India through history, trade and culture, epitomised by the *Kabuliwala* connection with the 'Pathans' or Pashtun moneylender and trader of dry fruits that is etched in the popular mind and film, and dominates the Indian 'image' of Afghanistan. Fortunately, these images eclipse those of Nadir Shah and Ahmad Shah Durrani and the long line of Central Asian Turks that came from Afghanistan and ruled much of India. The huge Persian influence on almost every aspect of the culture of northern India – statecraft, warfare, courts, language, architecture, music, painting, dress and faith – came to India from historic Khorasan, that includes Afghanistan. There is also the geographical and cultural continuity between the Hazaras of central Afghanistan and Kashmir and Ladakh.

This deep historical relationship in which India was not only frequently raided for plunder or conquest, but also was a seminal partner in trade and civilisational exchanges, has now been transformed into a strategic partnership that enjoys national consensus in both countries. The relationship has expanded to include sensitive areas like defence and intelligence sharing. Indeed, paradoxically, for a country that has been in almost continuous turmoil for the last 40 years, and one in the vortex of regional and great power politics since the Soviet military intervention in Afghanistan in 1979, the India-

Afghanistan relationship has, in welcome contrast to trends in India's relationship with many of its other neighbours, grown steadily over the last 16 years of democratic post-Taliban rule to become one of its strongest relationships in the region.

Today, this relationship stands cemented at all levels throughout Afghanistan by India's extraordinarily successful development partnership, scholarships for Afghan students in Indian universities, medical treatment and recreation for Afghan nationals in India, participation of Afghanistan's increasingly successful cricketers in the Indian Premier League, the popularity of Bollywood in Afghanistan, and strategic breakthroughs in connectivity through the Iranian port of Chabahar and an air corridor for Afghan products in the Indian market. A Partnership Council set up under a Strategic Partnership Agreement signed in 2011 held its second meeting in Delhi in September 2017.

In addition, from a country that was once viewed somewhat warily in the West as providing the rationale for Pakistan's obsessive interference and sponsorship of terrorism in Afghanistan, the new US policy for Afghanistan and South Asia unveiled by US President Trump in August 2017, publicly acknowledged India as a force for peace and development in Afghanistan while bluntly identifying Pakistan as the source of terrorism and instability.

Development Projects

India's development projects in Afghanistan valued at US $ 2 billion at Indian costs have played a key part in this. Few countries, including larger donors like the US, EU or Japan, can boast of as well as distributed *development* portfolio spanning almost every aspect of governance as India can. These include crucial infrastructure projects like the Pul-e-Khumri-Kabul power transmission line in the north, the 218 km Zaranj-Delaram road to the Iran border and eventually Chabahar port in the south-west, and the Salma Dam in the west, institution building as in the new Afghan Parliament and government capacity building through the Indian Technical and Economic Cooperation (ITEC), education and training as in the Afghanistan Agricultural Science and Technology University in Kandahar, earmarking of over 2000 seats per year under the Indian Council for Cultural Relations (ICCR), the ITEC and the Indian Council of Agricultural Research (ICAR) scholarships, military training in Indian defence training institutions, and small projects benefiting local communities in far flung border areas especially in eastern Afghanistan, directly.

These achievements are now being extended through a new generation of projects under an additional US$ 1 billion outlay announced by Prime Minister Modi covering drinking water and other projects crucial to the Afghans, and trade infrastructure and promotion initiatives, like Chabahar port and an air corridor, that will give Afghanistan greater access to the Indian market partially overcoming Pakistan's barriers to transit trade through its territory.

These have yielded good political dividends. Afghan leaders have frequently described Indian assistance to Afghanistan as far greater than the figures in terms of value for money, both financially and emotionally. For the Afghan people, they are symbols of India's good will and friendship that contrast starkly with Pakistan's destructive role in Afghanistan.

Nevertheless, as we look to the future from the perspective of mid-2018, Afghanistan stands at the proverbial crossroads. The first to strike the eye are the dangers and challenges.

Security Situation

From the security point of view, the previous year has been a particularly difficult year for Afghanistan with several high profile attacks by the Taliban, Haqqani network and the Islamic State, IS-K, or Daesh[1] against the government, security, civilian, religious and public targets throughout the year, including the National Assembly, Supreme Court, police, Shia mosques, Embassies, hotels and even hospitals. Except for a brief period after the placing of Pakistan in the 'grey-list' of the Financial Action Task Force (FATF) of the UN Security Council when there was a brief let up in high profile terrorist attacks, not even the more aggressive anti-Taliban Trump strategy has made any difference to the levels of violence in Afghanistan.

In 2018, there has been a spate of major attacks in Kabul and other places against public targets and events including Nowroz festivities, an ambulance, a humanitarian NGO, a voter registration centre, and two back-to-back suicide attacks on April 30 that killed 11 journalists. Together, they have, among them, already caused hundreds of civilian casualties and intense pain. Sectarian attacks attributed to the Daesh had increased. More and more, the Taliban and Daesh appear to be two sides of the same coin minted in Pakistan.

The Taliban continue to put pressure against prominent strategic district headquarters and towns in both the north and south of Afghanistan. According to the US Special Inspector General for Reconstruction of Afghanistan (SIGAR) and other estimates, the Taliban and other insurgents control approximately 57 per cent of the country. The Taliban have also announced their new annual Spring Offensive codenamed

1 Referred to henceforth generically as the 'Taliban' except where specified.

'Al Khandaq'. Al Omari and Al Mansouri were named after the now deceased Mullah Omar and Mullah Mansour in 2016 and 2017, on 25 April targeting US forces and their 'agents' but not explicitly Afghan security forces and legislative elections scheduled for October this year, in response to the Trump strategy, though as the attacks on voter registration centres in Kabul and elsewhere show, elections and civilians remain part of their operations.

The Afghan people have borne 10 years of war against the Soviets, seven years of internecine war during the Najibullah and Mujahideen interregnums, six years of oppressive rule of the Taliban, and 16 plus years of unrelenting suicide terrorism from madrasas, safe havens and sanctuaries across the Durand Line and US aerial bombardment and mistakes of the war on terror. Though they have coped with all these unbelievably heroically, they are now fed up with the violence. Terrorism fatigue is setting in. Unless it is addressed, it is difficult to predict which way it will lead, just as Mujahideen infighting in the 1990s paved the way for the Taliban.

Political Challenges

Yet, more challenging than the security situation where the security forces have at least been able to hold their own where it has really counted, beating back attacks on cities and most district headquarters, it is the political challenges that the Ghani-Abdullah government is facing that should be a cause of concern. While President Ghani has brought in a much-needed focus on governance, development and reforms that are supported by India and the West and those seeking a change from past ways of doing politics, they have also taken Afghanistan into dangerous political territory where politics is increasingly divided along tribal lines.

Powerful ethnic leaders like Vice President Dostum and the Governor of Balkh Province, Atta Mohammad Noor have been humiliated and been in open revolt for months with Dostum chafing in exile in Turkey, defying criminal charges, and Governor Noor's refusal to step down after his 'dismissal' by President Ghani, late last year followed by a public outburst against Chief Executive of the State Abdullah Abdullah, exposing internal fissures within the Jamiat. Political behaviour and discourse have taken an ugly turn raising the spectre of a return to the political violence of the early 1990's. Former President Hamid Karzai too is at odds with the government, challenging the government on critical issues including the Trump strategy. Moreover, democratic institutions have been undermined by lack of elections to the national Parliament for three years, and the district councils. These have finally been announced for October this year along with the commencement of the voter registration process on April 14.

The return of Hizb-e-Islami leader Gulbuddin Hekmatyar from Pakistan has altered and fractured the political balance and space in Afghanistan based on a tacit Bonn compact between a Pashtun President and the mainly Tajik-based Jamiat. With the Hizb-e-Islami back and on his side, President Ghani seems emboldened to pursue his reform agenda at the expense of ethnic and tribal leaders who still command vast loyalties. His efforts to nurture a new generation of progressive ethnic leaders to replace the generation of wartime leaders are still too early to take root in a highly traditional and patriarchal society. While admirable, these developments have the potential to put the post-Taliban compact and consensus under severe stress. In addition, on 28 February President Ghani made an unprecedented, fresh offer of reconciliation talks with the Taliban without preconditions along with political recognition, travel permits, release of prisoners and relocation of their families. Had the offer been accepted, it could conceivably have led to a peace process, but it could also have upset the ethnic balance in the government even more with as yet unpredictable consequences. Its effective rejection with the spring offensive leaves it in a limbo.

Hopeful Signs

Though negative developments over the past 40 years have been adding up, there have also been a number of hopeful signs and developments.

Governance

First, these headline stories and figures of casualties mask the considerable progress that Afghanistan has made over the last 15 years in terms of GDP growth, life expectancy, poverty reduction, education, health, especially maternal and child mortality, infrastructure and media freedoms. Sixteen years of democracy and international assistance have enabled a coming of age of a bright new generation aspiring to build a new Afghanistan free from terror and the tyranny of war-lordism.

Anti-war Sentiment

Second, two new developments in the Pashtun areas of Pakistan and Afghanistan emanating from the grassroots,[2] have injected fresh hope in an otherwise gloomy environment. First, sit-ins

2 Acknowledgement, 'Going Nationwide: The Helmand Peace March Initiative', Ali Mohammad Sabawoon, Afghan Analysts Network, April 23, 2018.

and spontaneous civil society protests, that included women, initially in Helmand, calling for a ceasefire and talks between the Taliban and the government under the slogan, 'Enough of War, We Want Peace', in response to a suicide car bomb attack at the provincial capital on 23 March that left dozens of civilians injured or dead, have entered their second month and spread to other Pashtun and non-Pashtun majority provinces covering some 16 or half of Afghanistan's provinces, from the north to south, and from the eastern provinces and Kandahar, to Bamiyan, Herat, Jawzjan, Balkh, Kunduz and Badakshan, and are acquiring the character of a country-wide and 'national' movement. A major civil society sit-in planned in Kabul, has been delayed citing security concerns.

While the local Taliban commanders were open to their demands, the leadership's response was negative and the government's reaction slow and confused. However, both the Meshrano-Jirga, the Elders Assembly (the upper house) and Wolesi-Jirga, the House of the People (lower house of the bicameral legislature) and the National Assembly of Afghanistan have expressed support for the Helmand demonstrations. A large gathering in Lashkargah planned to mark the first month of the movement had to postpone its resolve to march to Musa Qala, the district centre that serves as the unofficial 'capital' of the Taliban since 2015, pending a clear response from the government that they could take to the former. It is to be seen how they react to the new Taliban offensive. Meanwhile, the US and the Afghanistan National Defence & Security Forces (ANDSF) military operations against the Taliban and Daesh continue.

The sit-ins have been inspired in part by another people's movement across the Durand Line, the Pashtun Tahafuz Protection Movement (PTM) launched in Islamabad on

February 1 against torture and extra-judicial killings by the Pakistan Army following the suspicious killing of a young Pashtun shopkeeper by the police in Sindh that has electrified Pashtuns across the country. Though called off on 10 February after the government assurances that they would fulfil their demands, the hugely impressive peaceful protests led by the charismatic young Manzoor Pashteen, have resumed, most recently in Swat. The Movement has also had resonance in Afghanistan. A demonstration in support of the PTM, that also voiced support for the Helmand peace sit-ins, was held in Kabul but called off after nine days when a magnetic bomb, that no one claimed responsibility for, killed one protestor and injured 14. Notably, there are signs of the movement being emulated by Shias in Baluchistan who have also been victims of large-scale sectarian killings.

So far, news about both of these spontaneous peaceful people's movements have been sustained mainly by social media but downplayed or blacked out by mass media, and therefore perhaps not attracted much wider international attention than they deserve, including disappointingly in India. There is a risk that they will be derailed by outside agencies attempting to exploit, interfere or seek to make political capital of it.

Political

Third, it is to be seen if and how these promising stirrings of peace and resistance to violence emanating from the Pashtun grassroots can bear fruit in the coming months. Here too the conjunction of parliamentary and district council elections announced for October 2018 and Presidential elections in mid-2019 offer opportunities to channelise these civil society impulses in a peaceful political direction and a new political order though it must be admitted that the chances of them being overpowered or sabotaged far outstrip the hopes of success.

Such a process will also have to deal with the issue of reconciliation with the Taliban. The Helmand and PTM initiatives have opened the possibility of an authentic Afghan-owned, Afghan-led peace process rooted in the people and free from the clutches of Pakistan and other outside players with little understanding of Afghan realities. This should be allowed to flower, and the temptation *of outsiders* to step into it resisted, except insofar as to help create a more propitious environment for the government and local Taliban to talk.

It also offers the possibility of breaking out of a binary argument that since a military solution is not working, reconciliation with the Taliban, with all its implications, is the only other solution. This is a false dichotomy. Stronger efforts to politically defeat the Taliban have not been fully tested. The key to this is addressing local grievances and separating local Taliban commanders from their chain of command, finances and advisers outside the country who are preventing reconciliation at the ground level. Afghanistan does not have to accept an either/or choice between war and a retrograde order held up by criminal, terrorist and covert networks outside Afghanistan's borders—what the generation of Afghans who have grown up over the last 17 years reject, and what the sponsors of reconciliation talks abroad themselves would not accept.

Connectivity

Fourth, Afghanistan is being better connected with its neighbours and the region and beyond, opening prospects for trade and investment as never before. The up-gradation of the Chabahar port in Iran permitting trade with Afghanistan from

India and other countries bypassing and reducing Afghanistan's dependence on Pakistan has been a major breakthrough. Several consignments of donations of Indian wheat have already been shipped through this route and the Zaranj-Delaram highway built by the blood, sweat and tears of Indians - the Border Roads Organisation and Indo-Tibetan Border Force and Afghans alike. Similarly, an air corridor between India and Afghanistan, launched in June 2017 for the export of Afghan agricultural produce to India, has enabled over 2000 tons of fresh and dry fruits and 'hing', asafoetida valued at over US$ 40 million to be air-freighted from Kabul and Kandahar to Delhi and Mumbai over 82 flights by March this year.

To these have been added major new initiatives such as the 5-nation Lapis Lazuli Agreement signed by Afghanistan, Turkmenistan, Azerbaijan, Georgia and Turkey late last year connecting Afghanistan by land and sea to Europe, and the long anticipated inauguration of the laying of the TAPI gas pipeline from Turkmenistan via Afghanistan and Pakistan to India.

China too has proposed projects that link the China-Pakistan Economic Corridor (CPEC) to Afghanistan through various offshoots that would connect Afghanistan to Gwadar port. Though this adds to the challenge posed by the CPEC to us, it is a tempting and attractive prospect for Afghanistan. China is also leading a Five Nation Railway Corridor (FNRC) running from China through Kyrgyzstan, Tajikistan, Afghanistan to the Iranian ports of Chabahar and Bandar Abbas signed in Dushanbe in 2014 though it is behind schedule, as is another 7,200 km multi-modal International North South Corridor (INTC) backed by India intended to reduce transport time between India and Moscow from 40 days, through the Suez Canal, to 20 days that will also benefit

Afghanistan and Central Asia. Taken together, these projects have the power to change Afghanistan's economic future.

India's Role in Afghanistan's Future

India's policies in its neighbourhood are often criticised for being reactive, Pakistan-centric, and lacking strategic perspective and direction. There is a feeling that despite the deep historical ties, strategic importance and the successful rebuilding of India's relationship with Afghanistan post-Bonn, India has not been able to convert its intrinsic weight, positive attributes and political capital in Afghanistan into hard political influence as other countries are able to do with much less.

To some extent, this is valid. To overcome this, India will have to go beyond its current security-dominated vision of Afghanistan to one based on more long-term, fundamental and enduring attributes and goals, which are Afghanistan's strategic location, its economic potential, its territorial integrity, its political unity and regional realities.

First, the connectivity projects and initiatives described above are creating the pre-conditions to unlock Afghanistan's strategic location and economic potential as also that of Central Asia, based on sustainable development of its natural resources including minerals, hydrocarbons and hydropower, agro-horticultural and livestock processing, and new markets. India should be the first mover in developing these.

India should also be prepared to look at China's Belt and Road Initiative (BRI) connecting Central Asia and Afghanistan to the Arabian Sea that do not impinge on India's territorial integrity, augment access to and from Afghanistan and Central Asia especially through Chabahar, and contribute to its viability and economic prospects. In this light, as also in the 27 April

Modi-Xi Jinping informal summit in Wuhan, Afghanistan was identified as an area of India-China cooperation.

Second, India will have to move beyond its current largely trade and development-based relationship with Afghanistan to encourage, incentivise and cover risks associated with commercial Indian investment in Afghanistan, and our extended neighbourhood in general, as an arm of foreign policy especially along emerging connectivity routes, building on its pioneering 2013 initiative to organise the 1st International Investment Summit for Afghanistan in Delhi.

Indian industry should particularly develop, process and add value to Afghanistan, and the region's, natural resources – not merely extract and market primary agro-horticultural and related produce on which the majority of its people depend for livelihoods, but enhance its presence in the daily life of the Afghan people. Small investments in small enterprises, in light industries on a large scale through sustainable financing arrangements that do not lead to debt traps would generate employment, promote entrepreneurship, build a broad ownership base, raise productivity and revenues, and catalyse a virtuous cycle of investment, growth and sustainable development in Afghanistan in mutually beneficial partnerships that should bring incalculable political dividends. India should also be prepared to invest in the first and last mile connectivity to trunk routes, and environmental and water management to avoid and offset environmental damage. Security concerns should not deter such investments and will have to be factored into the strategy.

Third, any reading of India's history should make it clear that India will have to continue to invest in its security and defence on its western frontier for the near future, and investments in the security and defence of Afghanistan including the security of its own investments. Central Afghanistan, where India has an iron ore concession, that has still to be developed, can serve as a strategic 'fortress' for Indian investments westwards towards Iran as well as in other directions. We will also have to make a clear-eyed assessment of the implications of the appearance of China in Afghanistan and its various BRI routes through it via Pakistan and Central Asia to the Arabian Sea, for our security.

Fourth, we may have to be prepared to play a larger role in Afghanistan's politics, not interfering in its internal affairs but as a catalyst in preserving Afghanistan's internal unity in the face of external and internal threats.

Fifth, India should also complement its bilateral diplomacy with the US, with diplomatic initiatives on Afghanistan with all of its neighbours, especially Iran, Russia and China who are all more active in Afghanistan now. The recent Modi-Xi Jinping agreement to cooperate in Afghanistan could be built upon.

Conclusion

India's strategic vision for Afghanistan has been somewhat limited by contingent political and security factors including Pakistan's attempts to keep India away from Afghanistan and use it against us. So far, India has responded to recent challenges posed by Pakistan, the Taliban and its aftermath remarkably well despite handicaps of "geography, military capacity and excessive caution" through the skilful use of soft power. However, as India seeks to occupy its place in the 'Asian century', it must look outward, beyond its immediate horizon, to more long-term objectives and assets in its extended neighbourhood.

Afghanistan has been a formative factor in India's history. In the absence of ethnic, tribal, kinship, and past cultural ties, the strategic core of India's Afghanistan policy should be its location and economic potential that could serve as a hub and spoke in various directions, not just as a 'bridge' or 'roundabout'. Recent advances in regional connectivity offer the opportunity for India to go beyond its development and trade vision of Afghanistan to the use of outward investment as an arm of India's strategic thinking and foreign policy benefiting both India and its partners. These should be explored and exploited.

India's 'Act East Policy'

Relevance of Indo-Pacific Strategy

Rajiv Sikri

India's relations with its eastern neighbours revived with the launch of India's Look East Policy (LEP) in the early 1990s that led to annual India-ASEAN summits and India's membership of the East Asia Summit. While initially India's LEP focused on building economic relations with ASEAN, over time its geographic scope expanded and the security dimension gained prominence. China's rise and its aggressive behaviour towards its neighbours, including India, has made India's Indo-Pacific strategy essentially one of coping with the rise of China, which poses significant strategic challenges in India's immediate neighbourhood, including the Indian Ocean region. India's counter-strategy is to build-up partnerships with major maritime powers like the US and Japan. ASEAN remains at the centre of India's Act East Policy. Hopefully, China's leaders will understand the dangers in their current policies and not lead China into a great power confrontation. India too will have to rethink and reshape its policies towards its neighbours.

Historical Roots

IT IS generally thought that India started looking East only about a quarter century ago when the then Prime Minister, Narasimha Rao, proclaimed India's 'Look East' policy. However, that is not quite true, as for centuries India has looked East. There have been strong trade, cultural and people-to-people ties and contacts with its eastern and far-eastern neighbours. The reasons were not far to see. The lands to the East of India were fertile, prosperous and sustained large populations. The monsoon winds facilitated the movement of ships, sea faring vessels and boats between the Indian subcontinent and Southeast Asia. Thus evolved a vibrant Bay of Bengal community, where across this stretch of water, people moved back and forth easily, without inhibition.

One of the important features of this interaction was that it was largely peaceful. Apart from some forays by the Cholas into Southeast Asia in the 11th century, there was no attempt at empire building. These include the kingdoms of Srivijaya, Majapahit, Java and Bali (Indonesia), Ayutthaya (Thailand), Bagan (Myanmar), Kedah (Malaysia), Angkor (Cambodia) and Champa (Vietnam). The striking feature of all these kingdoms was their cultural-religious connection with India. All of them were Hindu or Buddhist kingdoms. However, it is important to note that all of them were well-established, large, confident kingdoms with local roots, quite autonomous of India.

During the colonial period, India's traditional pattern of interaction with Southeast Asia changed. On the one hand, the colonial powers broke the intra-Asian trade links and people-to-people connections in favour of a relationship between these erstwhile kingdoms turned colonies and the colonising European countries. At the same time, colonising Europeans took Indians as agricultural labourers and plantation workers to Southeast Asia, mostly as indentured labour, as a result of which a large Indian origin population mushroomed in countries like Malaya and Burma. Southeast Asia also played an important role in India's freedom movement, particularly as far as Subhash Chandra Bose's Indian National Army was concerned.

India's post-Independence Perspective

When India became independent, its leaders fully understood the importance of Southeast Asia for India. In a note on India's foreign policy recorded on 12 September 1948, Nehru said: 'We are most intimately concerned with South East Asia and we should therefore develop these contacts as much as possible. This means that we should particularly help in every way in the freedom of the countries of South East Asia and their closer cooperation with India in political and economic matters, and ultimately in defence. South East Asia would include Australia and New Zealand.... India is the natural leader of South East Asia if not of some other parts of Asia also.'

Sir Girija Shankar Bajpai, the first Secretary General of India's Ministry of External Affairs, shrewdly outlined a three-layered concept of security for India. The first, innermost, layer is from the Hindu Kush to the Irrawaddy, in other words from Afghanistan to Burma. Developments in this geopolitical space are of direct and vital interest to India. The second middle layer extends from the Straits of Aden and Hormuz to Singapore.

The Persian Gulf, northern Indian Ocean, Arabian Sea, Bay of Bengal and Southeast Asia fall in this category. The third, outermost, layer covers the expanse from Suez to Shanghai, or from West Asia to the Western Pacific. These three layers constitute India's immediate, extended and strategic neighbourhood respectively.

The importance of the Asian dimension of independent India's foreign policy was presaged in the Asian Relations Conference convened in New Delhi in March-April 1947, a few months before India itself became independent. Southeast Asia and East Asia continued to occupy a prominent role in India's foreign policy over the next decade or so. India's independence gave a fillip to the anti-colonial movements across Southeast Asia. India took a keen interest in the independence struggles of Burma and Indonesia: A conference was convened in Delhi in early 1949 and it played a prominent role in trying to resolve the Korean conflict; India was the Chairman of the International Control Commission in Indo-China; and, India was an active participant in the Bandung Afro-Asian Conference in 1955.

However, as the Cold War intensified and military blocs like SEATO were set up, India and the Southeast Asian countries found themselves on opposite sides. Other factors too contributed to India and Southeast Asia drifting apart. The Indo-China countries were engulfed in conflicts. Overland linkages with Southeast Asia, never easy because of the difficult terrain and poor communications, withered away as Burma became a closed society under military rule from 1962 onwards and the then East Pakistan, now Bangladesh, blocked transit after the 1965 war. India also focused on the greater opportunities in the West rather than in its relatively less developed eastern neighbours.

The imperatives for change in India's perspective, that led to Prime Minister PV Narasimha Rao's 'Look East' policy in the early 1990s were compelling and simultaneous in the context of the financial and economic crisis faced by India that led to a rethink about India's economic policy orientation; the desirability of plugging into the dynamic East and Southeast Asian economies; change in the global strategic environment following the end of the Cold War; and the consequent absurdity of regarding South Asia and Southeast Asia as separate strategic and economic theatres interacting only on the margins. ASEAN was the focus of India's 'Look East' policy in the 1990s. Progress in developing ties was halting and slow. India initiated a Sectoral Dialogue with ASEAN in 1992, and became a full Dialogue Partner and a member of the ASEAN Regional Forum (ARF) in 1996. But, ASEAN did not yet regard India as a credible serious partner. ASEAN's interest in India was limited and it was kept out of organisations like Asia-Europe Meeting (ASEM) and Asia Pacific Economic Cooperation (APEC) that were set up in the 1990s.

The year 1998 was a turning point. All countries, including ASEAN, Japan, Korea, Australia and New Zealand put relations with India on hold following Pokharan II. For the next 18 months or so, India's diplomatic energies were directed at handling the fallout from this development, and at the Kargil war with Pakistan. However, perceptions about India had changed during this period. There was the reality of India as a nuclear weapons power. India had also weathered the Asian financial crisis quite well. Unsurprisingly, once the dust had settled down, India was viewed as a major Asian power with the economic and military potential to be a partner in trying to balance China whose economic dominance was beginning to worry many Asian countries. Singapore's then Prime Minister Goh Chok Tong likened ASEAN to an airplane that could remain airborne and stable only if its two wings, China and India, were balanced.

ASEAN was also changing. Four new members were taken in between 1995 and 1999 – Vietnam in 1995, Laos and Myanmar in 1997 and Cambodia in 1999. Now, for the first time, India had a land border with ASEAN. India was also seen as a country with skills and assets that could help in the development of these four new member-states of ASEAN – the CLMV countries – with which it had close cultural, religious and historical ties.

The politics of India also changed. After the unstable coalition governments of the mid-90s, India got a stable government led by Prime Minister Atal Bihari Vajpayee. With the setting up of a Department for the Development of the Northeast Region in 2001, the Vajpayee government signalled its intention to give greater attention to the Northeast Region of India. Geography dictated that the development of the Northeast Region would depend greatly on the region's interaction with the CLMV countries and Thailand. This was an important trigger for the setting up of sub-regional organisations like BIMSTEC (which brings together India, Bangladesh, Nepal, Bhutan, Sri Lanka, Myanmar and the Maldives) and the Mekong-Ganga Cooperation (MGC) which groups India with the CLMV countries and Thailand.

India's 'Look East' Policy takes off

With this, India's 'Look East' policy began to acquire momentum. It also became two-pronged. The first prong reached out to the original, wealthier ASEAN countries-Thailand, Malaysia,

Brunei, Singapore, Indonesia, the Philippines – where the connectivity was by sea and the focus on trade and economic cooperation. The second prong was directed at the CLMV countries. Here, the focus was on developing land connectivity and reviving cultural and people-to-people contacts.

The year 2002 was a landmark year in India-ASEAN relations. ASEAN invited the Indian Prime Minister for the first-ever summit meeting with ASEAN leaders. It was at this meeting that India offered to conclude a Free Trade Agreement (FTA) with ASEAN, which gave credibility to India's 'Look East' policy and ensured that ASEAN-India summit meetings became a regular feature. The next five years or so saw intensive India-ASEAN engagement, both with the group as a whole as well as with individual ASEAN members.

In 2005, India became a founder member of the East Asia Summit. This was a most important development since it recognised India as an 'East Asian' power that had a legitimate role in community building and security in the region. In a psychological, political and strategic sense, this development bridged the gap between India and East Asia. One could say that this was the genesis of the concept of the 'Indo-Pacific' initiative.

Two developments during this period are noteworthy. First, while ASEAN remained at the heart of India's 'Look East' policy, the geographic scope of India's 'Look East' policy widened to include other countries in East Asia and the Pacific rim like Japan, South Korea, Australia and New Zealand. Relations with them expanded rapidly. Particularly noteworthy was the swift upturn in relations with Japan. Second, while economic cooperation remained a core area of cooperation – and free trade or comprehensive economic cooperation or partnership agreements were concluded or initiated with ASEAN and

BIMSTEC as well as with individual countries like Singapore, Japan, South Korea and Thailand – there was the beginning of cooperation in the security field, initially to counter terrorist threats, but later increasingly to counter Chinese threats.

The Chinese Vector in India's Look East Policy

So far, the Chinese vector was in harmony with the other elements of India's 'Look East' policy. In the early years of the 21st century, India and China relations were on an upward trajectory. High-level visits were regularly exchanged and trade was booming, even though it was heavily in China's favour. There was cooperation on many international issues. After the signing of the 2003 agreement on finding an 'early political solution' to the boundary question based on agreed political parameters and guiding principles and the 2005 agreement on establishing a 'strategic and cooperative partnership', a more hopeful future of India-China relations beckoned. Mid-2005 was the high point in India-China relations. Yet, notwithstanding statements about Asia having enough space for both China and India, the public rhetoric was at odds with practical reality. The lingering mutual suspicions found expression in the intensive diplomatic jockeying preceding the First East Asia Summit (EAS). China and some of its friends in the ASEAN tried to prevent India from joining the EAS but the other camp, where Japan and certain ASEAN countries played a leading role, managed to prevail in a touch-and-go affair. Henceforth, the China factor would be the dominant one in India's 'Look East' policy.

As India and the US drew closer following the agreement on the India-US nuclear deal, and Chinese self-confidence soared on the basis of its remarkable economic and military achievements, tensions began to rise in India-China relations. Other Asian countries as well began to worry about the rise of China. Under President Obama, the US too shook off its neglect of the region over the previous few years with its 'pivot to Asia', later termed as 're-balancing'. India and Japan accelerated their strategic embrace from 2007 onwards. Bilateral military cooperation intensified. The India-US Malabar naval exercises became a trilateral India-US-Japan affair. In 2007, Australia and Singapore also joined them, raising concerns in China about the emergence of a so-called 'Quad.' This was short-lived. New Governments that came to power in Japan and Australia, which deemed it prudent not to challenge the Chinese so openly, quickly dismantled this. Moreover, given their huge economic stakes with China, all the 'Quad' countries did not wish to convey an impression of being part of an anti-China coalition. The incipient Chinese challenge to the established order in the Indo-Pacific region was not seen as serious enough – at least not yet. But the contours of a new geopolitical structure in Asia were visible.

China's Aggressive Behaviour

The year 2008 marked a decisive turning point in China's attitude. On the one hand, the global financial crisis weakened the economic power and the moral authority of the West. On the other hand, China's success in holding the Beijing Olympics bolstered China's self-confidence. It felt that its time had come to regain its perceived place in the sun, and it began to behave like a great power intent on having its way. Its attitude towards other countries was marked by hubris, arrogance, insensitivity and intimidation. The earlier slogans of 'peaceful rise' and 'harmonious development' gave way to the 'China Dream,' which threatened to become a nightmare for many countries! From 2009 onwards tensions significantly rose between China and its East Asian neighbours, triggered primarily by China's aggressive moves to assert its territorial and maritime claims vis-à-vis a number of ASEAN countries in the South China Sea and vis-à-vis Japan over the Senkaku/Diaoyu islands. Unfazed, China continued its boorish and bullying behaviour. At the ARF meeting in July 2010, then Chinese Foreign Minister Yang Jiechi openly stated: 'China is a big country and other countries are small countries, and that's just a fact.'

The Philippines took its territorial dispute with China over claims to islands in the South China Sea to the International Arbitration Tribunal under UNCLOS, which ruled in favour of the Philippines in 2016. But China simply ignored the ruling and the Philippines, disappointed at the US unwillingness to come to its aid despite its treaty alliance with the US, thought it prudent to cut a deal with China. There was no unity within ASEAN on how to deal with China. As for Japan, China's muscular behaviour convinced the newly elected nationalistic Prime Minister Shinzo Abe that Japan should accelerate the ongoing process of building up its military strength.

Unmindful of mounting criticism, China relentlessly and swiftly continued to pursue its aggressive strategic moves. In the South China Sea, China consolidated its hold on the various islands and rocks by undertaking extensive land reclamation work and rapidly set up extensive military facilities at various locations in the South China Sea. The Chinese build-up in the South China Sea was worrying for India as well from a long-term perspective. If China could consolidate its position in the South China Sea, it could then move into the Indian Ocean with more confidence and thereby directly threaten India in its own backyard. There was also the danger that by controlling the South China Sea, China could create a counter choke point for the energy and trade SLOCs of China's adversaries.

India-China Relations Deteriorate

Chinese postures towards India also hardened. Some instances of this are: its claim to the whole of Arunachal Pradesh rather than just Tawang and objections to Prime Ministerial visits to the state; issuing of stapled visas to residents of Jammu and Kashmir and assertions that the India-China boundary was only 2000-odd kilometres long thereby questioning the status of Jammu and Kashmir as a part of India; and increasingly strident objections to the activities of the Dalai Lama and the so-called India-based Tibetan Government-in-exile.

While there was no serious incident on the border, the Chinese made it clear that, contrary to their thinking in 2005, they didn't envisage any early settlement of the border nor did they any longer consider themselves bound by the 2003 and 2005 agreements on how to handle the border issue. China also began to establish a robust presence in India's immediate neighbourhood with a base in Djibouti, another planned in Gwadar, and getting both Sri Lanka and the Maldives into debt traps through white elephant projects that would enable it to get long-term access to ports in both countries. China also consolidated its position in Nepal by exploiting the anti-India feeling that had been generated by the Madheshi blockade of the India-Nepal border for many months in 2015. India was wary and clearly worried but, perhaps its attention was focused on building up its relations with the United States and in handling various domestic political crises, that it underestimated the dangers of the looming strategic challenges posed by China.

It was not long before China turned up the heat on its borders with India. The standoff in the Depsang area of Ladakh-Aksai Chin in 2013 was the first instance of Chinese muscle flexing. When Prime Minister Modi came to power in May 2014, he tried to seriously explore the possibility of a cooperative relationship with China. However, Chinese intrusions into Chumar in Ladakh in September 2014, even as the Chinese President Xi Jinxing was on Indian soil, made it clear that China did not intend to give up its policy of keeping India under pressure on the border. By then, China had also launched its 'One-Belt One-Road' Initiative (since renamed as the 'Belt and Road Initiative'), an ambitious project intended to envelop various countries in Asia and Europe, as well as the Indian Ocean region into China's economic orbit and eventually into its strategic embrace. One of the key branches of this project, to which India had serious objections, was the China-Pakistan Economic Corridor, passing through Pakistan-occupied Kashmir.

For India, the severest crisis came in the summer of 2017 over Doklam near the India-Bhutan-China tri-junction. Fortunately, India held its nerve, did not give in to Chinese bullying and intimidation, and managed to prevent Bhutan from drifting into China's orbit. However, this was only a temporary reprieve for India, as the February 2018 Maldives crisis showed. Clearly, China was signalling to India that it intended to challenge India in its South Asian neighbourhood.

Maritime Dimension of India's Indo-Pacific Strategy

Recognising that it could not meet the Chinese challenge on its own, India sought to develop a countervailing force by working closely with the United States and the countries of

East and Southeast Asia. India signalled its growing strategic convergence with the United States by signing in 2015 a Joint Strategic Vision for the Asia-Pacific and the Indian Ocean that emphasised safeguarding maritime security, ensuring freedom of navigation and over flight, settlement of territorial and maritime disputes peacefully in accordance with international law, including UNCLOS. After much deliberation and considerable delay, India also signed with the United States a Logistics Exchange Memorandum of Agreement in 2016 that gives mutual access to designated military facilities for refuelling and replenishment.

India also accelerated its defence and security cooperation with the ASEAN and other East Asian countries through a reinvigorated 'Look East' policy, now called the 'Act East' policy. Japan, Vietnam, Indonesia and Australia came in for special attention. With Japan, the relationship was upgraded to a Special Strategic and Global Partnership, and with Vietnam to a Comprehensive Strategic Partnership. The key elements of the India-US Joint Strategic Vision were reflected in these relationships too. Trilateral maritime security mechanisms were established with the US and Japan, as well as with Japan and Australia. It is no coincidence that in five out of the six years between 2010 and 2015, the leaders of South Korea, Indonesia, Thailand, Japan and the United States were accorded the honour of being the Chief Guest at India's Republic Day celebrations.

In 2017, India shifted to another gear in its 'Act East' policy. The first important development was that the idea of the 'Quad' which had petered out in 2007 was revived with the meeting of senior officials of the four Quad countries on the margins of the East Asia Summit in Manila in November

2017, followed up by a meeting of the Naval Chiefs of the four countries at the Raisina Dialogue in New Delhi in January 2018.

India's rapidly growing defence and security cooperation with technologically advanced countries like the US and Japan has beefed up the Indian maritime capabilities. India is also now actively seeking military facilities across the Indian Ocean – in Oman, Seychelles, Mauritius and Madagascar. As a result of the agreement with the United States, India can make use of US facilities in Diego Garcia and, if an anticipated similar agreement with France fructifies, of French facilities in Reunion. India has also got access to Changi port in Singapore and has set up Satellite Tracking and Telemetry Stations in Vietnam and Indonesia. Defence and security cooperation is an important element in India's relationships with all ASEAN and Indian Ocean countries, even smaller countries like Cambodia and Brunei, and distant ones like the Philippines. It is noteworthy that Prime Minister Modi has accepted the invitation to be the Chief Guest for the 2018 Shangri-la Dialogue in Singapore. Truly, India's security is now intimately tied up with developments in the Indian Ocean and the Western Pacific regions. The Indo-Pacific strategic concept has become a reality.

India and ASEAN – New Directions

India also decided to give visibly greater attention to developing ties with the ASEAN countries. Signalling its commitment to the importance of ASEAN in its foreign policy, and to the unity and centrality of ASEAN in the region, India invited all the ASEAN leaders as Chief Guests for its Republic Day celebrations in 2018 to celebrate 25 years of India-ASEAN relations. The gesture was notable, but more significant was the decision of all ASEAN leaders to accept the invitation and be present on the occasion. Clearly, China and its policies were bothering them and their collective presence in New Delhi showed that they were looking to India to provide leadership in countering China. India used the occasion to reiterate that ASEAN was at the centre of India's 'Act East' policy.

This is not just symbolism. ASEAN acts as a buffer between the great powers of the region like China, Japan, the United States and India. The ASEAN region is also the link between the Indian and the Pacific Oceans – and between the individual members of the Quad. Thus, it is evident that there can be no meaningful Indian strategy for the Indo-Pacific region that does not take ASEAN into account. Currently, all regional economic and security cooperation structures have ASEAN at the core. From this perspective, an independent and united ASEAN is imperative to ensure that there's a stable regional architecture rather than one dominated by China. Significantly, maritime cooperation was the theme of the discussions at the India-ASEAN Retreat during the January 2018 Summit.

It will not be easy for India to dislodge China from its dominant position in the ASEAN countries. It has deep pockets and a rich and influential Chinese-origin population in these countries that can be used to further China's strategic interests. Yet India must make the effort. The three mantras that were seen during the 2018 India-ASEAN Summit, whose theme was 'Shared Values, Common Destiny', were culture, connectivity and commerce. Culturally, most ASEAN countries are much closer to India than to China. However, India has not been able to develop extensive people-to-people ties in the absence of good physical connectivity with ASEAN. The problem is not only poor connectivity between Northeast India and ASEAN, but also between Northeast India and the rest of India.

A much more cordial and cooperative atmosphere that has come in India-Bangladesh relations since Sheikh Hasina came to power in 2009 has helped to improve connectivity between India and the Northeast Region, and Bangladesh itself is keen to become an active participant in India's 'Act East' policy. India, for its part, also realises that Bangladesh's cooperation is critical for the optimal success of India's 'Act East' policy.

More than his predecessors, Prime Minister Modi has given much greater attention to the development of the Northeast region. Many road and other infrastructure projects, in particular the Trilateral Highway connecting India with Myanmar and Thailand that have been languishing for years are being speeded up. There are plans to extend it further to Laos, Vietnam and Cambodia. With SAARC in the doldrums, BIMSTEC has emerged as the more promising vehicle for regional cooperation. The Mekong-Ganga Cooperation is also a supplementary vehicle for regional cooperation with Thailand and the CLMV countries in soft areas like tourism and culture. But the Bangladesh-China-India-Myanmar initiative, which is strongly supported by China, has been put in cold storage, since India's priority is to enhance west to east, rather than north to south, connectivity.

India's economic relations with ASEAN are not proceeding as well as it was thought they might. Two-way trade is still only about US$ 70-75 billion. India is somewhat disappointed with the benefits from the India-ASEAN Comprehensive Economic Cooperation Agreement (CECA). It has paid a price in the FTA for goods where lowered tariffs have led to a rise in ASEAN exports to India, but the commensurate benefits have not accrued to India as anticipated in the domain of services and investment, where India feels it has an edge.

Learning from its experience with the India-ASEAN CECA, India is wary of giving concessions on trade without simultaneously getting agreement on services and investment in the negotiations under way for a Regional Comprehensive Economic Partnership (RCEP). Nor does India want to further expose its market to Chinese products. India wants a 'balanced' outcome to the RCEP negotiations. One weakness is that India is not part of the Asian supply chains. As in the case of the India-ASEAN CECA, where political considerations overrode the purely economic ones in arriving at the decision to go in for an India-ASEAN CECA, a similar judgment will have to be made by India on RCEP, where ASEAN is keen on an early agreement.

New 'Great Game' in the Indian Ocean

Even as it builds up its relations with countries near and far in the Indo-Pacific, India is well aware of the limitations of these partnerships and agreements in deterring China's activities that are harming India's interests. As the Doklam crisis showed, India had to tackle the Chinese threat alone. Nor should India count on countries like the US, Japan and the ASEAN to support India in its territorial dispute with China.

However, India cannot be passive and merely reactive if it truly aspires to be a 'leading' power that is prepared to make difficult choices and take risks. It is its vital interests that are at stake. With China already controlling the Eurasian landmass, after having got Russia to acquiesce to becoming a junior partner, China cannot be permitted to control the maritime domain too. Mackinder's thesis of a century ago that the

Eurasian 'Heartland' and the 'Rim-land' should not be allowed to be under a single power retains its strategic relevance today. If China cannot be challenged in the Eurasian land space, it must be checked on the seas.

Till a decade or so ago, it was believed that a new 'Great Game' was going to be played in Eurasia. That game appears to have been won by China – at least for now, this round at least. Now there is a 'Great Game' under way in the maritime domain, where it is imperative that China's ambitions to dominate Asia, and eventually the world, be thwarted. Keeping India strategically crippled is a key element in China's strategy, because India is the only other country in Asia that has the size, geographic location, population, as well as economic and defence potential to challenge China. Contrary to what China may have assumed, India is not prepared to accept a China-dominated Asian order. Not only was it the only major country to boycott China's Belt and Road Summit in May 2017, but it also spelt out its apprehensions about the model of development envisaged by China. This in turn has caused rethinking about the viability of some of the Belt and Road projects in many European countries, as well as neighbouring countries like Pakistan and Nepal. Prime Minister Modi has signalled that India has the political will to take on China, even though it carries considerable military and political risks.

The India-China competition in the Indian Ocean came to a head with the Maldives crisis in February 2018. President Yameen, whose policies have made it clear that he has been bought over by China and is willing to be a strategic pawn of China's, has ignored the call by India and many other countries to respect the Supreme Court judgment freeing political prisoners that include his political opponents. Instead, he has jailed the Chief Justice of the Supreme Court and a couple of other judges and imposed a State of Emergency that has been extended.

Amid calls by former President Nasheed for Indian intervention, China has cautioned India against taking any such step. In this way, an internal crisis in the Maldives has become an India-China issue. India has been put in a difficult position. Prime Minister Modi and President Trump have conferred, since the US too is concerned about a Chinese presence close to its base in Diego Garcia. At the time of writing, the situation is fluid. However, it is clear that India cannot sit by and do nothing while China takes over its strategic neighbourhood. This would blow a hole in its claim to be a net security provider in the Indian Ocean and South Asia, dent its reliability vis-à-vis Seychelles, Mauritius, Sri Lanka and the ASEAN states, and seriously question the credibility of the India-US strategic partnership and the nascent Quad. One would have to watch how India tackles the situation.

Future Prospects

China is proceeding from two reasonable assumptions. One is that no country will risk disruption of its ties with China for a confrontation that does not affect its core interests. The second is that no country by itself can be a match for China. However, there is the danger that China may be overplaying its hand. After some dithering, US President Donald Trump appears to have come to the conclusion that China poses a serious strategic challenge to US interests and therefore must be checked.

In recent months, India has become very active in building defence and security relationships with the Indian Ocean countries and ASEAN, including perhaps the sale of Brahmos missiles by India to Vietnam and US-2 amphibian aircraft by Japan to India. All Asian countries have realised that if India were to succumb to China, their prospect of staving off China's pressure would be extremely bleak. Should China not change course, a dangerous confrontation could well ensue. The situation is reminiscent of the 1930s when the other powers saw merit in appeasing Hitler's Germany till it went too far in invading Poland in 1939. Prudence would seem to dictate that China would like to avoid any conflict whose outcome is unpredictable. Any crisis could expose China's multiple fault-lines and weaknesses that could be potentially destabilising for China and politically fatal for its leadership.

Conclusion

However, one conclusion is inescapable. As China relentlessly and systematically works to get India's immediate neighbours out of India's sphere of influence, India too will have to reorient its policy towards them.

Prime Minister Modi's 'Neighbourhood First' policy was premised on Indian generosity towards its neighbours provided they respected India's security interests. While it has been successful vis-à-vis Bhutan and Bangladesh, it has not worked with Nepal, Sri Lanka and the Maldives. Nepal and the Maldives enjoy many unilateral concessions given by India in respect of trade, employment, travel etc. Perhaps the time has come for India to withdraw some of these concessions from countries that continue to act against India's interests. This would raise the costs for China in these countries and compel people in these countries to reflect whether the regimes they have elected or tolerated are serving the interest of the people. India could study and learn some lessons from the way Russia has handled relations with some of its recalcitrant neighbouring countries. Finally, India's Indo-Pacific strategy, which now essentially means coping with the challenge from China, should include elements that pro-actively create complications for China's Belt-and-Road Initiative.

Quadrilateral Security Dialogue

Anil Wadhwa

The Quadrilateral Security dialogue (Quad) saw a revival in 2017, after falling into disuse in 2007. The changed geo-political scenario in the Indo Pacific and China's aggressive actions in the South China Sea, leading to forcible occupation, and militarization of some of the disputed islands there, as also the relentless quest for port acquisition and setting up of bases and posts in the Indian Ocean littoral countries has been a major factor in the coming together of the Quad countries in order to preserve a rules based order. A free, open transparent and balanced Indo-Pacific region, where sovereignty and international law are respected and differences resolved through dialogue is the central pillar on the basis of which the Quad has come together. Centrality of the ASEAN must be respected in the Quads future actions. The Quad must have a concrete agenda of cooperation in order to sustain itself. This includes working on infrastructure and connectivity, security cooperation and dialogue including joint exercises, defence equipment and technology cooperation, collaboration in cyber security, anti-piracy operations, capacity building for Asia pacific countries, countering nontraditional threats to security maritime domain awareness and intelligence sharing. The Quad is not a military alliance directed against any country. Despite this, it will face pressure not to act in tandem, which must be resisted. The Quad process can be sustained through a regular dialogue mechanism through a formal process, with an agreed road map.

Born out of the Tsunami

THE QUADRILATERAL Security Dialogue or 'Quad' emerged as a consultative regional forum among democracies in 2004 following the tsunami of 2004 which struck South and South East Asia. The naval forces of USA, India, Australia, and Japan were the focus because they took the lead, and an ad-hoc coordinating mechanism was born to consult on regional challenges, in particular, in dealing with maritime emergencies and security threats like piracy. Together, the four countries contributed over 40,000 troops and humanitarian responders, in addition to planes, helicopters, and ships who assisted victims of the disaster. Three years later, the idea was resurrected when Japanese Prime Minister Abe, addressing the Indian Parliament, suggested a dynamic coupling of the Pacific and the Indian Oceans, and called for an 'arc of freedom and prosperity'.

The Quad enjoyed a brief revival when the four countries along with Singapore, held naval exercises in the Bay of Bengal in September 2007. The Quad fell into disuse for a while due to political compulsions brought to bear upon it. Some have argued that this was done to prevent the Chinese paranoia and prevent its military modernisation. However, rather than placate Beijing, if the Quad is to sustain itself, it must avoid similar situations at all cost, for its own credibility in the future. The reasons for the resurrection of this ad-hoc and loose grouping at Manila in September 2017, are many, but primarily, it is the changed geopolitics in the Indo-Pacific region.

THE QUAD COUNTRIES

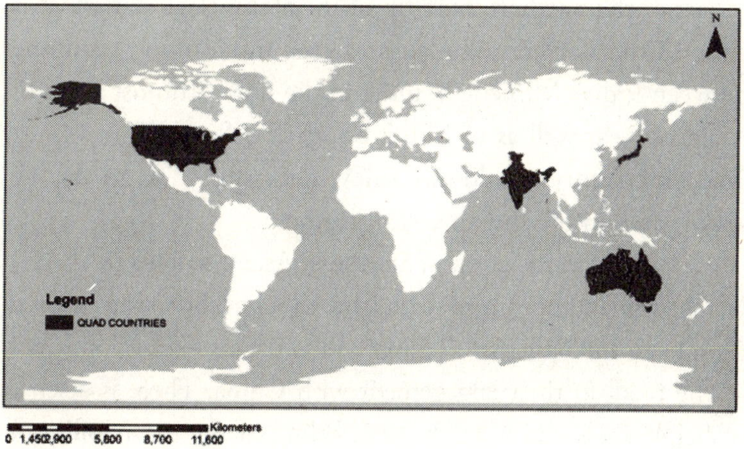

China has moved in aggressively to enter the geopolitical and economic space vacated by the United States in the Indo-Pacific region. Although all partners of the Quad are also cooperating with a rising and increasingly powerful China, it is using economic inducements and penalties, influencing operations, and implying military threats to persuade others to agree to its political and economic agenda. Its infrastructure and trade policies reinforce its desire for political dominance. China's assertive policy in the South China Sea has resulted in the occupation, transformation, militarisation and effective control over a large number of islands in the South China Sea.

In the Indian Ocean, China has been aggressively acquiring

port assets and potential bases including those in Myanmar, Bangladesh, Sri Lanka, Maldives, Pakistan and Djibouti. A 'joint Observation Station' supposedly proposed by the Chinese in Maldives is likely to have military capabilities along with provisions for a submarine base, identical to the one in Jiwani, near Gwadar in Pakistan. The Mukunudhoo Island in the Maldives where China will reportedly build the observatory is part of the northernmost tip of the archipelago nation. It is close to the northern sea lanes of communication – running between India's Minicoy Island and the northernmost atolls of Maldives – as well as to India's South and South West Coast. The observatory would also allow data collection to deploy submarines in the Indian Ocean region.

A divided Association of Southeast Asian Nations (ASEAN) has had to compromise with the thought of living with a dominant and aggressive China and is trying to develop 'rules of the road' in their engagement with China. There is a sense of helplessness and a heightened feeling of the inevitability of Chinese ascendancy in this situation. Chinese aggressiveness is driven by the need to acquire resources of oil, minerals, and other raw materials around the world. Its 'predatory' investments under the guise of Belt and Road Initiative have led to heightened concerns. The strategic assets are being acquired by China with its enormous trade surpluses. From the Chinese point of view, its sea lanes must be protected to ensure the continued flow of raw materials. China's competing claims with Vietnam, Malaysia, the Philippines, Brunei and Taiwan on islands and their associated economic zones within the South China Sea will continue, and economics, politics, and nationalism will continue to make this area a potential 'hotspot' for conflict.

Chinese traditional rivalry with Taiwan, its testy relationship with Japan, and the economic rise of South East Asia has also resulted in an enhancement of the strategic significance of this region. In the North East region of Asia, the North Korean regime has been steadily advancing its nuclear, cyber, and ballistic missile programmes. However, there are clear signs of a thaw and possibilities of tensions reducing following the visit of Kim Jong-un to China, the meeting between the North and South Korean leaders, as well as the much-awaited Summit between Kim Jong-un and President Trump, which script or not, did end with with fulsome declarations of a new friendship but just vague pledges of nuclear disarmament in June 2018.

The Sea Lanes of the World

The Indo-Pacific, therefore, has gained ascendancy as an area with important sea lanes of communication, as also a region where the world's major powers are involved. A free, open, inclusive transparent and balanced Indo-Pacific region, where sovereignty and international law are respected, and differences are resolved through dialogue can become a guarantee of enduring security and peace in the region.

The primary aim of the Quad is to enable regional security architecture for the maintenance of a rules-based arrangement. A revived Quad has had its first meeting in the new avatar at the level of middle level officers in Manila on November 12, 2017 who identified the need to address common challenges of terrorism and proliferation linkages impacting the region. The Quad members were supportive of upholding a rules-based order and respect for international law in the Indo-Pacific, ensuring freedom of navigation and over-flight, maritime security in the Indo-Pacific, peaceful resolution of disputes, and increasing connectivity consistent with international law and standards, based on prudent financing. Discussions will continue on the basis of shared values and principles but so far, the Quad has only spelt out objectives of different countries and a cautious approach, with Chinese pressure and displeasure in mind.

It is important that the Quad sticks to centrality of ASEAN as the pivot on which its Indo-Pacific strategy is based. Already, there is a lack of clear understanding in ASEAN about the 'Indo-Pacific' as a concept, and at the recent India–ASEAN commemorative Summit meeting in New Delhi, there was no widespread usage of the term by the ASEAN states. Led by President Jokowi, Indonesia called for an ASEAN meeting to study the concept and its implications for ASEAN. The ASEAN members agreed to be conscious of the evolving position of the Quad and to the new geopolitical situation in the region. While the ASEAN may be receptive to the 'free and open Indo-Pacific' idea proposed by the Quad, the priority for them is an inclusive and balanced cooperative framework in the Indo-Pacific. The Quad, therefore, needs to work with the ASEAN wherever possible.

It is understood that while the United States is having to counter the influence of China, which uses all means to shore up its influence and resources, and India continues to deal with a large and contested land border with China, which has been further complicated by the Chinese building the China Pakistan Economic Corridor (CPEC) thorough the disputed area of Kashmir for an outlet into Gwadar Port in Pakistan, Japan and Australia also feel the presence of the dragon in the room. China today has an interest in Australian assets, infrastructure, and influences its universities and politics. Japan has raised security concerns about China's intentions after a territorial dispute over the Senkaku Islands flared up in 2010.

The US pivot to Asia and its alliance system is under pressure because of the Chinese success in dividing the ASEAN countries by political influence and financial largesse for the weaker and poorer countries, in return for a controlling stake in their economies, politics and foreign policies.

Despite an International Court of Justice (ICJ) ruling in The Hague on China's aggressive actions in the South China Sea, China has managed to convince President Duterte of Philippines to pursue bilateral negotiations to settle outstanding issues. Its physical proximity in Asia and its geographical location has been used by China to convince the ASEAN countries that it is the force to deal within this part of the world rather than the United States. Economic dependence has been influencing many countries in the ASEAN to increasingly come under China's influence – especially projects under the One Belt One Road (OBOR) initiative – and countries like Laos and Thailand which are building high speed railways from Kunming in China to Malaysia and Singapore. China is matching the USA for military hardware and joint training exercises on cheaper terms. In this scenario, constructive and mutually beneficial projects, especially in infrastructure, between Quad members and ASEAN would offer an alternative, and benefit the Indo-Pacific as a whole.

Area of Influence

The idea of cooperation in the Indo-Pacific, therefore, by the Quad countries is not just centred on China. The Quad should have a practical agenda of cooperation. There are differing perceptions among the partners on what the Indo-Pacific encompasses geographically. The National Security Strategy of the United States, for example, identifies the Indo-Pacific as stretching from the 'West coast of India to the western shores of the United States' given the jurisdiction of US Indo Pacific Command (INDOPACOM). Others, especially India, have a different perception. India perceives the Indo-Pacific as stretching from the shores of the United States to the shores of Africa. Accordingly, the US Pentagon is considering enhancing the jurisdiction of INDOPACOM to cover the current jurisdiction of US Central Command (CENTCOM), which covers activities from the west coast of India to the African shores. Although Chinese actions have changed the geopolitical situation, countering China is not the sine qua non of Quad – it has to be a grouping with a larger purpose. In order to sustain itself, the Quad needs to build confidence and cooperation amongst itself and with its ASEAN partners, through the following measures:

- Maritime security and collaboration, addressing issues related to maritime challenges in the Indo-Pacific region, anti-piracy operations, joint escorts of international shipping, countering emerging maritime threats, force structuring, maritime domain awareness, intelligence sharing and white shipping information exchange.
- Improving infrastructure and connectivity in the wider Indo-Pacific region, China's Belt and Road Initiative is a means to have a greater say in international economic engagements by funding and building global transport and trade links with Asia and Europe. China has pledged US$ 124 billion for funding the plan. This January, China announced extending the initiative to the Arctic by developing shipping lanes opened up by global warming, to form a 'Polar Silk Road'. The

idea of an alternative infrastructure plan was discussed recently between Australian PM Malcolm Turnbull and President Trump. Australia and ASEAN agreed at their summit in March 2018 to establish a 'regional infrastructure pipeline of high quality infrastructure, to attract public and private investment'. Japan has already stated that it will use its Official Development Assistance (ODA) to promote a 'free and open Indo-Pacific Strategy' including 'high quality infrastructure' with the Asian Development Bank (ADB).

- India, under its 'Look East Policy' is funding the Trilateral Highway connecting its North East with Thailand via Myanmar by road. Thailand and Myanmar are also chipping in to this project. India has announced plans to align the project with the ASEAN Master Plan on Connectivity and to extend the trilateral to Laos, Cambodia, and Vietnam later. It is building the Kaladan Multi Modal Transport System which will again link India's North East with Myanmar and provide connectivity avenues to Bangladesh. The two policies can be aligned to create synergies for supply chains in the ASEAN.
- At the Africa Development Bank meeting in May 2017, there has been an attempt to spell out a strategy called the 'Asia Africa Growth Corridor', which will link economies, industries and institutions of Africa and Asia in an inclusive fashion. This will not be a state funded enterprise but will be led by the private sector drawing on existing links that both countries have with the region. A vision document has also been prepared by three leading think tanks of India, Japan, and ASEAN.

- Japan has also emerged as a major partner in India's efforts for the development of the North East Northeast and connectivity to ASEAN. It is towards this end the 'Japan India Act East Forum' has been set up, which will seek synergies between India's 'Act East Policy' and Japan's 'Partnership for Quality Infrastructure' located in the ADB and link it with Japan's 'Free and Open Indo-Pacific Strategy'.
- Strengthening cooperation with ASEAN and promoting discussions between strategists and experts.
- Security cooperation and dialogues, including joint exercises, (some analysts have identified the Malabar Exercises as a platform for defence engagement in the Indo-Pacific as a whole), defence equipment and technology cooperation in such areas as surveillance and unmanned system technologies.
- Collaboration in cyber security, information and communications technology, countering proliferation of Weapons of Mass Destruction (WMD) and terrorism.
- Coast Guard collaboration and mine sweeping technologies, anti-piracy operations, joint communications, deep sea mining and pollution control.
- Developing blue economy, collaborating and working together in maritime security capacity building for ASEAN and Pacific countries between themselves through groupings like India Ocean Rim Association (IORA), Indian Ocean Naval Symposium (IONS), and Western Pacific Naval Symposium (WPNS) to avoid overlaps and duplication of efforts.
- Jointly countering non-traditional threats to security like pandemics, help and rescue at sea, and

Humanitarian and Disaster Relief (HADR). Quad partners are already collaborating in these areas under the rubric of East Asia Summit.

In addition to shared concerns about Chinese actions in the South China Sea and the India Ocean, uncertainty about the US actions and staying power also motivates India, Japan and Australia to keep the United States engaged via this framework. The countries of the Quad have professed that it is not a military alliance, nor is it directed against anyone even though China and Russia today see it in a different light. Believing the Quad to be a containment strategy against China, scholars and academics in that country have immediately raised objections and cautioned the authorities to keep a watch on developments related to this grouping. Russian academics have even termed it the 'new NATO'. Any pushback on these grounds must therefore, be resisted. Contrary to what the Chinese Foreign Minister Wang Yi has said, the Quad is not a 'froth in the ocean' which can disappear easily.

Freedom of Navigation

While Japan and Australia have been aligned with the US for a while, they have not taken part in the US Freedom of Navigation Operations (FONOPS) around the contested territories in the South China Sea, which are continuously being militarised by China. India is unlikely to enter into a formal alliance, given the large, un-demarcated border with China and especially after the recent Wuhan Summit between Indian and Chinese leaders. Japan and China are also trying to improve their relations after a turbulent period with many political engagements slated for this year. An increasingly beleaguered Abe who had pushed through a parliamentary bill in 2015, which will allow Japan to reinterpret the pacifist Article 9 in the Japanese Constitution, faces public protests and pressure to step down. Australia, like other countries of the Quad, is heavily dependent on China in terms of bilateral trade and investments. Japan and Australia are dependent on China for as much as 22 per cent of their trade. At the end of 2017, China had invested as much as $1.18 trillion in the US debt market.

In any case, it is difficult to imagine that any of the Quad members would team up with each other to defend borders or enter into conflict which may arise in a dispute with China. The Quad is likely to remain, by nature, a loose grouping in the foreseeable future. Going forward, it can be imagined that the trilateral relationships that already exists among the Quad countries will be further strengthened. The Quad will continue to serve as a diplomatic grouping, which will stand up to a change in status quo by force. In the immediate phase, the Quad countries must continue to define the scope of the Quad, and refine what is being achieved through bilateral and trilateral agreements. The Quad will function with transparency, dispelling doubts about it being an alliance directed against any country. Threatening actions, objections and using the leverages at hand to scuttle joint action by the Quad will have to be resisted. A pay off or deference to commercial terms or political diktat must be rebuffed, and maritime ties strengthened amongst the partners for mutual benefit. The object must remain the creation of a multi-polar and increasingly connected Indo-Pacific, with due processes, to assure the mutual security of all stake holders.

The Quad, by coming together again, has signalled a revival to act in tandem in the Indo-Pacific. This process can be consolidated if the Quadrilateral Security Dialogue can be converted into a formal process, with regular meetings to coordinate cooperation in the security, economic, political fields with an agreed road map.

The Situation in West Asia

Sanjay Singh

The situation in West Asia is far from settled. The region is marred by conflicts in Syria and Yemen, extremist violence and widening sectarian division. There is no solution in sight for the Arab Israeli dispute and now the region is being buffeted by the increasing antagonism between Saudi Arabia and Iran. The political stasis in the region, the lack of opportunity for the population of some parts and frustrated aspirations of others, feed the instability. The major regional powers Iran, Turkey, Israel, Saudi Arabia and Egypt are unable to make a difference owing to their own problems. The regional instability attracts external intervention and global powers the US, Russia, China, Europe have inserted themselves into the region at its cost. This instability is of concern to India, given its extensive economic, energy and people to people ties with the region and calls for its greater attention.

The Aladdin Land

WEST ASIA conjures up contradictory images of holy sites, oil wealth and unbelievable opulence as well as strife, sectarian conflict, extremism and terrorist violence. The region is blighted, inter-alia by the continuing violence in Iraq, Yemen and Syria, the Palestinian-Israeli conundrum and the deepening divide between Iran and Saudi Arabia. Each of these will continue to have serious implications for the region and beyond.

The *Islamic State* (IS) has been defeated but not eradicated, just dispersed. Terrorist attacks by its followers and remnants could increase both in Iraq and Syria as well as in the countries where the foreign fighters of the Islamic State came from and to where they could return.

There are many causes for the emergence of the IS and other extremist groups. Firstly, lack of hope and economic opportunity in many parts of West Asia. Secondly, the widespread conflict that has afflicted parts of the region has led to a breakdown of state order in a number of countries. And thirdly, the widening sectarian divide between the Sunnis and the Shias. This has strengthened extremist forces professing jihad, which pose a challenge to nearly all types of state authorities, Islamic or otherwise.

Arab Spring, the term used to connote the uprisings in various countries of West Asia, which commenced in 2011, was fuelled largely by the aspirations of the people, especially the youth, attempting to change the political stasis that had existed in their countries for half a century. The authoritarian political order supported by conservative religious leaders, was challenged by those agitating for a reformed and moderate state and society. This challenge was often supported by the Muslim Brotherhood and its affiliates. However, except in **Tunisia**, these uprisings only led to instability, and in some countries unleashed a wave of violence, repression and civil war.

The developments in the regional battle zones give no cause for hope. The proxy war between Saudi Arabia with both Iran as well as the Muslim Brotherhood and the counterproductive actions by Israel and Turkey feed fuel to the fire. The great powers are again intervening in the region, further heating up the cauldron.

In Syria, the peace talks brokered by Staffan de Mistura, Special Envoy for Syria under UN auspices are not making any progress and the Russian-brokered Astana/Sochi peace process faces hurdles created by the US and its regional allies. The alleged use of chemical weapons by the Syrian regime, besides causing misery, spawns confrontation and provides justification for Western intervention, further raising existing tensions and diminishing any hope for peace.

Turkey, fully involved from the beginning in the 'troubles' in Syria, opened another front when its armed forces, backed by their Syrian opposition allies, the Free Syrian Army (FSA), entered Syria on 20 January 2018, and after making slow progress, finally took the northern Syrian town of Afrin from the Kurdish Militia. Turkey could perhaps house in this area the next stream of refugees, expected to flee from Ghouta and Idlib, areas from which the regime intends to next clear the Opposition.

The US now faces a difficult choice between supporting its Kurdish allies to safeguard its interest in maintaining a regional presence (about which in any case President Trump is ambivalent) and not alienating Turkey, its NATO partner. Russia, Syria and Iran, which exhibit a continuing commitment to their objectives, are not unhappy about this divide between

Turkey and the US, while Russia is developing a greater understanding with Turkey and is reportedly going to supply it the S-400 missile system.

Israel made its presence felt in the Syrian imbroglio when, in February this year it shot down an Iranian drone which was reportedly on a mission to drop bombs inside Israel. Israel, in its retaliatory attack on Syria, lost an F-16 aircraft, its first loss of a plane in combat since 2006. This is perhaps indicative of its loss of unchallenged control of the regional airspace and its vulnerability to Iranian/Hezbollah missiles. It is a situation that Israel will wish to correct.

Yemen, over which the Hadi-led Government has scant control, is in a state of chaos. The country has been divided into areas of influence of different tribal and political groups. The Hadi-affiliated national armed forces, the principal fighting force of the Government, which is supported by the Saudis and the Emeratis, has been bogged down in its fight against the Houthis and against Al-Qaeda militants in the south. The increasing divide and hostilities between the Southern Resistance Forces (SRF) and the Hadi Government and forces loyal to it, adds a new dimension to the chaos.

The Houthis are unlikely to be ousted soon from the capital Sanaa and the North or the port Hodeida and the West. The Saudis are frustrated by their inability to affect quick progress despite their extensive bombing in Yemen and the Kingdom itself has come under sporadic missile strikes from Yemen. A good augury is the reports that the Saudis and the Houthis are engaged in some form of talks in **Oman**. Revival of the peace process will need considerable effort from the new UN special envoy for Yemen, Martin Griffiths. To be successful it will require political accommodation between the Hadi and

Houthi forces, the shaping of a federal polity that will maintain national unity while providing freedom for local aspirations, the cessation of external intervention in the country and international political and financial support. Otherwise, the fratricidal war will continue endangering stability across the region.

Iraq seems to have stabilised after the defeat of IS in Mosul, but the situation remains fragile. The Government, led by PM Al-Abadi, has the onerous task of bringing the country's various communities together and ending the sense of discrimination felt by the Sunnis. The forthcoming elections in May this year will provide an opportunity to the country to put the past behind.

A look at how the major regional powers are faring is instructive:

Iran's influence further expanded in the region after the P5+1-Iran nuclear deal. Its economy has strengthened considerably by the removal of sanctions, ramping up of production and exports of oil and gas and renewed access to its funds banked abroad. The Chinese and some European countries have begun reinvesting in Iran. This deal, which amounts to Iran's suspension of nuclear activities but not an elimination of its nuclear capability was opposed by Israel and Iran's neighbours in the Gulf, who were alarmed by its increasing influence and support to its allies in Syria, Iraq, Lebanon and Yemen. While President Trump is determined to dismantle the nuclear deal in its present form, this may push Iran further towards China, which has a burgeoning economic presence in the country. Meanwhile, Iran in trying to expand its influence in the region has diverted scarce resources at the cost of its own domestic economy, consequently increasing the hardship faced by its people. Iranian currency is under great threat and has devalued considerably. The agitations in Iran earlier this year could be attributed to these growing economic difficulties. All this has compelled President Rouhani to urgently try and address the problems the country faces and prepare for those which may come in the wake of possible US action.

Turkey's freedom to continue projecting its leadership role in the region has been constrained by the instability in neighbouring Syria and Iraq and the waning of the fortunes of the Muslim Brotherhood and its own internal divisions. The ruling AKP party's agenda towards creating an all-powerful Presidency might have unintended consequences. The coup attempt in Turkey and President Erdogan's campaign against the Gulenists and other opponents has further complicated matters. Turkish aims may also be affected by its policy towards the Syrian Kurds, who with US support, were in the vanguard of the fight against the IS. There is growing turbulence in its own Kurdish areas. Turkey now requires re-adjustment of its policies towards its own as well as Syrian and Iraqi Kurds. Its relations with Israel remain difficult. Turkey is coordinating its position on Syria with Iran and Russia, but this creates tensions with the US. The presence of a large number of Syrian refugees in the country also gives rise to another set of problems.

The **Kingdom of Saudi Arabia** (KSA) was alarmed by developments during the 'Arab Spring' given the internal threat it faces from the Muslim Brotherhood (MB) and the Sahwa movement. Therefore, the weakening of the MB in Egypt under President Sisi was a good development for the KSA. On the other hand, the growing influence of Iran post the nuclear deal was a matter of concern for it. KSA faces a new threat to its southern borders from the instability in Yemen, challenge from Shia groups in the Eastern province and in Bahrain and a non-cooperative Qatar. The House of Saud also faces domestic criticism and internal dissent. Its policy of appeasing its own restive youth and clergy has limitations. Extremist groups like the IS and their ilk also threaten it. Crown Prince Mohammed bin Salman has gained considerable support for the Kingdom's regional ambitions from President Trump. He has taken a number of bold steps and outlined a new vision 2030 for the country. However, this is still a work in progress. Given KSA's growing financial requirements and diminished revenues from oil and gas, it will have to revisit its social contract with its own citizens and this may create new difficulties.

Egypt after being through a turbulent period during the 'Arab Spring' has stabilised under President Sisi, a twice-elected President backed by the military. It however faces considerable difficulty in addressing its growing economic problems, compounded by a fast-growing population and increasing water shortages due to reduced flows in the Nile. Under economic pressure, it has had to accept IMF's prescriptions, which may well put a brake on President Sisi's ambitious economic agenda. While President Sisi has marginalised the MB, he may not be able to eliminate it. Consequently, given its internal troubles, Egypt's role in addressing pan Arab issues and regional challenges will remain diminished.

Israel is militarily perhaps the strongest power in the region, with an advanced economy, technological prowess and considerable intelligence capabilities. But the **Palestinian issue** has boxed it in. It has become more and more recalcitrant in addressing the Palestinian issue. Its actions in Gaza and in creating new settlements have pushed the peace process into a cul-de-sac. It has leveraged 'Iran phobia' well, getting considerable support from President Trump on the Palestinian issue and greater understanding from the Kingdom of Saudi Arabia and its Crown Prince. But the Palestinian problem will not go away. Added to this is the chaos across its borders in Syria and the growing strength of the Hezbollah and increasing Iranian presence in the North.

To sum up, the instability affecting the region will continue and will attract growing foreign intervention, drawing in disgruntled elements from around the world. Muslim populations in different parts of the world cannot but be influenced by these events.

All this will threaten:

Firstly, energy security, possibly leading to higher prices eventually; though for the time being, oil and gas fields are fairly secure and in fact energy prices have fallen by more than half. Higher prices are not a certainty though, as there are contradictory trends, with oil prices coming under increasing pressure from various renewables, leading to diminishing revenues for states dependant on them and affecting their social contracts with their own people.

Secondly, sea lines of communication and trade through the Suez, Bab-al-Mandab, Gulf of Aden and the Straits of Hormuz, which are under threat from pirates and other extremist elements.

Thirdly, the region itself and beyond will be affected through further growth of radical and fundamentalist ideologies, sectarian conflict and terrorism. The employment of technology by radical cadres for the export of ideology through networks and social media is dangerous. There was gravitation of cadres from around the world towards West Asia owing to the success of the IS. This could reverse.

These developments have accentuated the conditions of disunity, weakness and vulnerability in the region into which Great powers as well as disgruntled elements will continue to be sucked in, further compounding the problem. The rift within the GCC is a manifestation of this.

The US will continue to be involved, one way or the other in managing developments in the region, especially where they impact on its own national interests. While much has been written about the shale gas revolution reducing the region's importance for the US, there is no getting away from the fact that the US, with bases in the region (5th fleet in Manama, Bahrain and USAF Centcom at Al Udeid Airbase in Qatar) and its Naval Support Facility in Diego Garcia, is presently the sole global power capable of effectively projecting force all over West Asia.

President Trump is making efforts to broker peace among Arab monarchies and obtain a settlement over **Qatar**, the hope being to once again unite the GCC countries against Iran, the US's principal enemy in the region. He has been very critical of the P 5+1 nuclear agreement with Iran and the fact that this has assisted Iran to become a 'regional power'. He wants the deal to be drastically revised, if not, the US is ready to abandon it. This, if it occurs, may push Iran further into alignments inimical to US interests.

The President's first visit abroad was to the Kingdom of Saudi Arabia and he has developed a special relationship with the Kingdom and its Crown Prince Mohamed Bin Salman. He, however, believes that countries of the region should assume a fairer share of the burden for their own security and seeks a more transactional relationship with them. How this will play out remains to be seen.

President Trump and his national security team have exhibited great support for Israel and Israeli Prime Minister Netanyahu. They are not putting any pressure on Israel to pursue the peace process and Trump has decided to move the US embassy to Jerusalem. This could be the death-knell for the two-state solution and lead to greater strife in Palestine.

Europe's energy interests are adversely affected by developments in the region, especially in the contiguous Maghreb. Many European nationals have come under the sway of extremist and terrorist ideologies. Europe also faces a growing refugee problem emanating from the instability in Syria, **Libya** and Afghanistan and owing to the rapidly growing population of the region and Africa, the fastest growing in the world. However, its appetite to interfere in the region, while diminished owing to its own troubles, has not completely abated.

Russia saw an opportunity in Syria and has inserted itself more forcefully into the region. Its profile has been enhanced by what it has been able to achieve in Syria and the cooperation it has extended over the oil and gas production and its pricing. It has been hosting a constant stream of visitors from the region seeking its cooperation, including from Iran, Turkey, Egypt, KSA and even Israel. Russia too faces a threat from extremists including the IS, especially in the Caucasus, given that over a thousand Chechens were in the region as cadres of Jihadist groups. Its actions in Syria are partly influenced by this as well as its desire to enhance its global standing.

The rise of **China**, the second largest economy in the world, and its efforts toward acquisition of comprehensive national power are sustained by an increasing consumption of energy and resources. This has led to burgeoning Chinese imports from and trade with West Asia and a growing economic presence underlined by the Central belt of the BRI being put in place through the region. This has been accompanied by its increasing maritime presence in the region and acquisition of naval facilities in the Indian Ocean Region. Authoritative Chinese studies recommend its greater politico-military engagement and participation in efforts towards promoting peace and security in the region.

The major Asian economies view the growing instability in the West Asian region with special concern, not least because they are heavily dependent on West Asia for their energy supplies. From the Asian perspective, Western military interventions in the region have been a major factor causing instability. It is estimated that about 90 per cent of Gulf oil and gas production will go to Asia by 2035. Asians also have very substantial trade relationships with the GCC countries and are implementing many multi-billion-dollar projects in the region.

India has a special interest in the Gulf and the broader region. Over 8 million of Indians live and work the region. The region provides around 70 per cent of India's oil and gas requirements as well as phosphatic fertilisers and urea essential for agriculture. It is India's largest economic partner with trade exceeding $100 billion annually and a growing investment partnership. A large number of Indians have faith-based links with the holy sites in the region and visit them on pilgrimages.

The year 2017 began with India reiterating the importance of the region by hosting the Crown Prince of Abu Dhabi as the chief guest at its Republic Day Parade. During the visit of Prime Minister Modi to UAE earlier this year, the two countries reaffirmed their abiding commitment to further consolidating their comprehensive strategic partnership. Prime Minister Modi has paid special attention to India's ties with the region.

Over the last four years he has visited KSA, Oman, Qatar, Jordan, Palestine, Israel, Iran, UAE thrice and Turkey for the G20 summit. Each of his visits have been marked by warmth and positive outcomes and matched by reciprocal visits. Every capital he has visited bilaterally sees India as a valued partner and seeks an enhanced political, economic, security and defence partnership with India.

Conclusion

India has developed bilateral institutional mechanisms with nearly all countries in the region to enhance cooperation in the fight against terrorism and extremism. It has defence and security cooperation arrangements with a number of countries in the region. The basic Indian approach has been non-prescriptive and to promote dialogue and moderation in the fight against extremism and the resolution of conflicts. It is important however, that India starts thinking beyond this, and examines possible options in playing a more robust role in the region.